The Catholic Catechism on Freemasonry

The Catholic Catechism on Freemasonry

A Theological and Historical Treatment on the Catholic Church's Prohibition Against Freemasonry and its Appendant Masonic Bodies

David L. Gray

Saint Dominic's Media
Belleville, Illinois

The Catholic Catechism on Freemasonry:
A Theological and Historical Treatment Against
Freemasonry and its Appendant Masonic Bodies

© 2020 David L. Gray
All Rights Reserved

Published by:
Saint Dominic's Media, Inc.
P.O. Box 8225
Belleville, IL 62222

www.saintdominicsmedia.com

Printed in the United States of America

2 3 4 5 6 7

BISAC Categories:
RELIGION / Christian Church / History
RELIGION / Christian Church / Canon & Ecclesiastical Law
RELIGION / Christianity / Catechisms

ISBN-13: 978-1-7321784-9-6 (Paperback)
ISBN-13: 978-0-578-64213-0 (Hard Cover)

That the Holy Spirit, the Spirit of Truth, would lead all hearts to love the orthodoxy of the Catholic faith

Our Lady of La Salette,
Pray for Us!

Saint Michael the Archangel,
Pray for Us!

Saint Maximillian Kolbe,
Pray for Us!

Saint Pope Pius X,
Pray for Us!

Saint Padre Pio,
Pray for Us!

Blessed Pope Pius IX,
Pray for Us!

Contents

Preface 7

My Background in Freemasonry 12

How to Use this Book 15

Chapter I – The Origins of Freemasonry 16

Chapter II – The Structure of Freemasonry 27

Chapter III – Freemasonry is a Religion 39

Chapter IV – *In Eminenti* (1738), Clement XII 50

Chapter V - *Providas Romanorum* (1751), Benedict XIV 66

Chapter VI – *Etsi Multa* (1873), Pius IX 97

Chapter VII – *Humanum Genus* (1884), Leo XIII 116

Chapter VIII – *Officio Sanctissimo* (1887), Leo XIII 164

Chapter IX - *Dall'alto dell'Apostolicio Seggio* (1890), Leo XIII 170

Chapter X - *Custodi Di Quella Fede* (1892), Leo XIII 200

Chapter XI - *Inimica Vis* (1892), Leo XIII 218

Chapter XII - *Praeclara Gratulationis* (1894), Leo XIII 228

Chapter XIII – The Epoch of Indifferentism 234

Appendix A - *Anderson's Constitution* (1723), GLofE 270

Appendix B – *Masonry Dissected* (1730), Samuel Pritchard 278

Preface

The Catholic Catechism on Freemasonry is my sincere effort at creating a clear, concise, and unrestrained guide to help Catholics and those responding to the call of Christ into His Church to understand the dogmatic (permanent) prohibition that the Catholic Church has against Freemasonry and its appendant Masonic bodies. This work is a historical and theological treatment of the Catholic Church's dogmatic prohibition against Freemasonry and its appendant Masonic bodies (sects) that have been in place since Pope Clement XII promulgated his Papal Bull *In Eminenti* on April 28, 1738.

While I value the efforts of Catholic Apologists like John Salza, author of *Why Catholics Cannot be Masons* and *Masonry Unmasked*, this book intends to propose a theological, rather than an apologetic, case about the irreconcilable difference between Catholicism and Freemasonry.

My perspective on Popular American Apologetics is that it frequently begins with an error that unintentionally but inevitably promotes indifferentism by framing their arguments under the errant presupposition that their opponent's case has some measure of merit and/or value.

The traditional structure of Popular American Apologetics is to present their opponent's argument and then explain why that argument is in error from the perspective of their faith tradition. In the case of Catholicism, the result of over three decades of creating an industry built on framing arguments in this manner with Protestantism is that we have made Catholicism an apparent equal to Protestantism, and by doing so, we have essentially told the world that Catholicism is just one idea out of many; that it is just a competing idea in a sea of ideas; that these Protestant arguments that we are presenting could be true, but you should trust us instead of them because our facts are more logical and reasonable than theirs.

The value that the science of Theology (the science of faith seeking understanding) has over the intellectual art of Apologetics (the art of presenting a reasonable defense of the subject) is that while Theology requires the assent of faith and reason, Apologetics, done well, can get away with the assent of reason alone. Apologetics does not solicit active belief but only asks that we conclude that its arguments are reasonable and logical. If those conclusions help to ignite a spark of faith, then that is a glorious grace. However, such grace is not necessarily necessary for Apologetics to succeed.

Moreover, Catholicism should never be put on the defensive and be forced to defend itself against lies. However, giving the leading voice to opposing ideologies and philosophies and then responding to those concepts according to what the Church teaches makes our faith look weak and dependent. It makes us look like the Protestant religion, which has difficulty explaining what it believes without inserting the point that Catholics are wrong about what they believe. While Protestantism and other anti-Catholic religions and philosophies need to lie about Catholicism to justify their existence, the One, Holy, Catholic, and

Apostolic Church needs nothing that belongs to the world to explain who She is in Christ.

Therefore, my work here intends to move away from the tendency of arguing with Freemasonry. I will sometimes explain Freemasonry's beliefs from their perspective. However, I will not engage or argue with it in the Popular American Apologetics sense. Freemasonry is just as much a religion as Protestantism. Similarly, it has nothing to contribute to Catholicism and does not deserve a seat at our table. On the contrary, my primary goal here is to clearly explain what has been the consistent teaching that the Catholic Church has made about Freemasonry since Pope Clement XII's 1738 Papal Bull *In Eminenti apostolatus specula* (The High Warning) and why all Catholics need to listen and obey the Church regarding this dogmatic teaching faithfully.

This work begins with a succinct explanation of the history and structure of Freemasonry and their appendant Masonic bodies. I will then explain the Legend of Hiram Abiff, the core mystery of Freemasonry, and how it connects with their history, structure, and central philosophy. I will also briefly touch on how people join the subordinate lodge, the Masonic degree obligations, and what goes on in their meetings. Most importantly, I will explain how Freemasonry is a fraternal religion. After this time, I will insert into this work a commentary on the nine Papal documents, two Canon Laws, and two documents from the Congregation from the Doctrine of the Faith that were written explicitly about Freemasonry. Through these documents, the reader will hear the Church speak from a magisterial and offensive position as the head of all Christians. My role as a commentator is to give historical, theological, philosophical, and ritualistic context from the perspective of Freemasonry.

Unless otherwise referenced, the times when I share elements from Freemasonry's rituals or teachings are drawn purely from my memory. I avoid, as often as possible, any reference to Masonic scholars simply because the diversity of their opinions regarding the ritual, allegory, and symbolism of Freemasonry does not add any weight whatsoever to the argument being made. Quoting what one scholar of Freemasonry has said about a topic is like quoting what one Protestant scholar has said. They all disagree with one another, and none of them have a deposit of faith or a definitive source of authority to draw from.

This, too, is a departure from previous works on this topic written by Catholics and Protestants that have relied on the opinions of people like Albert G. Mackey, Albert Pike, T. S. Webb, J. S. M. Ward, H. L. Haywood, and others. Every instance of reliance on such scholars presents another opportunity for a Freemason to distance himself from the arguments being made because those were just the personal opinions of someone who does not have the authority to speak for Freemasonry. Concerning the history of Freemasonry, I will cite high-quality and credible sources.

This book does not give a lengthy treatment about the appendant Masonic bodies, such as the Ancient & Accepted Scottish Rite (AASR), the Shrine (AAONMS or AEAONMS), the Order of the Eastern Star, etc., because, first, there are too many of these orders even to dare to address with substance. Secondly, being that all appendant Masonic bodies consist of only Freemasons, it is necessary to speak only of the root and foundation of the entire Masonic order.

The list of Papal documents that I am using does depart from the popular list, which includes documents such as *Ecclesiam a Jesu Christo* (1821), which concerned not Freemasonry but the Carbonari, which was never an appendant Masonic body and was never exclusive to Freemasons alone. Also excluded from my list are Papal documents that addressed the dangers of indifferentism (a core Masonic philosophy) and secret societies in general.

Preface

This group of documents is essential to the broader discussion on the prohibition of Freemasonry but is not exclusively about Freemasonry.

I want to thank Charles Madden O.F.M. Conv., author of *Freemasonry: Mankind's Hidden Enemy*, Saint Maximillian Kolbe's Knights of the Immaculata (Traditional Observance), John Salza, and the many other Catholics and Bishops Conferences down through the centuries who have spoken clearly and precisely about the dangers of Freemasonry and why Catholics are forbidden from joining, promoting, or associating with it.

As always, I thank you, O' Lord, for the gifts you have given me, especially my wife and daughters, who endure in patience with me.

Deum Verum,
David L. Gray
February 7, 2020, the Feast of Blessed Pope Pius IX

My Background in Freemasonry

I was what they called 'Raised to the Sublime Degree of Master Mason' at the age of twenty-two, and by the time I reached the age of thirty-two, I had earned some of the highest Grand Lodge appointments and had become an internationally known author, speaker, and authority on Masonic History; in particular on the subject of Prince Hall Freemasonry. My published books include *The Unveiling of the Third Preparation* (1995), *Inside Prince Hall* (2011), and *The History of the Most Worshipful Prince Hall Grand Lodge of Ohio F&AM 1971 – 2011: The Fabric of Freemasonry* (2012). The latter was a commissioned work I agreed to write objectively as a historian of Black American Fraternal History. As a Freemason, I had articles on the subject published in *The Masonic Voice* (Dr. Charles H. Wesley Masonic Research Society), *The Philalethes* (The Philalethes Society), *The Masonic Globe* (Blue Light Publishing), *Gleanings* (South Australian Lodge of Research), *Harashim* (Australian New Zealand Masonic Research Council), and *New South Wales Masonic Quarterly Magazine* (New South Wales Lodge of Research).

In addition to being a Past Master of a subordinate lodge, I held the elected offices of High Priest of a Royal Arch Chapter and Worthy Patron of an Eastern Star Chapter. I held appointed offices in a council of Royal and Select Masters, a Commandery of Knights Templar, and a Consistory of Ancient and Accepted Scottish Rite Mason (Sublime Prince of the Royal Secret - 32nd Degree). I was the first Prince Hall Freemason to be received as a member of the Ohio Lodge of Research of the predominately White Grand Lodge of Ohio F&AM (Free & Accepted Masons), where I was appointed Senior Deacon. I was also distinguished as a charter member and the first Editor-in-Chief of the Dr. Charles H. Wesley Masonic Research Society and elected as a Fellow of the Phylaxis Society.

Other unique honors and appointments bestowed upon me for my work in Freemasonry included receiving the Dr. Charles H. Wesley Certificate of Literature by the Phylaxis, a Certificate of Meritorious Service by the Phylaxis Society, appointed District Deputy Grand Lecturer for the Most Worshipful Prince Hall Grand Lodge of Ohio, chosen to be a Knight Zuri by the Knights of Freemasonry Universal, chosen as the 410th Freemason elected to the Masonic Brotherhood of the Blue Forget-Me-Not, and recipient of the Best Lecturer in the Entered Apprentice Degree 2nd and 3rd Sections by the Most Worshipful Prince Hall Grand Lodge of Ohio.

After spending my early adult life as a Deist and Agnostic, I came to definitely and unforgettably believe in the person of Jesus Christ in September of 2004. While I was trying to commit suicide by asphyxiation, I heard an audible voice that told me, *"I love you. I am here."* After soon realizing and accepting that it was, surprisingly, the voice of the Lord, who I, heretofore, thought was the leading fictional character of a fraud religion, from that day forward, I committed to following Jesus, which eventually led me to be Baptized a Protestant on August 28, 2005, and being Confirmed into the Catholic Church on August 8, 2006; the Feast of Saint Dominic de Guzman.

Since that time, I studied undergraduate Catholic Theology at Franciscan Steubenville (Ohio), earned a Master of Arts Degree in Theology from Ohio Dominican University (Ohio), published hundreds of essays on Catholic Theology, authored the books *Dead on Arrival: the seven fatal errors of sola-scriptura* (2011), *Cooperating with God: the Bridegroom's Prayer* (2012), *Cooperating with God: Life with the Cross* (2012), and *The Divine Symphony: an exordium to the theology of the Catholic Mass* (2018).

In 2017, I founded Saint Dominic's Media to publish books and media on Catholic liturgy, history, and the orthodoxy of the Catholic faith. My wife and three of my four daughters are also all converts to the Catholic Church, and we currently reside in the Greater Saint Louis, Missouri, area.

It was during the R.C.I.A process when I learned, from listening to the Eternal Word Television Network Radio, that Catholics cannot be Freemasons. After researching the subject further, I came to the same conclusion: that if I were going to become a Catholic, I could no longer be a Freemason. Since that realization, I have devoted myself to writing, speaking, and publishing videos on the subject as to why Freemasonry and its Masonic bodies are a danger and a threat to and irreconcilable with the Catholic Church.

How to Use this Book

Allow this Catholic Catechism on Freemasonry to enrich your understanding of why the philosophies and ideologies of Freemasonry are a danger to every soul under its influence and why the prohibition against Freemasonry has been a continuous and non-contradicted dogma of the Church since Pope Clement XII promulgated his Papal Bull *In Eminenti* on April 28, 1738.

It is true that as a mother, the Catholic Church loves us so much and cares for the destiny of our souls so tenderly that she warns us about approaching dangers and even forbids us at times to go down certain paths that She knows will lead to our ruin. Therefore, also allow this book to inspire you to speak in your Mother's voice, to encourage and warn your brothers and sisters to do what She says. For, as Christ Jesus said to His Apostles, whose successors are the bishops of the One, Holy, Catholic, and Apostolic Church they founded, *"He who hears you hears Me, and he who rejects you rejects Me, and he who rejects Me rejects Him who sent Me"* (*Luke* 10:16).

Chapter I | The Origins of Freemasonry

This chapter will trace Freemasonry's formal and derivational origins up to 1730. The objective of this chapter is not to give a complete account of the history of Freemasonry but to 1) describe its religious origins, 2) describe how it formally departed from those origins, and 3) give an account of the type of public information about Freemasonry that Pope Clement XII would have been disposed to know by the time he wrote his Papal Bull *In Eminenti apostolatus specula* (The High Watch) on April 28, 1738.

The Formal and Derivational Origins of Freemasonry

Freemasonry, as we know it today, consisting of thousands of jurisdictionally governed lodges that are subordinate to constitutionally formed Grand Lodges and working a philosophically engineered system of degrees and rites that are based upon the Masonic legend of Hiram Abiff, took rise on June 24, 1717, when at least four preexisting Masonic lodges in London, England[1] came together at the Goose and Gridiron Ale-house (tavern) in St. Paul's Church-yard to form a governing Grand Lodge; electing

---

[1] There is a dispute as to whether there were four lodges in attendance with some 'unattached' older Freemasons present, or whether there were actually six lodges in attendance that would account for all those who voted.

Anthony Sayer as their first Grand Master. The intent hereof electing a Grand Master, according to Anderson, was *"to choose a Grand Master from among themselves, till they should have the honor of a Noble Brother at their head."*[2] This first organizational meeting was preceded by one held in 1716 at the Apple Tree Tavern in Covent Garden, where they agreed to form a Grand Lodge.

The idea of a governing body over local lodges was an innovation in Freemasonry. While this 1717 organization was the first of its kind, by the time Pope Clement XII would publish his Papal Bull *In Eminenti apostolatus specula* on April 28, 1738, there would be Masonic Grand Lodges in England, Ireland, Scotland, France, Spain, Sweden, and even three in the new colonies (Massachusetts, Pennsylvania, and South Carolina). This small number of Grand Lodges does not account for the hundreds of subordinate lodges spread throughout Europe and North America that were beholden to them. There is no question about the fact that the creation of the Grand Lodge structure aided significantly in the explosive growth, longevity, and peace from within that the Masonic Order would enjoy for centuries to come.

Regarding the origin of these founding lodges, there is enough reliable evidence to state with a high degree of certainty that the organized stonemason guilds of Europe subsist in today's modern Grand Lodges of Freemasons. Moreover, the early stonemason guild's members were predominantly Catholics. It was these operative masons who were employed by the institutional Church and who were responsible for the building of the great and minor cathedrals, monasteries, shrines, and churches of Europe from the middle-ages and up to the sixteenth century. It was from these Catholic and Anglican stonemason guilds that

---

[2] Calvert, Albert Frederick. *The Grand Lodge of England, 1717 – 1917: Being an account of 200 years of English Freemasonry.* Herbert Jenkins Limited. London. 1917. 250.

craft Freemasonry today still maintains its structure, form, religiosity, and order.

One of the earliest pieces of evidence that demonstrates how closely aligned the early stonemason guilds were with the Catholic Church is found in the *Regius Poem*, which also goes by the name of the *Halliwell Manuscript*, so named after James Halliwell, who was not a Freemason but discovered this obscure text that had been donated to the British Museum in 1757 by King George II. In 1840, Halliwell delivered a paper on the *Regius Poem* entitled, *The Early History of Freemasonry in England*, and a wide notice of it took off from there. The *Regius Poem* belongs to a genre of literature known in Freemasonry as the 'Old Charges' or the 'Gothic Constitutions.' The purpose of these 'Old Charges' for the stonemason guilds was to function as a guide for their history, organization, duties, regulations, and the behavior of members. While the *Regius Poem* is not dated, it is purportedly (based upon linguistic evidence) to have been written between 1390 and 1450, with most recent scholarship putting it at more likely after 1425.[3] In the section of the *Regius Poem* pertaining to the Holy Mass and how to behave in the Church, it offers many stanzas that some faithful Catholics might appreciate, such as:

> In holy church leave trifling words
> Of lewd speech and foul jests,
> And put away all vanity,
> And say thy pater noster an thine ave;
> Look also that thou make no noise,
> But always to be in thy prayer;
> If thou wilt not thyself pray,

---

[3] Prescott, Andrew. *Some Literary Contexts of the Regius and Cooke Manuscripts*. University of Sheffield. Prescott argues that the Regius and Cooke manuscripts were reactionary documents that were produced by the stonemason guilds in response to a 1425 petition by parliament against the masons for "publicly violating and undermining the statues of laborers."

Hinder no other man by no way.
In that place neither sit nor stand,
But kneel far down on the ground,
And when the Gospel me read shall,

Fairly thou stand up from the wall,
And bless the fare if that thou can
When Gloria tibi is begun;
And when the gospel is done,
Again thou might kneel down,
On both knees down thou fall,
For his love that bought us all,
And when thou hearest the bell ring
To that holy sacrament,
Kneel you must both young and old,
And both your hands fair uphold,
And say then in this manner,

Fir and soft without noise,
"Jesu Lord welcome thou be,
In form of read as I thee see,
Now Jesu for thine holy name,
Shield me from sin and shame;
Shrift and Eucharist thou grand me both,
Ere that I shall hence go,
And very contrition for my sin,
That I never, Lord, die therein;
And as thou were maid born,
Suffer me never to be lost;
But when I shall hence wend,

Grant me the bless without end;

Amen! Amen! So mote it be!
Now sweet lady pray for me."

As its chief employer, it would have been natural for all the guilds associated with the life and duties of the Church to develop particular religious characteristics. For example, nearly every guild would have had a patron saint to whom they kept a candle burning day and night. Guilds would have had a priest and a chapel they supported and patronized. They would have also had their chaplain, even if it was not a guild devoted exclusively to religious purposes. These characteristics are still present in modern Freemasonry, whose lodges are said to be devoted to Saint John the Baptist and Saint John the Evangelist, whose feast days they celebrate on June 24 and December 27, respectively. The burning light for their patron saint has symbolically been replaced with what is known as the Three Great Lights (the Holy Bible, the Square, and the Compass) and the Three Lesser Lights (the Sun, the Moon, and the Worshipful Master of the Lodge).

For operative masons, the 'lodge' was a building near the worksite where they kept their working tools, took breaks, and ate dinner. The traveling masons contracted to work on a project did not sleep in the lodge but would have found rest in a nearby inn or other available lodgings. Masons who lived in or near the town where they were laboring would have returned home after a day's work.

Also, modern Freemasonry is indebted to its operative forerunner in governance and progression of degrees. Operative guilds were typically supervised by several wardens who were either elected by the assembly or appointed by the local mayor. Membership in a guild was obtained by a free-person voluntarily petitioning it for membership. If chosen, they were admitted to the guild under oath. The general membership classes were masters, journeymen (fellow crafts) who could also be a master and apprentices. As legal protections developed in parts of Europe, being an apprentice became a legally protected class in society because it involved indentured servitude, which by 1563 had been fixed to be seven-years. It was the responsibility of the apprentice's master to provide him food, shelter, training, supervision, and sometimes a wage and schooling for his apprentice. For their part, the apprentice was expected to pass proficiency tests upon examination to be promoted to journeyman eventually.

The oaths of obligation that we now find present in Freemasonry and the appendant Masonic orders are similar to the charges that an operative mason would bind himself to upon joining a guild. As described above in the Regius Poem, these charges were intended to impress upon the mason the manner by which he was to regulate his life. These charges upon the mason always outlined his duties, of which the first was his duty to God (i.e., belief in the dogma of the Church and rejection of all heresies); second, his duty to submit to the sovereignty and dictates of the King; third was his duty to his masters, his employer, and the master mason from whom he received his assignment. His duty to his master included not revealing to anyone his secrets of building, not sleeping with his wife, daughter, or maidservant, remaining peaceable, and not persisting in being disobedient or argumentative with his master, his dame, or any other mason. A mason was also charged to be upright in character, not to shame his master or the guild. He was not to commit fornication (including adultery), not to frequent inns and brothels, not to be out past 8 p.m., not to play card games except during the Twelve Days of Christmas. According to the Acts of Parliament, only noblemen were allowed to play cards for the rest of the year.[4]

The local craft guilds played a commercial and economic role in society. They were positively involved in every aspect of their member's lives. Members of guilds enjoyed the unique privilege of freedom (free-masons)[5] to travel so that they could provide their services to the Church and state. The guild provided them with safety, protection, and stability, covered burial costs for their deceased members, and provided for their surviving widow until her death. While a stonemason could work on some projects for his entire life, other itinerant masons had to travel dangerous roads to find work, and gaining rights to work in a new guild was essential. To facilitate safe travel, some operative stonemasons developed signs of recognition and credentials to distinguish one another. However, with the strong emergence of capitalism and manufacturing in the early nineteenth century, the guild system as we knew it eventually faded away, and their protected class status and privileges were abolished by European governments. However, over two centuries prior to that, operative stonemason lodges in Scotland and England had already begun transitioning into speculative lodges by accepting adult men who were not stonemasons into their ranks. From this point onward, these non-operative members were designated as 'accepted' masons. With more and more lodges transitioning completely to become speculative rather than operative guilds, everything we knew about craft guild operative masonry would live on in the craft lodge of Freemasonry.

---

[4] *Statutes of the Realm*, 23 Edw.III, c. 5-7; 24 Edw.III, c.I, 2.
[5] The term 'freemason' was earlier associated with skilled masons who worked with the softer and more chalky stone called 'freestone' that was found in many parts of Europe. The masons who worked with this stone were called 'freestone masons', which was often shortened to 'freemasons'.

Early Public Documents on Freemasonry

The document entitled *Constitutions of the Free-Masons. Containing the History. Charges. Regulations. &c. of that most Ancient and Right Worshipful Fraternity. For the Use of the Lodges* (see Appendix A) was written by Church of Scotland (Presbyterian) minister Reverend James Anderson (c. 1679/1680 – 1739) under the instruction and authority to amend by the leading members of Grand Lodge[6] (it was rewritten in 1738) for the newly founded Grand Lodge of England, and to standardize the rituals and practices of lodges subordinate to it. This constitution was based upon the aforementioned 'Old Charges' or 'Gothic Constitutions' and on the General Regulations, compiled by George Payne (the second Grand Master of the Grand Lodge of England) in 1720. Since this constitution was intended only for the governance of lodges subordinate to the Grand Lodge of England, it spread worldwide. It became a standard source document on regular Freemasonry. In 1734, it was reprinted by Benjamin Franklin in Philadelphia, Pennsylvania, making it the first Masonic book printed in America.

For this treatment on the origins of Freemasonry, two articles in Anderson's Constitution are essential to raise (bold added for emphasis):

I. Concerning GOD and RELIGION.

A Mason is oblig'd by his Tenure, to obey the moral law; and if he rightly understands the Art, he will never be a stupid Atheist nor an irreligious Libertine. But though in ancient Times Masons were charg'd in every Country to be of the Religion of that Country or Nation, whatever it was, **yet 'tis now thought more expedient only to oblige them to that Religion in which all Men agree, leaving their particular Opinions to themselves; that is, to be**

---

[6] See Appendix A for the full text of *Anderson's Constitution* of 1723.

good Men and true, or Men of Honour and Honesty, by whatever Denominations or Persuasions they may be distinguish'd; whereby Masonry becomes the Center of Union, and the Means of conciliating true Friendship among Persons that must have remain'd at a perpetual Distance.

VI. Of BEHAVIOR.
2. BEHAVIOR after the LODGE is over and the BRETHREN not GONE.

You may enjoy yourself with innocent Mirth, treating one another according to Ability, but avoiding all Excess, or forcing any Brother to eat or drink beyond his Inclination, or hindering him from going when his Occasions call him, or doing or saying anything offensive, or that may forbid an easy and free Conversation, for that would blast our Harmony, and defeat our laudable Purposes. Therefore no private Piques or Quarrels must be brought within the Door of the Lodge, far less any Quarrels about Religion, or Nations, or State Policy, **we being only, as Masons, of the Universal Religion above mention'd,** *we are also of all Nations, Tongues, Kindreds, and Languages, and are resolv'd against all Politics, as what never yet conduct'd to the Welfare of the Lodge, nor ever will.*

Given the very close relationship with the stonemason guilds and the Catholic and Anglican Churches, one might be surprised to discover that the founding document of modern Freemasonry shows such apparent hostility towards and the subordination of Christianity. To be sure, this was the so-called 'Age of Enlightenment,' and modern Freemasonry was ready to champion this century of philosophy by claiming to be the Universal Religion (defined as *"The Center of Union"*) by which all men can agree versus their opinions (i.e., their particular religion or denomination). Freemasonry was also ready to take the next step down the path of the Protestant reformulation of the faith that started two centuries before them in 1517.

While the serpent in the garden asked Eve if what God said was true, and the Protestants asked us if what the Catholic Church teaches is true, the Freemasons asked us, 'Is anything outside of yourself true?' Being that the seeds of relativism, secularism, indifferentism, and naturalism all lead to that same tree in the center of Hell called nihilism, it is exporting as teaching that not only do traditional morals, ideas, and beliefs have no value, but that institutions who promote those things need to be destroyed. Since it is true to say that Protestantism and Freemasonry are not the only institutions planting the seed of nihilism, it is also true, according to several Popes - most especially Leo XIII, that the world would not be in the desperate situation it is today if Freemasonry had not ever come.

Along with this public document, defining Freemasonry as a secular organization that is immersed in relativism, secularism, indifferentism, and naturalism, there was another public and widely distributed document that Pope Clement XII would have also been aware of and thought positioned this rapidly spreading organization as a threat to the Catholic Church. By 1738, at least eight exposés were written about Freemasonry,[7] but probably none more famous than *Masonry Dissected*,[8] written by Samuel Pritchard and printed in London in 1730. Pritchard styled himself as a late member of a constituted lodge and wrote *Masonry Dissected* (see Appendix B) to be an exposé that revealed in detail the rituals, obligations, and grievous punishments of each of the three craft lodge degrees of Entered Apprentice, Fellow Craft, and Master Mason.

---

[7] A Mason's Examination (1723), The Grand Mystery of Freemasons Discovered (1724), The Secret History of Freemasonry (1724), The Whole Institution of Free-Masons Opened (1725), The Grand Mystery of the Free Masons Discover'd, Wherein are the Several Questions Put to Them at Their Meetings and Installations, also Their Oath, Health, Signs, Points to Know Each Other by, etc. (1725), The Grand Mystery Laid Open, or the Free Masons Signs and Words Discovered (1726), The Mystery of Freemasonry (1730), Masonry Dissected (1730).

[8] See Appendix B for the full text of *Masonry Dissected*, by Pritchard.

Chapter II | The Structure of Freemasonry

The objective of this chapter is to give a general outline of the structure and governance of subordinate lodges and grand lodges and an even more general outline of other Masonic bodies. There is a distinction being made here between what is appropriately called 'Freemasonry' (pertaining to the craft degrees of Entered Apprentice, Fellow Craft, and Master Mason) and what is a Masonic (based – even very loosely - upon Freemasonry) appendant/affiliated/adopted body.

The Lodge and Grand Lodge Structure and Governance

The structure of the subordinate lodge[9] consists of five elected and required officers: Worshipful Master, Senior Warden, Junior Warden, Treasurer, and Secretary (in some jurisdictions, the Treasurer and Secretary could be the same person). The appointed officers most common in all subordinate lodges are Senior Deacon, Junior Deacon, Senior Steward, Junior Steward, and Tyler. Depending on the jurisdiction and size of a lodge, it might

---

[9] In tradition craft lodges have been called blue lodge for no formally defined reason. Other older traditional names have been 'craft lodge', 'ancient craft lodge', and Saint John's lodge.

have a Chaplain, Marshall, Director of Ceremonies/Ritual Director, Almoner, Organist, Orator, Historian, and several others. The officers in a Grand Lodge typically mirror those of the subordinate lodge. However, they may also include additional ceremonial offices, such as Deputy Grand Master who would be elected or appointed to that office prior to being elected as Grand Master, a Pro Grand Master to serve in the Grand Master's stead in situations where the Grand Master is a ceremonial office reserved for the nobility and an appointed district or regional officer to represent the Grand Master in a particular assigned locality.

Unlike the subordinate lodge, which exists at the will of the Grand Lodge and the Grand Master, each Grand Lodge is entirely autonomous from any other Grand Lodge. There is no such innovation in regular Freemasonry as an Arch Grand Lodge with other Grand Lodges beholden to it, and no Grand Master outranks another Grand Master. While the constitution of the Grand Lodge of England does establish the basis upon which modern Freemasonry was built, each Grand Lodge, even those springing from the Grand Lodge of England, has their constitution and by-laws that govern their existence. Nevertheless, the regularity of a Grand Lodge is generally determined by whether its constitution contains the central and core traditions of Freemasonry, such as requiring members to profess belief in one God and the autonomy of their Grand Lodge from other Grand Lodges.

Typically, elected offices are one-year terms, and once their term has been concluded from the highest office, they are given the honorary title of Past Master or Past Grand Master (some jurisdictions confer a Past Master Degree) and are referred to as such or as Worshipful Brother. While the working tools of a Master Mason are a Square, Compass, and, in some jurisdictions, the letter 'G' in the center (for the first letters of Geometry and the Grand Architect of the Universe), for his having governed the craft with wisdom, the Past Master is given the quadrant (or protractor) as a working tool to place under the square and is given the sun to place in the center.

The subordinate lodge takes from the craft guilds in requiring their new initiates to show proficiency in their current degree before they are fully recognized as such and before they can be voted on to be advanced to the following degree. Each Grand Lodge has its standards of what is required of the initiate to show proficiency. However, it could be having them memorize large portions of their initiation ritual and the catechism or as minimal as just memorizing the obligation of their current degree.

Regular vs. Irregular Freemasonry

Modern Freemasonry has divided itself into groups of Grand Lodges that define each other as either regular or irregular, based upon the standards of each. Generally, Grand Lodges that can trace their origin (having received a charter to function as a lodge) back to the Mother Grand Lodges of England (United Grand Lodge of England – 1813 after a merger with the competing Ancient Grand Lodge), Scotland, or Ireland, all enjoy mutual recognition with each other and allows their members to visit and participate in the life of each other's subordinate lodges. The clear exception to this rule is the Prince Hall Grand Lodges (consisting predominately of Black men), which was chartered by the Grand Lodge of England in 1784 but, due to racism against Blacks, still does not enjoy mutual recognition with a small number of Grand Lodges in the southern United States and some European countries, such as Germany. Outside of these bastions of White supremacy, Anglo Freemasons and Prince Hall Freemasons enjoy mutual recognition, visit each other's lodges, and participate with each other in social and civic activities.

Then there are those lodges and Grand Lodges that descend from the Grand Orient of France, who in 1877 rejected the 1813 constitution of the United Grand Lodge of England that obligated Freemasons to accept belief in 'The Grand Architect of the Universe (GAOTU).' Whereas the prior constitution of the Grand Orient of France stated, *"Its principles of Freemasonry are the existence of God, the immortality of the soul, and human solidarity. It considers liberty of conscience as an inherent right of each man and excludes no one because of his beliefs,"* its newly adopted constitution was revised to say, *"Its principles are liberty of conscience and human solidarity. It excludes no one because of his beliefs."* This change from their 1849 constitution, which previously stated that all Freemasons must believe in God and the immortality of the soul, now allowed non-theists and Atheists to be initiated in their subordinate lodges.

Yet, the idea that this difference between theism versus non-theism is why, to this day, the vast majority of Anglo Grand Lodges deem the Continental Grand Lodges to be irregular is false. This dispute has far more to do with politics and control than it does with membership criteria. A fair comparison to this Masonic disunity is the apparent separation between the Orthodox and Latin Catholic Christians, which had far more to do with the politics of the time than any theological excuses devised later. In the instant case, the Anglo Freemasons showed their hand of hypocrisy when they first denied membership to Indians (of Asia) because of their race, and then allowed Muslim Indians, but denied Hindu Indians on the grounds of polytheism, but later allowed them to join when it was conveniently interpreted that the various deities of Hinduism were just the personification of the characteristics of one God.

Moreover, the historical preference of the Anglo Freemasons was for people of brown skin complexions to have their own lodges rather than comingle with the 'superior race.' British Freemasonry was never intended to be an export for 'inferior' races to come into the universal fraternal religion because that would mean that they were their equals and truly their brothers. In the United States, that expression of Masonic racism took the form of not only separation due to race social construct but also the denial of Black Freemasons being accepted as 'regular,' even though the charter that Prince Hall's African Lodge #459/#370 received from the Grand Lodge of England in 1784 predates the charters of most Anglo Grand Lodges in the United States.

While that position to deny Black Freemasons in the United States the term 'regular' due to their race and history began to be no longer tenable towards the end of the twentieth century. Prince Hall Grand Lodges began to be recognized and accepted by Anglo Grand Lodges worldwide. Racism in Anglo Freemasonry has never enjoyed the global acknowledgment of it being 'unmasonic behavior' and incompatible with the principles of Freemasonry. Largely, Prince Hall Grand Lodges have followed the coercive advisement of the Grand Lodge of England to not exchange mutual recognition with any Continental Grand Lodges under the penalty of losing recognition from the Mother Grand Lodge.

No one should dismiss this feud primarily between the English and the French to define what Freemasonry is. It is merely a fraternal disagreement over whether Atheists can be initiated into their order. On the contrary, the central issue is the right to influence the world through Freemasonry. On a sublevel between the British and the French, this competition is as old as the Breton – Norman war. These countries have a long history of subverting and trying to outdo each other worldwide. However, the English calling the French Freemasons irregular was a mere trifle compared to the offense given to the English when France made

Cadbury carry a label on their products stating that it was not an authentic chocolate product (i.e., "Contains vegetable fats in addition to cocoa butter.") before it was allowed to be carried on French grocery shelves.

Nevertheless, this distinction between Anglo and Continental Grand Lodges is crucial in reading Church documents on Freemasonry. While all of Freemasonry presents a philosophical danger to the faith and dogmatic teachings of Christianity, and the initial English-export of Freemasonry as a spying agency was very troublesome, the political activism found in the Oriental brand of Freemasonry, as practiced in Italy, France, and South America has always been an immediate material and existential threat to the institutional Catholic Church.

There is a peculiarity afoot in Freemasonry when it comes to Anglo Freemasons attempting to distance themselves from the openly political and anti-Catholic machinations of the Continental Freemasonry because they are not 'regular' Freemasons, as if that phrase instantly discredits their expression of the Masonic principles. It is reminiscent of how some Muslims will attempt to discredit other Muslims whose reading of the Quran leads them to commit internal and external Jihad as if it instantly discredits their acts of terrorism because they followed the Quran literally. The fact is that all of Freemasonry shares the same Masonic principles, and those principles plot against the Church. Whether some Freemasons express those principles in public and the political sphere and others express them in their private relationships is only a difference in the accidents or the articulation, but not in the substance.

There are also small groups of upstart Grand Lodges that Anglo Grand Lodges also deem to be irregular because those Grand Lodges are operating without a charter from one of the Mother Grand Lodges. Grand Lodges in this group would also include lodges consisting of women (women Freemasons) and lodges consisting of men and women (co-Freemasonry). Prince Hall Freemasonry also hands out the label of irregularity to other predominately Black Grand Lodges who have descended from them by abnormal means or are upstarts.

There is nothing more critical in Freemasonry than tradition. Innovations are looked upon with great suspicion in Freemasonry, and change is prolonged to take hold. Holding fast to their ancient traditions, rejecting substantive deviations to their ritual, and celebrating fraternal xenophobia has allowed Freemasonry to avoid having many schisms and prevented upstart Grand Lodges, claiming to be regular Freemasons, from gaining any ground. A tradition for Freemasonry speaks as a type of deposit of their faith. Each Grand Master is a magisterial voice, infallibly and dogmatically interpreting the tradition as he wills, but never in a way that would void his authority. We still have Freemasonry because they are obligated to listen, love, and follow their tradition.

Masonic Bodies Outside of the Craft Lodge

Outside of the craft lodge degrees and, primarily, the Ancient and Accepted Scottish Rite, there is no global agreement between the Grand Lodges of Freemasons about what precisely constitutes a Masonic appendant body or whether Freemasons should be members of that claimed Masonic appendant body. Moreover, from country to country, there is a diversity of structures and governance of Masonic appendant bodies. Mistakenly, these Masonic bodies that sprung up at various times and places (primarily in the 1700s and 1800s) are frequently referred to as 'higher degrees.' However, each Masonic body is autonomous from the other. Each of them entirely depends upon the Grand Lodge to which they are appendant. Therefore, there is no 'higher degrees' between rites; instead, there are 'other degrees.' For example, in Freemasonry, there is no higher degree than Master Mason. In the Scottish Rite, there is no higher degree than Sovereign Grand Inspector General – 33rd Degree (Inspector General, the Southern Jurisdiction of the United States). In Scotland's Masonic Order of the Red Cross of Constantine, the highest degree is Prince Mason. To be sure, within each order or rite, there is a progression and a higher order of degrees, but this ranking does not crossover to any other order or rite, most especially to the craft lodge, which retains the privilege to suspend any of its members, thus proving that no other degree outranks a Master Mason.

In addition to appendant Masonic orders that are open to Master Masons, there are also what are called 'Affiliated' and 'Adopted' Masonic bodies such as the Shriners (Ancient Arabic (Egyptian for Prince Hall Freemasons) Order of Nobles of the Mystic Shrine), Order of the Eastern Star (Masters Masons and close female relatives), DeMolay International and Knights of Pythagoras for boys, Job's Daughters and International Order of the Rainbow Girls for girls, and many others.

Most appendant male Masonic bodies do not require their initiates to show proficiency in their current degree to receive the next degree in that house or order. For example, in the United States, it is more commonly the case for the 4th to the 32nd degrees of the Ancient and Accepted Scottish Rite to be conferred in large sections throughout a weekend or a couple of months without any requirement to show proficiency in each degree, but, of course, this too varies from jurisdiction to jurisdiction. For the most part, outside of the United States, the progression through the AASR takes a significantly longer. Moreover, in such jurisdictions, it is not expected that each initiate into the Scottish Rite will eventually become a 32nd degree, and those who receive the

33rd degree are incredibly rarer in number than one will find in the United States.

The commonality between the appendant Masonic bodies is that Freemasons do not have to belong to them, but only Freemasons can belong to them. Their appendage relationship to their jurisdictional Grand Lodge depends on them keeping their membership exclusive to Freemasons in their jurisdiction. Other similarities would include having initiation rituals, signs peculiar to each degree offered, secret handshakes for each degree, passwords for entry into the assembly, unique regalia, and oaths on the Holy book of a major religion.

Ridley notes that in Scotland, the freestone masons adopted a code word that only qualified master masons would know so that they could recognize each other and prevent entered apprentices from performing their work and receiving their wages. *"The code word became known as the 'Mason Word.' It was probably 'Mohabyn,'*[10] *which has links with the word 'marrow,' meaning 'mate' or 'comrade,' which was in use in Scotland until the nineteenth century."*[11] The operative masons in the southern English counties and the rest of Europe had no use for a code word because all freestone masons already knew each other.

Joining Freemasonry and Lodge Meetings

Most Grand Lodge jurisdictions still follow the tradition of the stonemason guilds, where outsiders were required to petition the guild to be accepted as an apprentice, and their petition

---

[10] According to Masonry Dissected by Samuel Pritchard (See Appendix B), the Master Mason's word issued in the third degree is "Machbenah," which signifies The Builder is smitten. Pritchard's 'Machbenah', Ridley 'Mohabyn', and the word 'Mahabone' that is found in most third degree rituals are all very similar.

[11] Ridley, Jasper. *The Freemasons: A History of the World's Most Powerful Secret Society.* Arcade Publishing. New York. 2011. 7-8.

was subsequently voted upon. It has historically been frowned upon and even forbidden for Freemasons to recruit new members. It was thought to be vitally important for new members to seek out membership on their own and come knocking at the lodge's door on their own free-will and accord. Yet, some jurisdictions have struggled to attract new members to offset their aging membership, affecting their subordinate lodge's finances and ability to function as required. In response to this problem, some Grand Lodge jurisdictions and appendant Masonic bodies have recently launched advertising campaigns to attract new members and make it easier to obtain membership in the appendant rites. One such event held in several Grand Lodge jurisdictions in the United States is often called a 'Degree Day' where hundreds of candidates, rather than participate in the conferral of the degrees, watch it being exemplified on a stage while they remain seated. In the Grand Lodge of Ohio, these 'Degree Days' have been taking place for over a decade and seem to have been proven successful, as it now boasts of having around 75,000 members spread across 450 subordinate lodges.

No one knows precisely how many Freemasons there are in the world, but by conservative estimates, there are somewhere under 2.5 million in the United States and about that same number throughout the rest of the world, of which the bulk of them are in Europe and in countries that either speak English or were heavily influenced by England; such as India, New Zealand, Australia, South Africa, and the Philippines. Freemasonry was outlawed by the China Communist Party but retained a small presence in nearby countries, such as Malaysia, Japan, and South Korea. Out of the continent of Africa's fifty-four countries, there are only seventeen Anglo Grand Lodges in operation. In many countries heavily influenced by the Islamic religion and who also reject so-called 'western ideology,' Freemasonry is considered a threat and has not been allowed to plant a firm footing. Even in countries with the largest Muslim populations, such as Indonesia and Pakistan, Freemasonry has been outlawed since 1961 and 1972, respectively. Inasmuch as Freemasonry claims to be the universal religion/brotherhood and the center of union by which all men agree, it has only been able to accomplish this goal in countries where there is not already a religion that has unified the citizenry. On the contrary, Freemasonry thrives wherever Protestantism and its seeds of division and confusion thrive.

Typically, subordinate lodges hold meetings either once or twice a month. One meeting of the month would be a regular business or communication meeting in which the routine events of any organization will take place, such as paying utility bills, collecting membership dues, organizing the fish fry next month, and issuing checks to donate to various charities. The second meeting would be a ritualistic meeting for the conferral of a degree. This meeting might be a regularly stated meeting or a special meeting that the subordinate lodge will ask their Grand Lodge to give them a dispensation to hold. Suppose it is a stated meeting, and no candidate can confer a degree. In that case, the subordinate lodge will use this time to either practice some portion of one of the degrees or listen to someone give a talk on some aspect of Freemasonry.

Grand Lodge jurisdictions usually require their subordinate lodges to meet a minimum of times during the year. Some lodges will 'go dark' for months when many members are on vacation, such as during the summer or winter months. A minimum number of members is required to be present for a subordinate lodge to be able to meet (i.e., a quorum). That number typically depends on which of the three degrees a subordinate lodge decides to open their meeting in. Grand Lodges typically have one formal Grand Lodge session a year, to which all members are invited. At these Grand Lodge sessions, new Grand Lodge officers might be elected, and programs and workshops will be held to advance the Grand Master's agenda. A Grand Master will also tend to require his District Deputies to hold a District Meeting once a year for all of the district's subordinate lodges to gather to discuss his agenda.

Chapter III | Freemasonry is a Religion

The purpose of this chapter is to demonstrate how Freemasonry is a syncretic fraternal religion according to what Freemasonry says about itself and the path to salvation that it conveys upon its candidates through its rituals (Sacraments).

Given that Freemasonry took rise from the stonemason guilds, which were very faithful to and friendly with the religion of their employers, it was natural for its philosophical system to retain much of that Christian character, inasmuch as it repurposed it to advance their agenda of indifferentism, relativism, secularism, and naturalism.

Generally speaking, most Freemasons will vehemently disagree that Freemasonry is a religion, simply on the uncritical opinion that:

1) Freemasonry does not have a dogma or theology;
2) Freemasonry does not have a magisterium to enforce orthodoxy;
3) Freemasonry does not confer sacraments; and
4) Freemasonry does not claim to offer a path to salvation through works, secret knowledge, or other means.

On the contrary, there are three senses by which we can verify that Freemasonry has not only a religious character or nature but that it is an actual religion: First, it incorporates syncretism, meaning that it has an established religious belief system that incorporates elements, practices, and traditions from other religions into itself. Second, as described in the 1723 *Anderson's Constitution*, Freemasonry is a replacement/substitute polytheistic religion that proclaims itself to be the *"Center of Union"* of all religions and to be that universal religion by which all men can agree. In this system, all other monotheistic religions are subordinate to Freemasonry's *"Universal religion,"* all members are obliged to call the God of their religion or their god the name or title, 'Grand Architect of the Universe.' Third, Freemasonry is a religion in form because it exhibits the five principal character marks of a well-established religion: 1. Posits that there is a God or gods, 2. Posits a Moral Law, 3. Offers sacraments or the means for their members to draw nearer to God/the gods or the means for personal betterment; 4. Intends for those sacraments or means to lead to a life after death, and 5. Has the ability on a global or local level to enforce or normalize tradition, regularity, moral law, and orthodoxy through an authority figure(s) and/or utilizing a magisterial interpretation of a sacred text. In the case of Freemasonry:

1) Freemasonry professes a named God (Grand Architect of the Universe), and it obliges its members to refer to their God as,
2) Freemasonry has a Moral Law that obliges all of its members to obey. The consequence of not obeying Masonic moral law may lead to either suspension or expulsion following the summary judgment of their Grand Master or by a trial in their lodge,

3) Freemasonry has Sacraments through which their mysteries and beliefs are conveyed or professed,
4) Through the working tools conferred on the initiate through their Sacraments, Freemasonry offers a path and means of self-improvement by which its members will be better enabled to reach an afterlife and
5) Grand Lodges act as a magisterial body that enforces tradition, regularity, moral law, and orthodoxy by granting or withdrawing recognition from other Grand Lodges.

Examining their Sacraments is the most central argument in proving that Freemasonry is a religion. The Sacraments of Freemasonry are the three degrees of Entered Apprentice, Fellow Craft, and Master Mason. Through these sacred rites and mysteries, the initiate is enlightened and given the working tools that will enable them to progress in their craftsmanship and become worthy of further advancement.

As speculative masons, the initiate is expected to understand how an operative mason would use their working tools to perfect their building craftsmanship and to apply those same principles to building themselves into a stone fit for that house not made with hands, eternal in the heavens.[12] For example, as an operative mason might use a twenty-four-inch gauge to lay and measure their work, the Freemason is taught to use that same gauge to lay and measure their day – to divide the gauge into three equal parts, where they will find eight hours for labor, eight hours for refreshment, and eight hours for rest. As an operative mason would use a level to make their work straight, the Freemason is taught that the level measures equality. It intends to give as a reminder that death is the great equalizer, and upon the level,

---

[12] Cf. Jn. 14:1-3, 2 Cor. 5:1-4, 1 Peter 2:1-8.

each mason travels to that *"undiscovered country from whose born no traveler returns."*[13]

What the fraternal religion of Freemasonry is offering through its Sacraments is a personal and self-determined path to salvation. This teaching that man can save man, not through supernatural means, but rather through naturalistic methods and personal effort is the heresy of Pelagianism revisited. Through its sacraments, Freemasonry is offering its initiates the autosoteric method of deliverance from immorality through personal freedom and due attention to moral discipline, which is the opposite of the Christian hetrosoteric delivery method that demands that man must be saved by another (namely, Jesus Christ).

Even the garments of Freemasonry have mysterious, religious, and sacramental significance. For example, as the operative mason would have covered the entire front of his body with lambskin to protect himself from debris and rough stones, the Freemason is taught that white lambskin apron represents *"purity of life and rectitude of conduct that is essential and necessary to gain admittance into that Celestial Lodge on High where the Supreme Architect of the Universe forever presides."*[14] The idea of a new white garment covering an initiate's body is not a concept lost on any religion. It is something that the stonemasons would have been familiar with from the Sacrament of Baptism in both Catholic and Anglican Churches where candidates for Baptism are clothed in white over-garments.

---

[13] "Undiscovered country" is a popular line from many lessons given on the meaning of the level in the Fellow Craft degree in Freemasonry that was borrowed from Hamlet. See: Marshall, Jeffery E., *Freemasonry and the Undiscovered Country.* http://www.themasonictrowel.com/Articles/Freemasonry/philosophy_files/freemasonry_and_undiscovered_country.htm (Retrived 11/19/2019).

[14] Mackey, Albert G. *Mackey's Revised Encyclopedia Volume 1.* The Masonic History Company, 1929.

At the near opening of each of the three craft lodge degree ceremonies, the initiate is brought in blindfolded to the center of the lodge and caused to knell in a manner unique to that particular degree and is told to repeat the words said to them. These words are their obligation pertaining to the degree that is about to be conferred upon them. In each degree obligation, the candidate promises to keep the secrets of that degree, under pain of some gruesome penalty, and with the help of their personal God. After they have made their obligation, their blindfolds are then removed. They are given the central secrets of that particular degree, consisting of the lights they see around the altar, the setting of the square and compass on an open Bible, the chapter and verse that the square and compass rest, and signs and tokens of that same degree. After this, the candidate is conducted around the lodge for inspection and further instruction.

It is not unknown for Freemasons to casually dismiss where the founding document of Freemasonry (*Anderson's Constitution* of 1723) twice calls it a 'universal religion' because each Grand Lodge (though springing from the Grand Lodge of England whose founding constitution that is) is independent, autonomous, and has their constitution that does not call Freemasonry a universal religion. Yet, hypocritically, they will refer to *Anderson's Constitution* to point out the longstanding rule that *"no private Piques or Quarrels must be brought within the Door of the Lodge, far less any Quarrels about Religion, or Nations, or State Policy,"* as proof that Freemasonry is not a religion.

Their central argument in opposition to Freemasonry being a religion is that because Freemasonry forbids its members from speaking about religion during a lodge meeting, Freemasonry must not be a religion. On the contrary, this high sophistry completely misses the mark. Again, if Freemasonry is a syncretic religion that has subordinated every other religion under itself and refers to each man's personal God as the polytheistic Grand Architect of the Universe, confers sacraments, obligates its members on the holy book of their choice, and incorporates all types of other religiosity. It does not need to bring up any other religions, because it is a religion unto itself. Arguing that Freemasonry is not a religion because its members are not allowed to speak of other religions during the lodge meeting is like saying Catholicism is not a religion because the Priest never speaks about Protestantism during his homily or that Islam is not a religion because the Iman never mentions Judaism during his Friday sermon at Jummah. Such an argument is entirely illogical and flies in the face of basic reason.

It is an unfortunate happenstance that Freemasonry has, for the past three hundred years, marketed itself as a mere fraternity and cleverly dogged, through word manipulation, claims that it is a syncretic fraternal religion. Unfortunately, religious scholars and religious studies programs have missed out on the research analysis opportunity that such an admission would have presented to the world.

Like Judaism, Freemasonry also avoids the feminine because it does not have a female voice or image of their Grand Architect of the Universe. As a religion, Freemasonry should be classed as a Protestant denomination, one that similarly inveighs against the Catholic Church, and one that has given birth to other Jesus Christ-professing religions, such as Mormonism. Some might decline to call Freemasonry a Protestant religion because it never explicitly mentions Jesus Christ in the Craft Lodge degrees. However, there should remain no question once we consider all of the implicit allusions to Christ that are found in the degrees. Freemasonry may be the only mainstream Protestant religion that started as a guild of Catholic tradesmen, and that in itself should be something intriguing for religious studies programs to dig deeper into.

The idea of a syncretic fraternal religion is also unique to study because Freemasonry proposes a gnostic type of revelation. The central question that religious studies pose to every religion is, 'What did it bring that was new?' Even as one of the thousands of Protestant denominations, should that question be asked of Freemasonry, I believe the new thing or renewed thing that it has brought to the world was a pagan polytheism under the guise of a fraternal-based syncretic monotheism. Again, that in itself is something interesting to study.

The Legend of Hiram Abiff

Being that the guilds of Europe were popularly known for their public plays,[15] it was not surprising that Freemasonry would also move to convey its mysteries through myth, drama, pageantry, and allegory in a manner that explains to their initiates how their religion came to be. The legend of Hiram Abiff at King Solomon's Temple appears to be an amalgamation of various legends down through the ages together with a Biblical text to fit into the theme and purpose of the Master Mason degree, which is to signal to the candidate that the work of a Master Mason is never over until his labors on earth are completed. He finally receives his reward/his wages in Heaven. During the third degree, the initiate is also obligated to know about some of the important intricacies of the building of King Solomon's Temple,

---

[15] The Mason's Company of Newcastle were required by their charter to act out the play *The Burial of Our Lady Saint Mary the Virgin* on Corpus Christi Day every year. The Mason's Company of Chester acted with the Goldsmith' Company in *The Destroying of the Children by Herod*. Ridley, Jasper. *The Freemasons: A History of the World's Most Powerful Secret Society*. Arcade Publishing. New York. 2011. 9. Lane, *The Outwith London Guilds of Great Britain*, 5, 9, 17-18.

such as the names, dimensions, and ornamentation of the pillars outside the Temple.

According to the myth of Freemasonry, there were fifteen Fellow Crafts at the building of King Solomon's Temple, who were given charge over the other Fellow Crafts and Apprentices. When the building of the Temple was nearly complete, the fifteen began to sense that they might be cheated out of 'the secrets of a Master Mason' (password and signs that will give them a higher wage in Continental Freemasonry) that had been promised and organized a conspiracy to obtain them by any means necessary; even violence. When the hour came to execute their grand scheme, twelve of the fifteen recanted of the machinations, but the others, Jubelo, Jubela, and Jubelum, more savory than the other twelve, moved forward with their impious designs to take what had been promised them and which they felt entitled to.

Knowing their master, Hiram Abiff had a pattern of retiring at the hour of high twelve to devote himself to the Most High; they went to lay in wait for him at the temple's east, north, and south entrances. After Hiram Abiff finished his devotions, he attempted to return to his labors by entering through the south entrance. He was accosted by the first ruffian who used a heavy plum rule working tool to threaten his life should he not disclose to the ruffian the secrets of a Master Mason. Hiram Abiff did not lie when he told the ruffian that the secret was only known to three people in the world: himself, Hiram, the King of Tyre, and King Solomon, and by obligation, he would not divulge the secret, even if it cost him his life. Instead, Hiram pleaded with the ruffian that if he would be patient, he would receive what was promised to him once the building of the Temple was completed. Not satisfied with this answer, the ruffian aimed a violent blow at the forehead of Hiram but missed, striking his right temple instead. Hiram fell on his left knee and found a way to escape to the North entrance, where he was accosted by a second ruffian who wielded a level as an instrument of death and demanded from Hiram Abiff the secrets of a Master Mason. After Hiram refused this ruffian the same as the first, this one attempted to land a fatal blow on his Master by striking him on the left temple. Hiram fell this time on his right knee but was able to flee to the East entrance, where the third ruffian was stationed. After refusing to divulge the secrets of a Master Mason this third time, this villain, armed with a heavy maul, used it to deliver Hiram a fatal blow to his forehead.

Having killed their Master, the Jubelo, Jubela, and Jubelum now have to figure out what to do with the body. They decided to bury it under a pile of rubble for now but later moved it outside of the city and buried it in a shallow grave that they marked with a sprig of acacia.

The next day, King Solomon is confused about why the craftsmen are wandering around the temple and not working. The workmen tell King Solomon that they are wandering because there are no building plans on the drawing board; therefore, they do not know what to do. Alarmed at this news, King Solomon sends out a group of Fellow Crafts in search of him. It just so happens that one of the search parties finds the sprig of acacia on top of a pile of rubble and a body underneath it. After investigating their corpse, they discover that it is the slain body of their Master, Hiram Abiff. They also found the three ruffians hiding nearby, for they had been unable to escape because they did not have the password to leave the country. Upon returning to the temple, the ruffians confess their crimes, are taken away, and never heard from again. Seeing the body of Hiram Abiff lying lifeless on the ground, King Solomon attempts three times to raise him from the dead, but each time, his grip slips, and he cannot raise him. Now that one of the only two of three people in the entire world who knew a portion of the secrets of a Master Mason is dead, King Solomon decrees that the secrets of a Master Mason are lost and replaces them with substitutes. In Continental Freemasonry, the secrets are not lost. However, so that no one ever again tries to obtain them unlawfully, King Solomon orders them to be buried under the Temple, inscribed on Hiram's grave. He then creates a substitute for them instead.

If King Solomon had raised Hiram Abiff from the dead, Freemasonry could never have been charged as being a denier of the supernatural. However, he was not, nor does Freemasonry rely on any source of truth beyond what can be known by the five human senses. This aspect of Freemasonry compelled Pope Leo XIII, in his encyclicals *Humanum Genus* and *Custodi Di Quella Fede,* to declare that naturalism is a core principle of the Masonic sect.

Some appendant Masonic bodies continue to build upon this emblematical myth outside the subordinate lodge. For example, in the Mark Master Degree (often called the 4th Degree), which in some jurisdictions is an autonomous house and in other systems is part of the Royal Arch or Holy Royal Arch houses, the candidate learns that before Hiram Abiff's assassination, he was charged to make a 'keystone.' This 'keystone' has significant meaning for the lessons that his degree intends to convey. Wherever the Ancient & Accepted Scottish Rite (AASR) is an appendant body of a Grand Lodge, only their 4th to 33rd Degrees are worked in that jurisdiction; that is, if a candidate for their rite is already a Master Mason, they will not have the 1st through 3rd degrees conferred upon them again. However, the AASR works a version of the Legend of Hiram Abiff in their Master Mason degree.

The History of Prohibitions Against Freemasonry

Chapter IV | In Eminenti

P ope Clement XII (1730 – 1740) was born Lorenzo on April 7, 1652, and into the Corsini aristocratic family that had produced at least one cardinal of the Catholic Church in every generation for one hundred years. They even had a saint in the family: Saint Andrew Corsini, a Carmelite friar and Bishop of Fiesole.

Lorenzo was educated at the Collegio Romano at the University of Pisa. After his father and his cardinal uncle died in 1685, he renounced his inheritance as the eldest son and entered the clergy. By 1690, he was the Archbishop of Nicomedia, and in 1706, Pope Clement XI made him a Cardinal. Later, Pope Benedict XIII elevated him to the headship of the Holy Office of the Inquisition. After Benedict XIII died in 1730, a four-month-long conclave ensued, which finally elected Lorenzo, who then took the name Clement XII in honor of his benefactor. He was seventy-eight then and would exercise his Petrine ministry until his death on February 6, 1740.

Pope Clement XII's first year in office was highly productive. He worked to repair the finances of the Church, which were ruined by his predecessor, by bringing to trial and imprisoning Cardinal Coscia for embezzlement and forcing Benedict XIII's other assistants to repay the monies they had stolen. To further refill the papal coffers, Clement XII relaunched the lottery system, issued paper money, taxed imports, and created a free-port at Ancona. He also drained marshes and built aqueducts. By year two of his papacy, he became blind and bedridden with gout and a hernia. He would spend the rest of his Pontificate governing from his bed, but no less ambitiously, thanks to the assistance of his nephew Neri Maria Cardinal Corsini (1685 – 1770).

One of the most lasting actions of Pope Clement XII's papacy was issuing his Apostolic Constitution *In Eminenti apostolatus specula* (The High Watch) on April 28, 1738. This constitution (issued as a 'Papal Bull') is the basis upon which the Catholic Church's objection to Freemasonry is built and grounded. This Constitution sets forth the precise reasons for how Freemasonry plots against the Church, why it is a danger to the faith, and why Catholics are forbidden from joining, associating with, or promoting it and any of its appendant bodies.

Every Catholic Christian needs to comprehend the condemnations and prohibitions that Pope Clement XII outlined in *In Eminenti* because they are dogmatic, lasting, permanent, irrefutable, and reflect the core principles of Freemasonry as it is practiced in every sect and Grand Lodge, whether Anglo or Continental, regular or irregular.

In Eminenti apostolatus specula
(The High Watch)
Pope Clement XII - 1738

(numbers (#) added to the paragraphs)

CLEMENT, BISHOP, Servant of the Servants of God to all the faithful, Salutation, and Apostolic Benediction.

Since the divine clemency has placed Us, Whose merits are not equal to the task, in the high watch-tower of the Apostolate with the duty of pastoral care confided to Us, We have turned Our attention, as far as it has been granted Us from on high, with unceasing care to those things through which the integrity of Orthodox Religion is kept from errors and vices by preventing their entry, and by which the dangers of disturbance in the most troubled times are repelled from the whole Catholic World.

(1) Now it has come to Our ears, and common gossip has made clear, that certain Societies, Companies, Assemblies, Meetings, Congregations or Conventicles called in the popular tongue Liberi Muratori or Francs Massons or by other names according to the various languages, are spreading far and wide and daily growing in strength; and men of any Religion or sect, satisfied with the appearance of natural virtue, are associated with one another in a union, according to their laws and the statutes laid down for them, by a strict and unbreakable bond which obliges them, both by an oath upon the Holy Bible and by a host of grave penalties, to an inviolable silence about all that they do in secret together. But it is in the nature of crime to betray itself and to show itself by its attendant clamor. Thus these aforesaid Societies or Conventicles have caused in the minds of the faithful the greatest suspicion, and all prudent and upright men have passed the same

judgment on them as being depraved and perverted. For if they were not doing evil they would not have so great a hatred of the light. Indeed, this rumor has grown to such proportions that in several countries these societies have been forbidden by the civil authorities as being against the public security, and for some time past have appeared to be prudently eliminated.

(2) Therefore, bearing in mind the great harm which is often caused by such Societies or Conventicles not only to the peace of the temporal state but also to the well-being of souls, and realizing that they do not hold by either civil or canonical sanctions; and since We are taught by the divine word that it is the part of faithful servant and of the master of the Lord's household to watch day and night lest such men as these break into the household like thieves, and like foxes seek to destroy the vineyard; in fact, to prevent the hearts of the simple being perverted, and the innocent secretly wounded by their arrows, and to block that broad road which could be opened to the uncorrected commission of sin and for the other just and reasonable motives known to Us; We therefore, having taken counsel of some of Our Venerable Brothers among the Cardinals of the Holy Roman Church, and also of Our own accord and with certain knowledge and mature deliberations, with the plenitude of the Apostolic power do hereby determine and have decreed that these same Societies, Companies, Assemblies, Meetings, Congregations, or Conventicles of Liberi Muratori or Francs Massons, or whatever other name they may go by, are to be condemned and prohibited, and by Our present Constitution, valid forever, We do condemn and prohibit them.

(3) Wherefore We command most strictly and in virtue of holy obedience, all the faithful of whatever state, grade, condition,

order, dignity or pre-eminence, whether clerical or lay, secular or regular, even those who are entitled to specific and individual mention, that none, under any pretext or for any reason, shall dare or presume to enter, propagate or support these aforesaid societies of Liberi Muratori or Francs Massons, or however else they are called, or to receive them in their houses or dwellings or to hide them, be enrolled among them, joined to them, be present with them, give power or permission for them to meet elsewhere, to help them in any way, to give them in any way advice, encouragement or support either openly or in secret, directly or indirectly, on their own or through others; nor are they to urge others or tell them, incite or persuade them to be enrolled in such societies or to be counted among their number, or to be present or to assist them in any way; but they must stay completely clear of such Societies, Companies, Assemblies, Meetings, Congregations or Conventicles, under pain of excommunication for all the above mentioned people, which is incurred by the very deed without any declaration being required, and from which no one can obtain the benefit of absolution, other than at the hour of death, except through Ourselves or the Roman Pontiff of the time.

(4) Moreover, We desire and command that both Bishops and prelates, and other local ordinaries, as well as inquisitors for heresy, shall investigate and proceed against transgressors of whatever state, grade, condition, order dignity or pre-eminence they may be; and they are to pursue and punish them with condign penalties as being most suspect of heresy. To each and all of these We give and grant the free faculty of calling upon the aid of the secular arm, should the need arise, for investigating and proceeding against those same transgressors and for pursuing and punishing them with fitting penalties.

Given at Rome, at Saint Mary Major, in the year 1738 of Our Lord.

Paragraphs 1 – 2:
In paragraphs 1 and 2, Pope Clement XII delineates the four interconnected errors of Freemasonry and his motives behind forbidding Catholics from associating with it in any positive manner:
1. Freemasonry is an error, vice, danger, and a disturbance in the Catholic Church; being such, the Orthodox Religion needs to be kept free from it, lest it (Freemasonry) breaks into the household of God like thieves and like foxes seeking to destroy the vineyard.
2. Freemasonry caters towards/relies on/was established on the appearance of natural virtue (i.e., indifferentism) and its own law. It obligates men by an oath on the Bible and by a host of grievous punishments and silence about what they do in secret together.
3. Being that the meetings of Freemasonry take place in secrecy, they lack transparency and cause rumors. Due to this, the faithful have great suspicious about it.
4. Societies like these disturb the peace of the temporal state and the well-being of souls.

Paragraph 1:

In paragraph one, Pope Clement XIII defines Freemasonry. First, he notes the diversity and breadth by which Freemasonry is spreading rapidly throughout Europe, and then immediately names the first error by which men are casually entering into association with this order, writing, *"and men of any religion or sect, satisfied with the appearance of natural virtue, are joined together..."* The subordination of religious differences (in particular, the minimizing of the truth of the Catholic faith) under the appearance of being united under the common standards of decency, honesty, and probity is, at a minimum, an immoral effort at ecumenism but more than likely it is an evil effort at indifferentism. Gathering multiple religions together under one arch-religion is not fraternity; it is syncretism.

Pope Clement XII also hints at the 1723 *Anderson's Constitution* declaration on Freemasonry being the *"universal religion"* by rightly discerning that Freemasonry subordinates religious differences by establishing their own *"laws and the statutes laid down for them, by a strict and unbreakable bond which obliges them, both by an oath upon the Holy Bible and by a host of grave penalties, to an inviolable silence about all that they do in secret together."* Here, Clement XII notes the irreconcilability between Catholicism and Freemasonry in regard to its laws and statutes. Being that the Catholic Church has its own laws and statues that she obliges her children to obey, it is impossible for a Catholic to obligate themselves to obey a different and distinct body of laws and statues under the coercion of secrecy and grave penalties.

Having to choose between obeying the laws and precepts of the Church or those of another entity is not a position that Catholics should ever place themselves in. For example, it may be the case that a subordinate lodge may summon a member to a lodge meeting, but on the same day of the summons, the Catholic might be required to participate in a solemn feast day. Now, this person has a choice; if they fail to appear at the lodge on the call of a summons, they may face expulsion from the Masonic order, but if they fail to appear at the Holy Mass, they incur grave sin.

While there are many civil offices in which a Catholic might make an oath on the Bible, those duties should never conflict with their duties to God, neighbor, and self. Nor should they be exercised in secret, lest they stir up the appearance of scandal and bring disrepute upon one's Church, community, and household.

By the time Clement XII promulgated *In Eminenti apostolatus specula*, Freemasonry had been banned in the Netherlands, Sweden, and Geneva. It had also been suppressed and persecuted in parts of Spain, Portugal, France, and Italy. *"... in several countries these societies have been forbidden by the civil authorities as being against the public security, and for some time past have appeared to be prudently eliminated."* Therefore, Pope Clement XII is not acting arbitrarily here, even though, as the Shepherd of all Christians, he has the right to exercise such care. Rather, he is signaling that there is a maturing sense of the faithful that Freemasonry is *"depraved and perverted."*

Paragraph 2:

This paragraph is divided into three sections: 1) An explanation as to why it belongs to the Apostolic duty to keep watch over the Lord's Household; 2) A statement on how the decision was arrived at collegially, not arbitrarily; cardinals of the Catholic Church were consulted, and research into the works of Freemasonry was conducted, and 3) A statement on his Apostolic authority to dogmatically decree Freemasonry to be condemned and prohibited forever.

The dogma of the infallibility of the Pope when speaking *ex-cathedra* (literally, from the throne – i.e., from his chair, from the seat of Peter) would not be defined until July 18, 1870, at the First Vatican Council. It was on that day the Church taught and defined this pre-existing practice[16] as a divinely revealed dogma that the Roman pontiff speaks *ex-cathedra*, when:

---

[16] Most Catholic theologians agree that Blessed Pope Pius IX's 1854 encyclical *Ineffabilis Deus* (The Immaculate Conception) is a one clear example of a pre-Vatican I exercise of a Pope speaking *ex cathedra*.

1. In the exercise of his office as shepherd and teacher of all Christians,
2. In virtue of his supreme apostolic authority, and
3. He defines a doctrine concerning faith or morals to be held by the whole church.

When these three things occur, the First Vatican Council taught that the Roman Pontiff *"possesses, by the divine assistance promised to him in blessed Peter, that infallibility which the divine Redeemer willed his church to enjoy in defining doctrine concerning faith or morals."*

By virtue of this teaching being consistently and explicitly repeated by seven different Popes after it was first promulgated by Pope Clement XII (including in two Canon Laws)[17] over the span of nearly two and a half centuries, it is not arguable that *In Eminenti apostolatus specula's* prohibitions against Freemasonry rightly belongs in the body of dogmatic teachings of the Catholic Church. Yet, as to whether this Apostolic Constitution was another pre-Vatican I exercise of Papal infallibility is arguable. Clement XII does meet most of the criteria that the First Vatican Council set forth, such as: *In Eminenti* does define what Freemasonry is, it does remind us of Pope Pius XII's 1950 encyclical *Munificentissimus Deus* in regard to how other bishops were consulted on the matter prior to its promulgation and how there is an appeal to the sense of the faithful, it does make a clear statement on Apostolic authority, and it does argue through defining terms that this prohibition against Freemasonry is a matter of

---

[17] *In Eminenti apostolatus specula* (1738) - Pope Clement XII, *Providas Romanorum* (1751) - Pope Benedict XIV, *Etsi Multa* (1873) - Pope Pius IX, *Humanum Genus* (1884), *Officio Sanctissimo* (1887), *Dall'alto dell'Apostolicio Seggio* (1890), *Custodi Di Quella Fede* (1892), *Inimica Vis* (1892*)*, *Praeclara Gratulationis Pune fois encoreublicae* (1894) - Pope Leo XIII, *Une Fois Encore* (1907) – Pope Pius X, 1917 Code of Canon Law No. 2335 – Pope Benedict XV, 1983 Code of Canon Law – Pope John Paul.

faith and morals. The only criteria that it is missing, in comparison to how it was exercised by Blessed Pope Pius IX *(Ineffabilis Deus* – 1854) and Pope Pius XII, is that it was not issued from the literal throne of Saint Peter (*ex-cathedra*) at Peter's Basilica; rather, it was promulgated from the throne of Saint Mary Major.

Nevertheless, the condemnations and prohibitions against Freemasonry and *"whatever other name they may go by"* that are found in this Constitution are to be permanently (*"valid forever"*) binding upon all Christians (*"the Lord's household"*). In addition, there are no distinctions of Freemasons or Masonic sects made in this constitution, based upon their region, country, nationality, constitution, regularity, or irregularity.

Paragraph 3:

In this section, Pope Clement XII exercises his authority as Shepherd of all Christians. The precision here by which he refuses to leave any ground to negotiate or enter into ecumenism with Freemasons is historic for Papal documents but not unknown to the sacred Scriptures. *Psalms* 1:1-3 also informs us not to hold company with evildoers. The Apostle Saint Paul warned the Thessalonians to *"abstain from every form of evil"*[18] and instructed the Church at Corinth to remove from their Church the man who was living with his father's wife.[19]

Not only are all of the faithful, of every state, grade, condition, order, dignity, and pre-eminence, both clerical and lay, forbidden from becoming Freemasons, but they are not even allowed to promote the Masonic order, receive Freemasons into their home, hide them (e.g., they are fleeing persecution), or to be associated with them in any way. Public servants or those who

---

[18] 1 Thess. 5:22.
[19] Cf. 1 Cor. 5:2.

have authority over buildings are not allowed to have Freemasons meet in their facilities. The faithful are not allowed to give any public or secret encouragement or support to the Freemasons – directly or indirectly. If anyone is found not staying entirely away from Freemasons and their institutions, that person could be excommunicated *latae sententiae* (i.e., automatically by virtue of the act itself, incurred at the moment of the offense and *"without any declaration being required"*). Moreover, the only way one can be absolved from this grave sin is at the hour of death or by the Pope himself.

According to the 1983 *Quaesitum Est*, which will be discussed later, it is still the case today that *"The faithful who enroll in Masonic associations are in a state of grave sin and may not receive Holy Communion."* However, according to the 1983 Code of Canon Law (Canons 1364 – 1399), the only grave offenses that merit *latae sententiae* ex-communication reserved to the Apostolic See are: *"one who throws away the consecrated species or, for a sacrilegious purpose, takes them away or keeps them"*; *"a person who uses physical force against the Roman Pontiff"*; *"both the bishop who, without a pontifical mandate, consecrates a person a bishop and the one who receives the consecration from him"*; *"a confessor who directly violates the sacramental seal"*; and a confessor who absolves *"an accomplice in a sin against the sixth commandment of the Decalogue."*

Therefore, according to Canon Law and Church teaching, enrolling in the Masonic order still merits a *latae sententiae* excommunication, but it can now be resolved through the Sacrament of Penance and Reconciliation by a Priest, which is the same remedy today for those who procure a completed abortion or *"an apostate from the faith, a heretic or a schismatic."*

From *In Eminenti* till today, there has never been a change in the Church's prohibitions against Freemasonry, since the remedy to cure those afflicted by this sin of grave matter has been made more readily available and accessible through a Catholic priest.

Paragraph 4:

In this section, Pope Clement XII moves to enlist every resource available inside the Church and in the secular space (e.g., local police) to squash the heresy of Freemasonry wherever it is found and rid the Catholic Church of all Freemasons. No matter the person's *"state, grade, condition, order dignity or pre-eminence . . . they are to pursue and punish them with fitting penalties."*

Three years prior to the Catholic Church issuing this prohibition against Freemasonry, a proclamation was issued at The Hague on December 12, 1735, by the President and Council of Holland, Zeeland, and Friesland stating that *"certain persons here at The Hague, under a specious pretense of belonging to a so-called Fraternity of Freemasons, meeting together under a Grand Master,"* had formed an illegal association; for *"it is in no way to be supposed that the study of architecture is the sole and principal object of their meetings."* The proclamation cited that the fundamental objective behind these secret meetings was faction and debauchery, and, for this reason, they are illegal. The action required by this proclamation called for law enforcement authorities to prevent such meetings from being held, and anyone who allowed a room in their house to be used for a Freemason's meeting was committing an offense.[20]

The Netherlands, by this time in history, had become predominately Calvinist, and, therefore, the issue here with this as-

---

[20] Proclamation of the Council at The Hague, December 12, 1735 (Early Masonic Pamphlets, 333-334). Ridley, Jasper. *The Freemasons: A History of the World's Most Powerful Secret Society.* Arcade Publishing. New York. 2011. 49.

sociation of Freemasons did not involve a religious objection; rather, the objection was one of politics. Freemasonry was principally thought to be an English export. Since the so-called 'Glorious Revolution' of 1688, England had a parliamentary government that observed the rule of law over the sovereign rule of a monarch. For this reason, Freemasonry would continue to be viewed with high suspicion, even in Protestant countries, until the revolutions against monarchial rule would sweep through the rest of Europe.

As a borderless and secret association with its own laws and governance, the Freemasons always maintained friends, even within its pack of enemies, by initiating into its ranks prominent noblemen, enforcers of the law, and influencers of society throughout Europe. One such instance was Charles Sackville, Earl of Middlesex (soon to be Duke of Dorset), who formed the first lodge of Freemasons in Florence during the final year of his grand tour (from 1731 to 1733). Charles was a Protestant, but the lodge members he formed were primarily English Catholics who had fled to Florence over their support of the House of Stuart and James II and his efforts to restore religious toleration to Catholics.

As they were called, these English Jacobite (Lat. Jacobus for James) Catholics were responsible for establishing several lodges throughout Italy. Among the most prominent was Charles Radclyffe, Earl of Derwentwater, who was beheaded in December of 1746 as a traitor to England over his role in the Jacobite rebellion the previous year. Even though many influential Freemasons occupied offices in the English government that could have intervened and saved their lodge brother from capital punishment, their loyalty to the country and their hatred of Catholics prevailed over their obligation as Freemasons to protect each other.

By 1736, in Paris, France, the number of Freemasons in the city had increased to nine different lodges. Among those numbers were the Prince of Cinti, all the Dukes of France, and even the Count of Maurepas.[21] By March 29, 1737, the police of Paris had forbidden taverns and meeting houses from hosting Masonic meetings due to a *"great Feast"* that had caused a noticeable degree of property damage.[22] In contrast, the Florentine Freemasons were much quieter. However, in 1737, they had earned a visit by the Holy Inquisitor, who was sent there by Pope Clement XII to prosecute them at the request of the Duke of Tuscany. This persecution went nowhere after Francis Stephen, Duke of Lorraine, succeeded him upon death that same year. Francis's initiation into Freemasonry at The Hague in 1731 had been widely reported in the press in England.

Pope Clement XII's first two motives behind *In Eminenti apostolatus specula* clearly concern Freemasonry's threat to Catholicism's worldview through its promotion of indifferentism, secularism, and relativism. The Catholic Church firmly holds that she alone was established by Christ Jesus, through His Apostles, to be the center of union of all people and that there is no salvation outside of His One, Holy, Catholic, and Apostolic Church. Juxtaposed to this orthodoxy of the faith is the teaching of Freemasonry that it is a 'universal religion' and the *"Center of Union, and the Means of conciliating true Friendship among Persons that must have remain'd at a perpetual Distance."*[23] Both of these concepts cannot be true, and there is not enough space in God's creation for them to mutually coexist.

---

[21] Read, Will. The Church of Rome and Freemasonry. Ars Quator Cornoatorum Transactions. Vol 104. (1991).
[22] Ibid.
[23] Anderson, James. *Constitutions of the Free-Masons. Containing the History. Charges. Regulations. &c. of that most Ancient and Right Worshipful Fraternity.* 1728. Article I.

Aside from Pope Clement XII's two religious objections, two others concern the threat that Freemasonry poses to the temporal state as a parliamentary ruled-English export.

3. Since the meetings of Freemasonry take place in secrecy, the lack of transparency causes rumors. Due to this, the faithful have great suspicious about it.
4. Societies like these disturb the peace of the temporal state and the well-being of souls.

Evident in these final two errors is a rational and well-placed fear about what these Englishmen and their sympathizers were meeting about in secret. For all the outsiders knew, Freemasonry was an English spy agency. The English spies worked with their sympathizers in these secret lodge meetings to plot a revolution. In these secret meetings, they could be stirring up passion about a world without monetary rule. This brand of circulating gossip and rumors surrounding these secret meetings of Freemasons was disturbing the peace of the temporal state and the well-being of souls.

Even Pope Clement XII's nephew, Neri Maria Cardinal Corsini, showed some degree of allegiance or favor towards the Freemasons in writing to his uncle, in the wake of *In Eminenti*, a letter to assure him that Freemasonry in England is merely an innocent amusement.[24] However, if Pope Clement XII sympathized with the intentions of the House of Stuart to restore Catholicism in

---

[24] Scanlan, Matthew. *The Pope and the Spy.* Freemasonry Today. Issue 25. Summer 2003. "In a letter written in the wake of the bull, the Cardinal emphasizes that he found that freemasonry in England was nothing more than an "innocent amusement", but that in Florence it had degenerated into a "school of atheism" and clearly identified Stosch as the man responsible for such degeneration." Baron Philip von Stosch was trusted agent of King George II and worked as a spy paid by Holland. In 1720 he was sent by Britain to Rome to spy on the James Stuart of the exiled House of Stuart, and would eventually made his headquarters in Florence, Italy.

England and viewed Freemasonry as a Protestant-like export from England, Corsini's letter would have fallen on deaf ears.

The immediate outcome of *In Eminenti apostolatus specula* is that the prohibitions against Freemasonry were enforced in all of the Papal States (also called the Republic of Saint Peter) in Italy and many Catholic countries, lodges were dissolved, and the Supreme Sacred Congregation of the Roman and Universal Inquisition began to appointment commissioners throughout Europe to investigate individuals who were reported to have ties to Freemasonry. Some of these individuals were cleared of all charges against them. In contrast, others were excommunicated, tortured, imprisoned, banished, and sentenced to serve as slaves in the galleys. Some were even sentenced to death for the grave sin of heresy.

Nevertheless, Freemasonry would continue to spread throughout the world. Wherever you found Englishmen and/or Protestantism, lodges of Freemasons would follow, and for the next three centuries, the Catholic Church would continue to follow these findings of Pope Clement XII and reaffirm her perspicuous positions against Freemasonry, most especially in regards to the charge of Freemasonry having a plotting indifferentism towards all monotheistic religions; in particular towards the true faith of Catholicism.

Chapter V | Providas Romanorum

Pope Benedict XIV (1740 – 1758) was one of the strongest theologians to ever pass through the Seat of Peter. The depth of his many works of theological prose and wit even won him the admiration of the French deist (by reason, not by faith) philosopher Voltaire, who dedicated his play *Mahomet the Prophet* to Benedict XIV in writing, *"To the head of the true religion, a writing against the founder of a false and barbarous religion."*[25]

Born Prospero Lorenzo Lambertini in Bologna, Italy, on March 31, 1675, some of his significant accomplishments as Pope included revising the calendar and martyrology, laying down guidelines on beatifications and canonizations, refuting Saint Thomas Aquinas' finding that the relics of Christ's blood could not be authenticated, originating the papal 'encyclical' letter, and establishing guidelines on mixed marriages between Catholics and Protestants to require an oath on the part of the non-Catholic partner to raise their children in the Catholic faith and that such marriages could not take place within the liturgy of the Holy Mass because the couple could not receive communion together.

---

[25] Coulombe, Charles A. *A History of the Popes: Vicars of Christ*. MFJ Books. New York. 2003. 384.

Despite enjoying such an impeccable reputation as a leader and a theologian, Pope Benedict XIV could not escape the rumors that he and some of his cardinals had been initiated as Freemasons.[26]

In the Kingdoms of Spain and Naples, there was a growing need to act more strongly against the threat and infiltration of Freemasons. The constitution of Pope Clement XII against Freemasonry was only thirteen years old. However, it was old enough for some to raise doubts about its validity because his successor had not affirmed it since he took office on August 17, 1740. Therefore, the Kings of Spain and Naples pressed upon Pope Benedict XIV to affirm *In Eminenti apostolatus specula* in some manner that would give them ecclesial backing to continue the work to suppress Freemasonry.[27]

Following the promulgation of *Providas Romanorum*, the Kings of Spain and Naples issued decrees suppressing Freemasonry. In countries that had previously ignored *In Eminenti*, this new Constitution was also disregarded.

---

[26] Benimeli, José Antonio Ferrer. *La masonería española en el siglo XVIII.* Siglo Veintiuno Editores; 2a ed. corr edition. 1986. 97.
[27] Ibid., 107, 118 - 120.

Providas Romanorum
(Roman Providence)
Pope Benedict XIV - 1751

Bishop Benedict, servant of the servants of God.
A perpetual memory.

We consider it a duty, with a new intervention by Our authority, to uphold and confirm - in so far as correct and serious reasons require - the provident laws and sanctions of the Roman Pontiff Our Predecessors: not only those laws and those sanctions whose vigor or process of the time or for the carelessness of the men we fear it is possible to slow down or to extinguish, but also those that have recently obtained strength and full force.

1. In fact, Clement XII, Our Predecessor of Happy Memory, with his own Apostolic Letter of April 28 of the year of the Incarnation of the Lord 1738, the eighth year of his Pontificate - Letter addressed to all the faithful and which begins In eminent - condemned for always and forbade some Societies, Unions, Meetings, Meetings, Conventicles or Aggregations commonly called of the Freemasons or des Francs Maçons, or otherwise called, already then widely diffused in certain Countries and that now more and more increase. He forbade everyone and individual Christians (under penalty of excommunication to incur ipso facto without any declaration, from which no one could be absolved by others, except at the point of death, other than the Roman Pontiff pro tempore) of attempting or daring to enter such companies, propagate them or give them favor or shelter, hide them, register to them, to join or intervene, and more, as in the same Letter more widely and more widely is contained. Here is the text.

[*In Eminenti apostolatus specula* is inserted here in the body of *Providas Romanorum*)

3. But since, as far as we have been told, some have had no difficulty in affirming and publicly disseminating that the said excommunication penalty imposed by Our Predecessor is no longer operative because the relative Constitution has not been confirmed by Us, as if it is necessary, for the Apostolic Constitutions to maintain validity, the explicit confirmation of the successor;

4. And having been suggested to Us, by some pious and God-fearing people, that it would be very useful to eliminate all the subterfuges of the slanderers and to declare the uniformity of Our soul with the intention and the will of the Predecessor himself, adding to its Constitution the new vote of Our confirmation;

5. We certainly, until now, when we have benignly granted absolution from the excommunicated excommunication, often first and foremost in the past year of the Jubilee, to many faithful who are truly repentant and sorrowful for having transgressed the laws of the same Constitution and which they assured from the heart to move away completely from similar societies and conventicles, and that for the future they would never have returned; or when we granted the Penitentiaries delegated by Us the power to give absolution in Our name and with Our authority to those who resorted to the Penitentiaries themselves; and when with prompt vigilance we did not fail to see to it that the competent judges and tribunals proceeded in proportion to the crime committed against the violators of the Constitution itself, which was actually carried out several times; we have certainly provided arguments that are not only probable but completely evident and unquestionable, through which the dispositions of

the Our soul should have been understood and the firm and deliberate willing consent with the censorship imposed by the aforementioned Clement Predecessor. If a contrary opinion were to spread about Us, We could surely despise it and remit Our cause to the just judgment of Almighty God, pronouncing those words that were once recited in the course of the sacred functions: "Grant, O Lord, we pray you, that We do not cure the slanders of perverse souls, but having crushed the same perversity we plead that You do not allow us to be afflicted by unjust slanders or enveloped by cunning adulation, but rather that we love what You command ". Thus reports an ancient Missal attributed to San Gelasio, Our Predecessor, and that from the Venerable Servant of God Cardinal Giuseppe Maria Tommasi was inserted in the Mass which is called Against slanderers.[28]

6. However, so that it could not be said that We had imprudently omitted something, in order to easily eliminate the pretexts for lying liars and to close their mouths; having first heard the advice of some Venerable Our Cardinal Brothers of the Holy Roman Church, we have decreed to confirm the same Constitution of Our Predecessor, word by word, as reported above in a specific form, which is considered to be the widest and most effective of all: we confirm, we validate, we renew and we want and we decree that it has perpetual strength and effectiveness for Our sure science, in the fullness of Our Apostolic authority, according to

---

[28] Mention here is made of an "ancient Missal attributed to San Gelasio," which is referring to the so-called Gelasian Sacramentary – only second to the Verona Sacramentary as being the oldest known books on the Latin/Western liturgical rites. The Gelasian rite was a mixture of the older Roman and Gallican rites. This rite ceased being worked with the issuance of Pope Hardian's Sacramentary that he created at the request of Charlemage to unify the liturgy in the empire. Yet, apparent from this constitution, there are some prayers against slander from it that were reinserted into the liturgy of Trent in some Churches.

the tenor of the same Constitution, in everything and for everything, as if it had been promulgated with Our motu proprioand with Our authority, and had been published for the first time by Us.

7. In truth, among the very serious reasons of the aforementioned prohibitions and condemnations set forth in the aforementioned Constitution there is one, by virtue of which men of any religion and sect may unite with one another in such Societies and Conventicles; it is clear what harm can be done to the purity of the Catholic religion. The second reason is the closed and impenetrable promise of secrecy, by virtue of which hides what is done in these meetings, to which the sentence that Cecilio Natale, with Minucius Felix, allegedly put in a very different case: "The honest things always love public light; the wicked are secret." The third reason is the oath with which they undertake to observe inviolably this secret, as if it were lawful for someone, questioned by legitimate power, with the excuse of some promise or oath to avoid the obligation to confess all that is sought, to know if in these Conventicles something contrary to the stability and the laws of the Religion and the Republic is done. The fourth reason is that these societies oppose civil sanctions no less than the canons, bearing in mind, in fact, that in accordance with civil law all the colleges and meetings formed without public authority are forbidden, as we read in the *Pandects* (book 47, title 22, De Collegiis et corporibus illicitis), and in the famous letter (n. 97 of the book 10) of C. Plinio Cecilio, who, reports that it was forbidden for his Edict, according to the commandment of the Emperor, that the Aetheries were held , that is that they could exist and reunite Companies and meetings without the Prince's authorization. The fifth reason is that in many countries the aforementioned Societies and Aggregations have already been proscribed

and banned with laws of Secular Princes. Finally, the last reason is that among the prudent and honest men the aforementioned Societies and Aggregations were blamed: in their judgment, anyone who enrolled in them was accused of blasphemy and perversion.

8. Finally the Predecessor himself exhorts the Bishops, Prelate Superiors and other Ordinaries of the places in the above Constitution not to neglect to invoke the help of the secular arm if it is necessary for the execution of this provision.

9. All these things, even individually, are not only approved and confirmed by Us, but also recommended and enjoined on Ecclesiastical Superiors; but we ourselves, through the debt of the Apostolic solicitude, invoke with our present letter and with deep affection seek the help and help of Catholic princes and secular powers - being the same supreme princes and mayors elected by God as defenders of the faith and protectors of the Church - so that it will be their responsibility to work in the most effective way so that the Apostolic Constitutions may be given due respect and absolute obedience. This brought to their memory the Fathers of the Council of Tridentine (sess. 25, chap. 20), and much earlier the Emperor Charlemagne had very well declared it in his Specifications (tit. I, chap. 2), in which, "In no way can we know how those who are unfaithful to God and disobedient to his priests can be faithful to us." Consequently, he imposed on all the Presidents and Ministers of his provinces obliging all individuals to give due obedience to the laws of the Church. He also committed very serious penalties against those who neglected to do this, adding among other things: "Those who in these things (which does not happen) will be found negligent and transgressors, know that they will not hold honors in our Empire, even

though they are ours children; nor will they have a place in the Palace, neither with us nor with our faithful will they have society or community, but rather they will pay the penalty in the distresses and in the constraints ".

10. We also want the copies of the present, even if printed, signed by the hand of some Notary public and bearing the seal of a person constituted in Ecclesiastical dignity, the same faith is given that would lend itself to the Letter if it were exhibited or shown in the original.

11. To no one therefore, absolutely, is it allowed to violate, or with fearless daring, contradict this page of Our confirmation, innovation, approval, commandment, invocation, request, decree and will. If anyone dared so much, know that he will incur the indignation of Almighty God and the Holy Apostles Peter and Paul.

Given in Rome, at Saint Mary Major, on March 18 of the year of the Incarnation of the Lord 1751, the eleventh year of Our Pontificate.

Paragraph 1:

In this section, Pope Benedict XIV explicitly confirms that his predecessor's condemnation against Freemason associations promulgated in In Eminenti apostolatus specula is *"for always"* and for *"everyone and individual Christians."* The condemnation is not only for being initiated into the society of Freemasons but also for those supporting them, sheltering them, hiding them, affiliating with them, intervening for them, and more. The penalty for doing these things is *ipso* facto/latae sententiae excommunication. This section is followed immediately by inserting the complete text from *In Eminenti apostolatus specula.*

Paragraph 3 - 4:

In these paragraphs, Pope Benedict XIV states that the motive for writing *Providas Romanorum* is because there is a contention being circulated by *"slanderers"* that intends to create subterfuge by claiming that *In Eminenti apostolatus specula "is no longer operative"* because the new pontificate has not confirmed it. This is a claim that Benedict XIV measuredly disputes by quipping, *". . . as if it is necessary"* for an Apostolic Constitution to maintain is validity by being explicitly confirmed by the succeeding Pope. The idea that a Papal document such as *In Eminenti* that promulgates things to be forever true (i.e., dogmatic) should expire after the document's author dies or resigns from the Papacy is ludicrous. How could a thing be dogmatic if it dies or loses its truth over time?

Paragraph 5:

Here, the Pontiff continues to show how his actions have always been in continuity with his predecessor on this issue. He notes that in the previous year, he offered the faithful the opportunity to receive absolution for the sins associated with the prohibition against Freemasonry by giving the authority to *"penitentiaries"* (i.e., a priest who has the faculties to administer the Sacrament of Penance and Reconciliation) to grant absolution for the sins that *In Eminenti* reserved to the purview of Supreme Pontiff alone. He also states that he *"did not fail to see to it"* that competent judges and tribunals proceeded *"in proportion to the crime committed against the violators of the Constitution itself, which was actually carried out several times."*

Pope Benedict XIV views it as slanderous that some would hold that his Pontificate is friendly towards Freemasonry. For this, he invokes a prayer against slanderers found in the ancient Gelasian liturgy, *"Grant, O Lord, we pray you, that We do not cure the slanders of perverse souls, but having crushed the same perversity we plead that You do not allow us to be afflicted by unjust slanders or enveloped by cunning adulation, but rather that we love what You command."*

Paragraph 6:

In this paragraph, Pope Benedict XIV states that the reason for including the entire text of *In Eminenti* into the body of this constitution was because it was considered to be *"the widest and most effective"* method to confirm, validate, and renew the prohibition against Freemasonry was by the decree of Apostolic authority that it is the perpetual teaching of the Church. Benedict XIV's use of the universal 'We' of the Church intends to bring his voice in continuity with the voice of his predecessor but also with all the bishops of the Church in his present age and the future. Bringing *In Eminenti* into this constitution gives it the same weight as if it *"had been promulgated with Our motu proprio and with Our authority* [that is, by our own accord and authority], *and had been published for the first time by Us."*

Paragraph 7:

In this section, Pope Benedict XIV restates the reasons found in *In Eminenti* for the prohibition against Freemasonry due to these six issues:

1. Indifferentism and false ecumenism: the Catholic Church's central and most powerful theological argument against Freemasonry is that the idea of men of any

religion and sect binding themselves together in a brotherhood and uniting together under the name of one generic god harms the purity of the Catholic religion. Benedict XIV believes, as all Catholics should that there is something truly exceptional about Catholicism that needs to be preserved and not treated like a prostitute and shared with mixed company as if she is equal to or lesser than them.

2. Inviolable secrecy: Freemasons not only take vows never to disclose the secrets of a Master Mason, but they also meet in secret with one another. *"The honest things always love public light; the wicked are secret."* Benedict XIV draws upon this quote from the Catholic writer Marcus Minucius Felix, a second or third-century Latin-speaking writer and lawyer from northern Africa, demonstrating how well-read he is. In his apologetic dialogue *Octavius*, he is represented by his character Ottavio, who challenges Cecilio Natale (Caecilius) over his pagan beliefs in adoring the god Serapis. Cecilio would like to invite Minucio to judge their controversy, but he declines to be a religious umpire. The dialogue is crafted in such a way as to give Ottavio a stronger argument. However, Cecilio is too proud to admit defeat. This was a peculiar quote for Benedict XIV to use because Cecilio made it against Christianity. After all, Christians cannot even see their God; they have *"no altars, no temples, and no acknowledged images."*

3. Subversive secrecy: Freemasons take these oaths are subversive to society because they oblige Freemasons to avoid making a good confession. This objection points back to the political problem of Freemasonry being an

export from England that may be intent on causing revolution and disruption to the monarchial system. Secondarily, it is also a religious objection because such secrecy could invalidate the conferral of the Sacraments on a person.
4. Meetings violate the law; there were laws in place throughout European countries that required permits for groups to meet. Owners of meeting facilities were expected to ensure that people meeting in their facilities had permission to gather there. Such as laws even in the United States today, where groups need a permit to hold public marches and parades. On university campuses, organizations must meet specific standards to hold meetings on school property. While this objection to Freemasonry meeting illegally may no longer be applicable in most parts of the world today, it does not then, thereby, invalidate any of the other errors.
5. A sense of the faithful; there was a growing sense outside of Protestant Europe that Freemasonry was a danger and a threat. Here, Pope Benedict XIV confirms that even thirteen years later, our prohibition against Freemasonry is still in harmony with where the public is on this issue. Again, the world is much bigger today than it was in 1751. However, it is true that wherever Protestantism and religious indifferentism are accepted as the norm, Freemasonry can be legally practiced.
6. Scandal: the final reason for the prohibition is that Catholics view those who belong to Freemasonry as blasphemers and heretics. It is still true today that faithful Catholics know that Catholics who are enrolled in the Masonic orders are living contrary to the faith and are committing a sin that is of grave matter. To see people

like these receive the Holy Eucharist and participate in the life of the Church (without correction) causes scandal and actual harm to other's spiritual life.

Paragraphs 8 - 9:

In these sections, Pope Benedict XIV reiterates the call that Pope Clement XII made to require all the Bishops, Prelate Superiors, and Ordinaries to enforce these prohibitions against Freemasonry and *"to invoke the help of the secular arm if it is necessary for the execution of this provision."* He then goes a step further to call upon the help of Catholic Princes and secular powers by the authority of his office and their duty to God to be *"defenders of the faith and protectors of the Church,"* according to the Council of Trent's Eighth Decree on the Reformation concerning the immunities, liberty, and other rights of the Church that are recommended to Secular Princes. If that were not enough, Benedict XIV recalls Emperor Charlemagne's charge to obligate all of the faithful to be obedient to the laws of the Church under pain of severe penalty.

Paragraphs 10 – 11:

In paragraph 10, Pope Benedict XIV requires that every recipient of this constitution have it signed by a notary and attach their seal of office thereto. Then, in Paragraph 11, he commands that no one shall violate or contradict any part of this constitution. If anyone should dare to, they will *"incur the indignation of Almighty God and the Holy Apostles Peter and Paul."* In this way, Benedict XIV ends *Providas Romanorum* with a dire warning of a grave penalty similar to how the servant John ended the account of his *Revelation*.[29]

---

[29] Cf. Rev. 22:18-19.

Providas Romanarum would be the final Papal document that explicitly and specifically addressed the error of Freemasonry until Pope Pius IX's *Etsi Multa* in 1873. Until then, four documents would address the broader subject of secret societies,[30] as others had cropped up around Europe and the Americas that were exercising similar philosophies and political agendas as Freemasonry, such as the Carbonari.[31] Three documents attacked the heresy of indifferentism,[32] which is the first objection that Catholicism has to Freemasonry.

The critical instance of Pope Leo XII's (1823 – 1829) 1826 *Quo Graviora* followed a similar format to *Providas Romanorum* by including the text of *In Eminenti, Providas Romanorum, and Ecclesiam a Jesu Christo* to demonstrate that the prohibition against Freemasonry and the Carbonari is a permanent (dogmatic) teaching of the Church. It also invoked the wrath of Ss. Peter and Paul, as did *Providas Romanorum*. Distinct from the three previous documents, *Quo Gaviora* was issued from the Seat of Peter, together with all other factors included, qualifies it as having met the future criteria of being an infallible pronouncement of a Supreme Pontiff. Also distinct was the fact that *Quo Graviora* not only repeated the prohibition against Freemasonry and the Carbonari, but it also extended that same prohibition to all secret societies then present in 1826 and all those that will come in the future that rise against the Catholic Church:

> *"Since matters are in such a state, We judge it to be the Character of our Office to Condemn these clandestine sects again, and in such a manner indeed that no one of them can boast*

---

[30] *Quo Graviora,* Pope Leo XII (1825), *Traditi Humiltati,* Pope Pius VIII (1829) and *Qui Pluribus,* Bl. Pope Pius IX (1846).
[31] *Ecclesiam a Jesu Christo,* Pope Pius VII (1821).
[32] *Mirari Vos,* Pope Gregory XVI (1832), *Inter Multiplices,* Bl. Pope Pius IX (1853), and *Quanto Conficiamur Moerore,* Bl. Pope Pius IX (1863).

that they are not encompassed by Our Apostolic Pronouncement, and under this pretext lead careless and less sagacious men into error. Therefore, from the Counsel of Our Venerable Brethren, the Cardinals of the Holy Roman Church, and also by Our own motion indeed with Our certain knowledge and mature consideration, We forbid forever under the same penalties which are contained in the Letters of Our Predecessors already reported in this Our Constitution, which Letters We expressly confirm, that all secret societies, those which now are and those which perhaps will afterwards sprout out, and which propose to themselves against the Church and against the highest civil powers those things which We have mentioned above, by whatever name they may finally be called."

Despite the efforts of the Catholic Church to protect the faithful and to expose evil for what it is, the world would continue to see Freemasonry spread in every country where Protestantism and indifferentism had been normalized.

Freemasonry Seduces Mozart and Haydn

One of the great early successes of Freemasonry outside of England, where it was most welcomed, was Vienna, Austria, through the strident efforts of Joseph II, Holy Roman Emperor. Although his Catholic father, Emperor Francis I (Holy Roman Emperor in title only), had been a Freemason, his mother, Maria Theresa, ruled as sovereign for forty years after succeeding her father, Emperor Charles VI, who died in October 1740, and had faithfully implemented the Catholic Church's prohibition against Freemasonry;. However, police in her Austro-Hungarian Empire declined to pursue aristocrats who were known to be Freemasons.

With a Holy Roman Emperor comes a court, which becomes a magnet for those seeking influence and wealth. As the court at the imperial capital of Vienna began growing in fame and influence, it also grew in affection towards Freemasonry under Joseph II, which was partly due to a child-like reaction to them being punished for so long. Free of the suppression of Maria Theresia, Freemasonry was now all the rage. Even the symbols of Freemasonry found their way onto women's clothing, and wearing white gloves like the Freemasons became fashionable.

Freemasonry in Vienna was known for its gathering together of intellectuals and artists. Such notable Catholics who had become Freemasons in Austria include composer and virtuoso pianist Johan Nepomuk Hummel, mineralogist and metallurgist Ignaz von Born, composer, conductor, music teacher, and violinist Leopold Mozart, Angelo Soliman (born Mmadi Make in around the Gulf of Guinea Africa), Wolfgang Amadeus Mozart, and Joseph Haydn. Also notable among this group was the composer, conductor, and teacher Alexander von Zemlimsky, whose parents were Catholic, but he was born a Jew due to his parents converting to Judaism, the religion of his great-grandmother.

The most curious of all the notable and apparently 'faithful' Catholics in Austria at that time who decided to reject Church teaching and become Freemasons was Joseph Haydn. Known as the father of Symphonic form and of the String Quartet,[33] Haydn often prayed the rosary to help him compose his symphonies. Jones notes that when Haydn became a Freemason, it was *"fashionable to do some amongst the Viennese aristocracy, bourgeoisie, and mercantile classes, an admixture of society that Haydn had already encountered in the emerging salon culture of the*

---

[33] Rosen, Charles. *The classical style: Haydn, Mozart, Beethoven* (2nd ed.). Norton. New York. 1997. 43-54.

decade, and he would have viewed it as a natural extension of that milieu."³⁴

According to Masonic lore, Wolfgang Amadeus Mozart played a role in seducing Haydn into Freemasonry. The society that the older composer thought he was joining is described in this 1785 petition letter to join the lodge Zur Wahen Eintracht:

"The advantageous opinion I formed about the Freemasons awakened in me, a long time ago, the sincere desire to join this Order with its humanitarianism and wise principles. I turn to you, Sir [the master of ceremonies of the lodge], in the hope that through your kind intervention at the Lodge of which you are an honored member, you may be able to further my sincere wish."³⁵

If Haydn had been duped, as many have, in thinking he was joining a social organization that does philanthropic work after his initiation as an Entered Apprentice, what he then heard might have taught him the truth about what Freemasonry actually practices. After the lodge meeting had been concluded, the brethren gathered together for a meal, and it was at that time when a toast was offered by Joseph von Holzmeister, Chief Clerk of the Imperial War Ministry, in which he noted his new brother's accomplishments in music and attempted to demonstrate how musical compositions are aligned with the principles of Freemasonry, in saying (**bold** added for emphasis),

"Brother Initiate had created a new order in the orchestra . . . If every instrument did not consider the rights and properties other instruments, in addition to its own rights, if it did not often diminish its own volume in order not to do damage to

---

³⁴ Jones, David Wyn. *The Life of Haydn*. Cambridge University Press. New York. 2009. 120.
³⁵ Jeffers, Paul H. *Freemasons: Inside the World's Oldest Society*. Kensington Publishing Corp. New York. 2005. 71.

the utterances of its companions, the end, which is beauty and harmony, would not be attained. I know of no more dignified, no more delightful concept than a society of upright men, each driven to drink from the spring of wisdom to find truth and share it with others for the common good – a Society where shining and enlightenment does not give rise to jealousy but is rather a source of emanation where the manly handclasp is the sign of a heart expanded by much greatness, not the mask of false friendship where man may open his heart to man without having to fear prejudice, hate or intrigue. A society in which the meetings give joy to every member – an event to which each one looks forward with pleasure and leave with deep satisfaction.

Harmony can be, indeed must be, the characteristic of the order as a whole. It must be the center-point of each Lodge – the essential strength through which beauty is defined in the whole of nature: without it nature itself must fall, and the starry firmament must sink with the each into chaos. You newly elected Brother Apprentice, know especially well the designs of this heavenly gift of harmony. To praise all her charms to you would be superfluous. ***I content myself if, in this brother talk, I have awakened in you the desire to remain steadfast to your Goddess (Harmony) in this circle, new my brother, to you.***"[36]

Whether it was that clear exposition of heresy in Holzmeister's toast that awakened Haydn to the conflict that the paganism of Freemasonry has with the truth of Catholicism or the fact that he was just too busy with his music to be bothered with carrying on with the lodge, Haydn never attended another meeting

---

[36] Ibid., 72.

at lodge Zur Wahen Eintracht again, and by 1787 had been dropped from their membership roster.

The story was dramatically different for Wolfgang Amadeus Mozart, who found friends and a home in Freemasonry. His famed Masonic opera *The Magic Flute* was created in concert with Johann Emanuel Schikaneder, who wrote its libretto as propaganda for Freemasonry. However, it was not the only work of Mozart intended to exemplify his religious fraternity's ideals. In the same year that *The Magic Flute* was released and became very popular in Vienna, Mozart fell ill and died at home on December 5, 1791, at 35. The rumors circulating after his death were that he had been murdered, perhaps by his wife and her lover, by the husband of Mozart's mistress, or by the Freemasons who were angry that *The Magic Flute* revealed their secrets.

Along with the works of Masonic music left unfinished by Mozart, it was also his Catholic requiem mass. However, it was completed in early 1792 by Catholic Franz Xaver Sussmayr for the Requiem service for the wife of Count Franz von Walsegg.

The Illuminati and the Rosicrucians

Next door to Austria in Bavaria, another sworn enemy to the Catholic Church was forming. Just as lodges of Freemasons originally consisted of Catholics, so too was the Illuminati started by an ethic Jew who was a Baptized Catholic and a Canon Law professor at the Jesuit-run University of Ingolstadt in Bavaria.[37] On May 1, 1776, Adam Weishaupt and four students established the 'Perfectibilists' (later renamed the 'Illuminati') with the Owl of Minerva as their symbol.

---

[37] The Society of Jesus (Jesuits) had been dissolved in 1773 by order of Pope Clement XIV but, thanks to having accumulated substantial wealth, were still active throughout the world as owners of corporations and as independent educators.

Weishaupt seemed to want to build something like Freemasonry with a system of degrees, secret handshakes, and passwords, but to *"put an end to the machinations of the purveyors of injustice to control them without dominating them."*[38] In short, Weshaput was attempting to collect a small group of men who would act as puppet-masters to overthrow the Catholic Church, governments, and monarchs so that the Illuminati could usher in a new world order. The Illuminati's most tremendous success was infiltrating Freemasonry and gaining control of numerous lodges through which they redesigned the first three degrees and elevated the most promising Master Masons into the Illuminati. They also successfully recruited aristocrats, clerics, university professors, doctors, and lawyers.

While the Illuminati wanted to tear down and reconstruct the world as it was, their enemy was the Rosicrucians, who were more inclined to a Protestant-flavored brand of mysticism and philosophy. This secret society envisioned a world that was friendly toward monarchial rule but was also influenced by philosophy, science, reason, and magic. The Rosicrucians had been around since the early seventeenth century. However, they had won significant influence in Germany and used it to weaken the Illuminati there.

The Masonic United States of America

Given their reputations for having subversive political agendas, the Freemasons and the Illuminati were often the first groups people blamed for the revolutions breaking out throughout Europe and America. Indeed, there were many Freemasons who fought with the revolutionaries in France (1789 – 1799), and of the fifty-six signers of the Declaration of Independence (July

---

[38] Dülmen, Richard van Dülmen. *The society of the enlightenment: the rise of the middle class and enlightenment culture in Germany.* Polity Press. Cambridge. 1992. 110.

4, 1776), at least ten of them were Freemasons[39], and many more fought in the war against Great Britain (1775 - 1783). On top of that, eight of the first twenty-five Presidents of the United were Freemasons.[40] Suppose Weishaupt's idea of 'the few influencing the many' proved effective. In that case, it is reasonable to believe that these groups may have been responsible in some way for these revolutions. However, no irrefutable evidence, such as lodge meeting minutes, has been found to prove such a claim.

From its founding, the United States of America was influenced by the principles of Freemasonry, particularly the concept of freedom found in its *Declaration of Independence*. Although Thomas Jefferson, who drafted the Declaration of Independence, was not a Freemason, he worked closely in France with Gilbert du Motier, Marques de Lafayette, a Freemason and a French aristocrat and military officer. With the recommendation of his Masonic Brother Benjamin Franklin, Lafayette went on to command American troops during the American Revolution. Afterward, he returned to France, where he played a vital role during the French Revolution of 1789 and the July Revolution of 1830.

"We hold these truths to be self-evident, that all men are created equal, that they are endowed by their Creator with certain unalienable Rights, that among these are Life, Liberty and the pursuit of Happiness..." This opening line of the preamble of the Declaration of Independence is an appeal to reason and natural

---

[39] According to Masonic researcher Paul Bessel (http://bessel.org/decl-mas.htm - retrieved 12/06/2019). William Ellery, Benjamin Franklin, John Hancock, Joseph Hewes/Howes, William Hooper, Thomas McKean (perhaps), Robert Treat Paine, Richard Stockton, George Walton, William Whipple.

[40] George Washington, James Monroe, Andrew Jackson, James K. Polk, James Buchanan, Andrew Johnson, James A. Garfield, and William McKinley. The others who are known to have been Freemasons include Theodore Roosevelt, William H. Taft, Warren G. Harding, Franklin D. Roosevelt, Harry S. Truman, and Gerald Ford.

law as evidence by which man comes to know that he was created by a nameless Creator and given three rights that cannot ever be revoked. Those three rights are (1) life, (2) liberty, and (3) the pursuit of happiness. Here, we see traces of the nameless Grand Architect of the Universe and what Freemasonry values most: freedom from political, religious, and military oppression. According to Masonic teaching, political oppression, religious darkness, and military tyranny can be extinguished by the power of the three great lights of Freemasonry.

Out of this darkness, the Entered Apprentice is first brought to light. However, before he is given that opportunity, he must first announce that he is free. He must be a free-man and not an enslaved person, and he must come to knock at the lodge's door on his own free will and accord. Then, upon initiation, he learns that one of the tools of an operative Entered Apprentice is chalk, which for the Freemason symbolizes freedom; that is, the ability to draw his lines within the bounds of Freemasonry. This freedom is freedom from religion and from adhering to religious laws, revealed truth, and dogma. For, the religion of Freemasonry already has its own revealed truths, laws, and authority that are higher and a more noble calling than the lower religions to which it subordinates itself. What is truly self-evident in this context is that the freedom proposed by Freemasonry and by the Declaration of Independence always devolves into indifferentism, relativism, secularism, and naturalism.

In this way, the First Amendment of the *Constitution of the United States*, *"Congress shall make no law respecting an establishment of religion, or prohibiting the free exercise thereof..."* is yet another import from Freemasonry to promulgate the idea of freedom from religion, freedom from state and the church having a relationship (thus keeping Freemasonry free from religious persecution), and everything pertaining thereto. Truly, the ideas of freedom from religion and separation of church and state found in the First Amendment read remarkably similar to the ideas found in the first article of Anderson's Constitution:

I. Concerning GOD and RELIGION.

A Mason is oblig'd by his Tenure, to obey the moral law; and if he rightly understands the Art, he will never be a stupid Atheist nor an irreligious Libertine. But though in ancient Times Masons were charg'd in every Country to be of the Religion of that Country or Nation, whatever it was, yet 'tis now thought more expedient only to oblige them to that Religion in which all Men agree, leaving their particular Opinions to themselves; that is, to be good Men and true, or Men of Honour and Honesty, by whatever Denominations or Persuasions they may be distinguish'd; whereby Masonry becomes the Center of Union, and the Means of conciliating true Friendship among Persons that must have remain'd at a perpetual Distance.

In this first article, Freemasons are obligated to separate themselves from the religion of the state and to set themselves apart from the religion of 'opinion' altogether. Freemasonry does not deny that man needs religion. However, it finds it more expedient to establish in itself a new religion "in which all Men agree". It will, thereby, become their *"Center of Union."* Pope Leo XIII also saw the intimate relationship between this form of Masonic-inspired government and the principles and desires of Freemasonry. In his 1884 *Humanum Genus,* Leo XIII called it an expression of 'naturalism.'

The Masonic Republic of France

In France, Thomas Jefferson served as a consultant to Freemasons Abbé Sieyès, Marquis de Lafayette, and Honoré Gabriel

Riqueti, Comte de Mirabeau, in their drafting of the *Declaration of the Rights of Man and of the Citizen* (1789). Like the *Declaration of Independence* and portions of the *Constitution of the United States*, the seventeen articles of this revolutionary document are grounded in naturalism and the 'enlightenment' principles of personal autonomy, freedom from religion, and freedom from the State having a relationship with religion.

The *Declaration of the Rights of Man and of the Citizen* was the first revolutionary document of its kind. It was also the most irreligious and anti-Catholic thing ever produced by Freemasons to press a revolution inspired by the principles of Freemasonry, namely, indifferentism, naturalism, and freedom from religion. More than the First Amendment of the *Constitution of the United States*, several articles of the *Declaration of the Rights of Man and of the Citizen* are a wholesale adoption of *Anderson's Constitution* and a rejection of the authority of Christ and His Church.

> ***Article I*** – *Men are born and remain free and equal in rights. Social distinctions can be founded only on the common good.*
>
> ***Article II*** – *The goal of any political association is the conservation of the natural and imprescriptible rights of man. These rights are liberty, property, safety, and resistance against oppression.*
>
> ***Article III*** – *The principle of any sovereignty resides essentially in the Nation. Nobody, no individual may exercise any authority which does not proceed directly from the nation.*
>
> ***Article IV*** – *Liberty consists of doing anything which does not harm others: thus, the exercise of the natural rights of*

each man has only those borders which assure other members of the society the fruition of these same rights. These borders can be determined only by the law.

Article V – The law has the right to forbid only actions harmful to society. Anything which is not forbidden by the law cannot be impeded, and no one can be constrained to do what it does not order.

Article VI – The law is the expression of the general will. All the citizens have the right of contributing personally or through their representatives to its formation. It must be the same for all, either that it protects, or that it punishes. All the citizens, being equal in its eyes, are equally admissible to all public dignities, places, and employments, according to their capacity and without distinction other than that of their virtues and of their talents.

Article X – No one may be disturbed for his opinions, even religious ones, provided that their manifestation does not trouble the public order established by the law.

Article XI – The free communication of thoughts and of opinions is one of the most precious rights of man: any citizen thus may speak, write, print freely, except to respond to the abuse of this liberty, in the cases determined by the law.

Article XII – The guarantee of the rights of man and of the citizen necessitates a public force: this force is thus instituted for the advantage of all and not for the particular utility of those in whom it is trusted.

Article XVII – *Property being an inviolable and sacred right, no one can be deprived of private usage, if it is not when the public necessity, legally noted, evidently requires it, and under the condition of a just and prior indemnity.*

It was soon realized during the Reign of Terror what the *Declaration of the Rights of Man and of the Citizen* meant by imposing these rights. Even twenty-days before the National Constitution Assembly adopted the final article, all tithe gathering by the Catholic clergy was abolished. Two months later, on October 10, 1789, the Assembly seized and sold all the land and property belonging to the Catholic Church. The following year, the Assembly passed the *Civil Constitution of the Clergy* that attempted to subordinate the Catholic Church in France to the French government. As the French Revolution continued, so was its true desire to strip any vestiges of Christ Jesus out of France. Churches were desecrated, destroyed, and sold; holy icons, sacramentals, and statues were smashed; priests and religious were exiled and executed. In the place of the Catholic Church, France erected the Cult of Reason and the Cult of the Supreme Being. The French celebrated the Festival of Reason in place of Catholic Holy Days.

When the French Jesuit Priest Augustin Barruel wrote in his 1797 *Memoir Illustrating the History of Jacobinism* that a conspiracy was laid afoot long ago by Voltaire and a cabal of other agents, including many Freemasons and their ideological allies (i.e., those influenced by Masonic philosophy; the Masonic Lobby), set out to overthrow monarchial rule and destroy the Catholic Church and its religious orders, it read like a fantastic tale. Those who hated what was taking place in France were quick to agree that it was the Grand Orient of France (Continental) Freemasons who were to blame. The Anglo Freemasons were justified in their rejection of the Continental's perceptible political activism. Those who suspected Barruel was writing a version of history that his new English friends wanted to hear were happy enough to dismiss his claims as ordinary fiction.

Yet, the fact of the matter was that the French Revolution targeted the Catholic Church for destruction, but Freemasonry was not targeted. Catholic and religious priests were exiled and murdered, but Freemasons were not. Catholic Churches were being desecrated, destroyed, and sold, but Masonic lodges were left untouched. Freemasonry still existed in the new France, but the Catholic Church did not. While the bells of the Catholic Church were made silent, loud and clear was heard the chant *"Liberté, Liberté chérie"* from *La Marseillaise*, the national anthem of France, which was written in 1792 by French Freemason Claude Joseph Rouget de Lisle. Very few people should ever think that such an anti-Catholic revolution was merely coincidental and spontaneous.

The Anti-Masonic Party of the United States

Along with George Washington, Lafayette, and Baron von Steuben, at least half of the remaining soldiers in the Revolutionary Army were Freemasons. However, as we will see with Europe's revolutions and America's Civil War, Freemasons would fight each other on both sides. In the instance case, Freemason Paul Revere is juxtaposed with this Masonic Brother Benedict Arnold.

At this point in history, Freemasonry was so ingrained into what was accepted as being normal, acceptable, and fashionable in American society that no one questioned why George Washington took his oath as the first President of the United States on a Bible that was provided to him by Jacob Morton, who was the Worshipful Master of Saint John's Lodge No. 1 of the Grand

Lodge of New York.[41] On September 18, 1793, George Washington assisted Joseph Clark, Grand Master of the Grand Lodge of Maryland, in the public Masonic cornerstone laying ceremony to construct the United States Capitol building. The depths to which Masonic thought influenced every aspect of the foundations and tapestry of the United States of America are permanent and should never be dismissed as not having lingering side effects.

Before the promulgation of *Etsi Multa* in 1873, an anti-Masonic movement swept across the United States in the form of a political party called the Anti-Masonic Party. From 1828 to 1840, this party pushed back against the heavy influence that Freemasons had gained in the business, judicial, and political spheres. The instigating event that propelled the organization of this movement was the mysterious disappearance of William Morgan, a bricklayer from western New York who was thought to have broken his Masonic vow of secrecy by speaking out against his religious fraternity and preparing to write an exposé about it. Starting as a single-issue party, by 1828, the Anti-Masonic Party had expanded its platform to include nationally financed internal improvements in conjunction with a protected tariff to assist in faster economic development, which was a position that the National Republican Party also shared. The Anti-Masonic Party competed very successfully as a third-party option in Pennsylvania, New York, Vermont, Massachusetts, Ohio, and Rhode Island until mid-1830. By 1840, most Anti-Masonic Party members had become absorbed by the Whigs, a stronger political party sharing their broader goals.

---

[41] This same King James translation of Bible, consisting of the Deutero-Cannonical books, was used for the inaugurations of Warren G. Harding, Dwight D. Eisenhower, Jimmy Carter, and George H. W. Bush. It was also been used in the funeral procession of George Washington and Abraham Lincoln.

The Carbonari

In Italy, the Carbonari (Italian for "charcoal makers") rose up from 1800 to 1848 with an anti-Catholic world-view. Their goal was to facilitate the creation of a constitutional monarchy or a republic by inciting revolution through their vast network of independent cells operating throughout the country. The Carbonari was never an appendant Masonic body or consisted exclusively of Freemasons. However, they did allow Freemasons to enter their organization as masters rather than apprentices (the only two degrees/grades offered). Under explicit, precise, and harsh terms, Pope Pius VII, in his September 13, 1821 constitution *Ecclesiam a Jesu Christo* (Church of Jesus Christ), condemned the Carbonari as being destructive, criminal, and dangerous and placed it under the same prohibitions and grave penalties as his predecessors had placed Freemasonry.

In 1859, *The Permanent Instruction of the Alta Vendita* was published, purportedly by a still-existing Sicilian sect of the Carbonari, offering a strategic blueprint on infiltrating and destroying the Catholic Church. It was essential to both Pope Pius IX and Pope Leo XIII for all Catholics to know the contents of *Alta Vendita*, which says in part (**bold** added for emphasis):

*"The Papacy always exercised a decisive action over the fate of Italy. With the arm, the voice, the pen, the heart of its countless bishops, friars, nuns and faithful of all the laity, the Papacy finds people everywhere ready for sacrifice to martyrdom, to enthusiasm. Wherever he wants to evoke it, it has friends who die and others who strip for love of him. It is an immense lever of which only some Popes have understood all the power. (And even they who do not, they have served only to a certain extent). Today it is not a question of restoring this momentarily weakened power to our service: **our ultimate goal is that of Voltaire and the French revolution:***

that is, the complete annihilation of Catholicism and even of the Christian idea, which, if it remained standing above the ruins of Rome, would later be its perpetuation. But in order to reach this goal more certainly and not prepare ourselves for disillusionment that will prolong indefinitely or compromise the success of the cause, we must not listen to these French boasters, to these nebulous Germans, to these melancholy Englishmen who believe they can kill Catholicism now with an obscene song, now with a sophistry, now with a trivial sarcasm hanging around like the English cottons. Catholicism has a life that resists those things. It has seen far more relentless and terrible adversaries; and the evil taste of blessing the grave of the angriest among them is often taken with his holy water. Therefore, let our brothers of those countries find their own excesses of anti-Catholic zeal: let us make fun of our Madonnas and our apparent devotion. With this passport (of hypocrisy), we can conspire with all our comfort and come, little by little, to our purpose.

Therefore, the Papacy has been, for the past seven hundred years, inherent in our Italy. Italy cannot breathe, nor move without the permission of the Supreme Shepherd. With him, it has the hundred arms of Briareus; without him, it is condemned to a compassionate impotence, divisions, hatreds, hostility from the first chain of the Alps to the last ring of the Apennines We cannot want such a state of affairs: we must seek a remedy for this situation. The **Pope, whoever he is, will never come to the secret societies, it is up to the secret societies to take the first step toward the Church and towards the Pope, with the aim of winning them both.**

The work we are about to do is not the work of a day, nor a month, nor a year. It may last many years, perhaps a century, but in our ranks the soldier dies and the war continues."

Chapter VI | Etsi Multa

Blessed Pope Pius IX (1846 – 1878) remains the longest-serving Pontiff in the history of the Catholic Church; that is, depending upon what year we agree that Saint Peter began his tenure. Aside from the longevity of his Papacy, Pius IX was also one of the most intriguing and interesting Popes in the history of the Church.

Born Giovanni Mastai-Ferrett on May 13, 1792, in Sinigaglia, Italy, he was ordained a priest in 1819 and, in 1823, was sent by Pius VII to Chile to assist with the nuncio there. By 1840, Giovanni had been appointed a cardinal by Pope Gregory XVI, whom he succeeded as Supreme Pontiff on June 16, 1846. He took the name Pius in honor of Pius VII, one of the Catholic Church's most formidable politicians and the one who had encouraged Giovanni in his vocation despite his bouts with epilepsy.

The conclave in 1846 was dominated by liberals who wanted to give control of the Papal States over to laypersons and break from several other longstanding traditions. For their part, the minority conservative block wanted to continue the approach of Gregory XVI, who clung to the Monarchial Papacy tradition. In Giovanni, the liberals believed they had a man who viewed the Church and the world as they did, particularly a Pope who wanted to decentralize Church authority and extend more rights to local bishops and the laity. Given the soft and merciful hand he had exercised as Archbishop of Spoleto, such was a reasonable belief.

Perhaps the most challenging aspect of Pius IX's papacy was the revolutions of 1848 that swept across Europe just two years after his election to the Throne of Peter. In every country, except for Russian, Spain, and the Scandinavian countries, the movement of discontent and revolution spread and was intent on toppling governments. As these revolutions began to break out in Palermo, Sicily, on January 12 and reached Paris, Berlin, and Milan by March, people knew that the Freemasons had conspired with them.

For decades before 1848, the Grand Orient Freemasons in France had been openly engaged in political activities designed to advocate for the import of democratic rule. In 1847, many Masonic banquets were held around France where the keynote speakers, Odilon Barrot and Adolphe Cremieux, were demanding the resignation of Prime Minister François Guizot.[42] In Germany, lawyer, journalist, and anti-Semite[43] Eduard Emil Eckert cited in his 1852 book *The Masonic Order in its True Meaning* an article from a German Masonic journal from 1848, which read, *"Democracy is a child of masonry and we must recognize it as our child. It is our business to bring up this child to wisdom, strength, and beauty."* After the uprising in France had ended, the Grand Orient issued a statement in which they attempted to distance themselves from the murder of the Paris' Archbishop Monsignor Denis

---

[42] Ridley, Jasper. *The Freemasons: A History of the World's Most Powerful Secret Society.* Arcade Publishing. New York. 2011. 206.
[43] Kappen, Jimmy. *The conspiracy of Freemasons, Jews, and communists. An analysis of the French and German nationalist discourse (1918 – 1940).* In Second International Conference on the History of Freemasonry. Edinburgh, UK. 2009.

Auguste Affre. However, later that year, the Masonic journal *Le Franc-Maçon* called its readers to vote for the liberal poet Alphonse de Lamartine for Prime Minister because he believed in *"the scared words, Liberty, Equality, Fraternity."*[44]

Even the Pope was not spared from the revolutionaries' demands, as they demanded that he declare war on Austria. Given that Vienna considered Pius IX an enemy, given his implementation of liberal policies, his plea that they voluntarily cede the Italian providence was rejected with prejudice. On November 15, 1848, Pius IX's prime ministers were assassinated, and two days later, the Swiss Guards were disarmed. This was quite the turn of events for a Pope who, just two years previously, was unrelentingly cheered by liberals but was now teaching him that the more you give liberals, the more they will feel entitled to take.

On November 24, 1848, Pius IX disguised himself as a priest and fled Rome to Gaeta, where he found protection under the Neapolitan king. While the Pope was in exile, a Roman Republic was declared in which just a shadow of the dreams of Freemasonry, the Illuminati, and the Carbonari were all realized. From its declaration on February 9, 1849, until the French army reestablished the Holy See's temporal power on July 3, 1849, anti-Catholicism and indifferentism ruled the day. Good Friday was celebrated in the Roman Republic with a massive fireworks display and Saint Peter's Basilica desecrating. The constitution of the Roman Republic allowed for all religions to be practiced freely, and capital punishment was abolished.

The General and Minister of War of the Roman Republic was a career revolutionary named Giuseppe Maria Garibaldi (the so-called 'father of Italian independence') who had become a Freemason in 1844 in the Grand Orient of France, and in 1860 was invited to become the Grand Master of the Grand Orient of Italy;

---

[44] Ibid, 207.

an office in which he served with distinction from 1862 to 1868. Ridley states, *"On more than one occasion, he [Garibaldi] openly stated that he was an Atheist."*[45]

Louis Napoleon was very friendly with the Freemasons. He used their global network to advance his agenda, and, in turn, they used his influence to advance their Masonic program. However, it was ironic that the army he sent to overthrow the Roman Republic and restore the Pope was led by a Freemason, General Charles Oudinot.[46] Napoleon's interest in being the defender of the Pope was to win favor with faithful Catholics.

After settling a truce with the French, Garibaldi withdrew from Rome with his 4,000 troops. Then, by 1850, he was in New York visiting Masonic lodges, *"where he met several supporters of democratic internationalism, whose minds were open to making socialist thoughts their own and gave Freemasonry a strong anti-papal stand."*[47]

Pius IX returned to Rome a year after the French restored his rule. However, the fight for Italian unification continued for another twenty years. Unfortunately, several swift defeats against the French by the German unification forces in the Franco-Prussian War of 1870 caused Napoleon III to withdraw his troops from defending Rome. With Napoleon taken prisoner at Sedan, King Victor Emmanuel II, the first king of united Italy, took advantage of his opportunity and seized Rome. By September 20, 1870, the only property that the Catholic Church had left to claim was the Vatican. It would not be until 1929 that the Vatican recognized the Kingdom of Italy by signing the Lateran Pacts.

---

[45] Ridley, Jasper. *The Freemasons: A History of the World's Most Powerful Secret Society.* Arcade Publishing. New York. 2011. 220.
[46] Ibid, 208.
[47] http://freemasonry.bcy.ca/biography/garibaldi_g/garibaldi.html (retrieval date - 12/7/2019).

With no property by which he could gain revenue and refused to accept a monthly stipend from Italy, in 1871, Pius IX appealed to the laypeople worldwide and *"other persons of good will"* to provide financial support to the Roman See. This collection became what is known today as 'Peter's Pence.'

Aside from presiding over the loss of Papal territories, three of the most lasting accomplishments of Pius IX were the promulgation of his 1854 encyclical, *Ineffabilis Deus*, on the Immaculate Conception of the Virgin Mary, approving the unanimous request of the America bishops that the Immaculate Conception be invoked as the Patroness of the United States on February 7, 1847, and convoking the First Vatican Council in 1869 where Papal Infallibility was defined.

Now, given that Pius IX had published several very strong encyclicals against indifferentism, modernism, secret societies, and Freemasonry,[48] it is odd that he had been accused of being a Freemason himself. The case of him being a Freemason is most certainly connected to him being a liberal as Archbishop, as well as early on in his Papacy, and given that he was planted into that position by the liberal block of the Church, some of whom may have been infiltrators. While it is clear that Pius IX had liberal leanings until he learned that liberalism leads to nihilism, it does not necessarily mean that he earned that leaning by being made a Freemason.

A cleverly contrived story cited in several credible Masonic publications and books to prove that Pius IX is a Freemason relies on a story that states Giovanni Mastai-Ferretti had been initiated

---

[48] *Qui Pluribus* (against the dangers posed by secret sects, rationalism, pantheism, socialism, Communism and other popular philosophies) – 1846, *Quanto Conficiamur Moerore* (against indifferentism and other false doctrines) – 1863, *Qunta cura/Syllabus of Errors* (condemnation of 80 modern errors including liberalism in every political form, indifferentism, naturalism, communism, secret societies, and Bible societies) – 1864, and *Etis Multa* (against Freemasonry) – 1873.

an Entered Apprentice, passed to the degree of Fellow craft, and raised to the sublime degree of Master Mason on August 15, 1839, in lodge Eterna Catena, of Palermo, Italy during his youth – this, according to the testimony of two Freemasons who were his enemies; Giuseppe Maria Garibaldi and Victor Emanuel II, King of Italy and Grand Master of the Grand Orient of Italy. In 1873, the Grand Orient of Italy held a Masonic trial and expelled Pope Pius IX.[49] As far as this story having any measure of credibility, we know for sure that in 1839, the year of his supposed initiations, Giovanni was still working in the northern Italian city of Imola, which is a very long distance from Palermo - a city on the island of Sicily. While it is possible that the future Pope could have secretly traveled that long-distance and secretly spent time there just to become a Freemason, there is no reason to believe that story based solely upon the testimony of two accusers, given their character faults and their hatred of the Catholic Church.

A story carrying more circumstantial weight that Pope Pius IX was at most a Freemason and at minimum one of their ideological allies (albeit we would still have to ignore his Papal pronouncements against Freemasonry), is the fact that he donated a stone block of marble from the Temple of Concord in Rome to be used in the construction of the interior wall of Washington's Monument in Washington, D.C. The donated stone never ended up being used for the monument because it was supposedly stolen on the night of March 6, 1854, by nine men who were sympathizers of the defunct Anti-Masonic Party.

The grave problem with the stone donation is that the Washington Monument is a Masonic edifice whose ceremonial cornerstone was laid by Freemasons during their dedication ritual. The Vatican, along with several Masonic lodges, donated stones for

---

[49] https://freemasonry.bcy.ca/biography/pius_ix/pius_ix.html - (retrieved 12/08/2019).

the construction of this Masonic edifice that is dedicated to George Washington,[50] who is not only the first President of the United States but also the country's most revered Freemason, and someone whom Pius IX called a "great"[51] man. Therefore, it is suspicious that the Pontiff of a Church that forbids any promotion, association, or encouragement under pain of excommunication, directly or indirectly, of Freemasons would donate a stone for constructing a Masonic building dedicated to a Freemason. If Pius knew what that building was to be used for and how it would be dedicated, he excommunicated himself by donating that marble stone.

There is the argument from speculation that Pope Pius IX may have heard that the Americans were constructing a building for their first President. He was reaching out as a monarch with a friendly gesture to show good-will and to build closer relations. Nevertheless, given the other inconsistent and confusing gestures of Pius IX, such as sending a portrait of himself to Confederacy President Jefferson Davis, while telling the American bishops that the American Civil War was 'destructive'[52] while signing off on a letter from the Holy Office in 1866 that repeated Saint Thomas Aquinas teaching that it is not contrary to the natural and divine law for an enslaved person to be sold, bought, exchanged, or donated,[53] it may just simply be the case that Pius

---

[50] The tradition, of which Pius IX may have been aware, that George Washington died a Catholic, according to Father Leonard Neale, SJ, and that he maintained Catholic traditions, such as signing himself with the Sign of the Cross before meals, oftentimes attending Holy Mass, and forbidding the burning in effigy of the Pontiff on 'Pope's Day' (Shoda, Richard W. *Saint Alphonsus, Closures, and Continuity 1956 – 2011.* Dorrance Publishing. Pittsburg, Pennsylvania. 2014. 23.), does not minimize the gravity that the George Washington Monument is a dedicated Masonic edifice.
[51] *Longinqua* (Catholicism in the United States), 1895, 4.
[52] Doyle, Don H. *The Cause of All Nations: An International History of the American Civil War.* Basic Books. New York. 2015. 257-70.
[53] Holy Office, Instruction 20, June 1866

IX was offering the world a feeble imitation of Pius VII by trying to politic himself into being an enemy of no one and a friend to everyone.

An argument is also to be made that Pius IX may not have known a great deal about the Masonic involvement in George Washington's Monument in light of his choice of words in a private letter to Archbishop of Paris, George Darboy, on November 26, 1865, in which he severely admonished the prelate over the funeral Mass of Bernard Pierre Magnan (Marechal Magnan), who was the Marshal of France and the Grand Master of the Grand Orient of France until his death on May 29, 1865.

The politics of the situation was that in January 1862, Napoleon III issued an imperial decree that gave him the authority as Emperor to appoint the Grand Master of the Grand Orient of France, and his first choice was Magnan.[54] Such was the dependent relationship between Napoleon and the Freemasons, who needed each other for political survival. Darboy also felt that he needed the protection of Napoleon III, and, therefore, to deny the Emperor's chosen one his last rites and a request from the Freemasons to offer Magnan his last Masonic rites might have put Darboy in Napoleon III's crosshairs.

As for Pius IX, the politics of France were of no concern to him whatsoever. Not only did Darboy grant Magnan absolution posthumously and preside over a Masonic funeral rite, but he flatly lied about the whole affair:

"In fact, we cannot conceal from you, venerable brother, that our grief and astonishment was very great when we heard that you had presided at the Obsequies of the Marechal Magnan, Grand Master of the Order of Freemasons, and given a solemn absolution when the Masonic Insignia were

---

[54] Ridley, Jasper. *The Freemasons: A History of the World's Most Powerful Secret Society.* Arcade Publishing. New York. 2011. 212.

placed on the cataphalque; and that the members of that condemned sect with decorations, and the same insignia, were ranged around the cataphalque.

In the letter which you addressed to us on the 1st of last August, you assure us that these insignia had not been seen by you, nor by your clergy; that, in one word, they were unknown to you in any manner; but you knew very well, venerable brother, that the dead man had during life had the misfortune to fulfil the charge of that proscribed sect, vulgarly called by the name of the *' Grand Orient," and consequently you might have easily foreseen that the members of that sect would assist at his funeral; and that they would take care to make a parade of their insignia.

You ought therefore in your religious position to have maturely weighed these considerations, and to have been on your guard on the occasion of this Funeral, in order not to have caused by your presence and co-operation the astonishment and profound grief which all true Catholics have felt on this occasion. You cannot be ignorant that masonic societies, and all other associations of the same iniquitous character, have been condemned by the Roman Pontiffs,* our predecessors, and by ourselves, that even severe penalties have been enacted against them. These impious sects, having different denominations, are, in fact, all linked together by their mutual complicity in the most criminal designs, all being inflamed with the most intense hatred of our holy religion and the Apostolic See, and are endeavoring by the dissemination of pestilential books, to injure them in many other ways, by perverse maneuvers and by every kind of devilish artifice to corrupt all over the world both morality and *belief, and to destroy all honest, true, and just opinion; to spread throughout the universe these monstrous opinions; to conceal and propagate the most detestable vices, and every conceivable rascality; to shake the power of all legitimate authority, and to compass the overthrow, if it were possible, of the Catholic Church, and of civil society, and to drive God Himself out of heaven.*

Now we cannot pass over in silence the accounts that have reached us, that such erroneous and pernicious opinions have been accredited by you, namely, that the acts of the Apostolic See do not engender any obligations, at least, not until they have been clothed by a warrant for their execution from the civil power."

It should be noted that Darboy and Pope Pius IX had a long and challenging relationship, primarily due to the latter's strong belief in the sovereignty of the Papacy and the former's equally strong belief in the autonomy of bishops. It was primarily due to this divergent position and Darboy's liberal tendencies that he was never made a Cardinal by Pius IX. Ironically, Darboy's friendliness towards the Freemasons did not even save his life after being taken hostage and executed by them and Socialists during the reign of the Paris Commune revolutionary government (March 18 to May 28, 1871).[55]

Therefore, given Pope Pius IX's treatment of Darboy over his presiding over a Masonic burial rite for one of their Grand Masters, it does not seem likely that Pius himself would intentionally join in with the Freemasons to honor George Washington with a

---

[55] Leighton, John. *Paris Under the Commune: Or, The Seventy-Three days of the Second Siege; with Numerous Illustrations, Sketches Taken on the Sport, and Portraits (from the Original Photographs)*. Hachette Livre. Paris, France. 2018. 346.

Masonic monument. Suppose Pius IX had ever been initiated a Freemason. In that case, no credible evidence exists that such an association made a positive impression on him.

Nevertheless, nineteen years after the 'Pope's Masonic Cornerstone Scandal' and twenty-seven years after the beginning of his Papacy, Pope Pius IX promulgated *Etsi Multi*, in which he outlined all the dangers that were threatening the Catholic Church from within and from without in Europe.

The primary issue being addressed in this encyclical is *Kulturkampf* (i.e., culture struggle), a sweeping series of anti-clerical reform laws in Germany, Switzerland, Austria, Italy, and Belgium. These news laws were primarily attempting to seize the state control of education out of the hands of the Catholic Church and to control ecclesial appointments.[56] Pope Pius IX believed that Freemasons and the philosophy of Freemasonry were generally responsible for *Kulturkampf*.

Before he gets to paragraph number twenty-eight, where he explains the dangers of Freemasonry and how it is responsible for *Kulturkampf*, Pius IX addresses the events of recent persecutions against women religious *"driven from their houses"* in a hostile manner, the new anti-Catholic laws and religious persecution in Switzerland and Germany, the German endorsement of the Old Catholic Church (*"openly support those recent heretics who call themselves Old Catholics"*), the excommunication of Joseph Hubert Reinkens, who was elected Bishop of Germany for the Old Catholic Church.

---

[56] One of the earliest Papal documents concerning state government attempts to usurp control of education away from the Catholic Church was Pope Pius VIII's encyclical *Litteris altero abhinc* (Two Years Ago), which was promulgated on March 25, 1830. In this document, he does not mention Freemasonry by name. Pius VIII also promulgated *Traditi Humilitati* the year prior, which addressed the harm and machinations of secret sects in general.

In this challenging encyclical, Pope Pius IX draws from Scripture, the wealth of Church teaching, and pious writers, such as Saint Cyprian of Carthage, Saint Ambrose, Saint Augustine, Saint Peter Chrysologus, Saint Boniface, and Saint Leo the Great.

Etsi Multa
(Although Many)
Blessed Pope Pius IX - 1873

28. Some of you may perchance wonder that the war against the Catholic Church extends so widely. Indeed each of you knows well the nature, zeal, and intention of sects, whether called Masonic or some other name. When he compares them with the nature, purpose, and amplitude of the conflict waged nearly everywhere against the Church, he cannot doubt but that the present calamity must be attributed to their deceits and machinations for the most part. For from these the synagogue of Satan is formed which draws up its forces, advances its standards, and joins battle against the Church of Christ.

29. Our Predecessors, as watchers in Israel, denounced these forces from the very beginnings to rulers and nations. Against them they have struck out again and again with their condemnations. We Ourselves have not been deficient in Our duty. Would that the Pastors of the Church had more loyalty from those who could have averted such a pernicious plague! But, creeping through sinuous openings, never stinting in toil, deceiving many by clever fraud, it has reached such an outcome that it has burst forth from its hiding places and boasts itself lord and master. Grown immense by a multitude of followers, these nefarious bands think that they have been made masters of their desire and have all but achieved their goal. They have at last achieved what they have so long desired, that is, that in many places they obtained supreme power and won for themselves bulwarks of men and authority. Now they boldly turn to this, to hand over the Church of God to a most harsh servitude, to tear up the supports on which it rests, and to attempt to distort the marks by which it

stands out gloriously. What more? They would, if possible, completely wipe it out from the world after they had shaken it with frequent blows, ruined it, and overturned it.

30. Since these things are so, venerable brothers, apply all your effort to protect the faithful committed to your care against the snares and contagion of these sects. Bring back those who have unhappily joined these sects. Expose especially the error of those who have been deceived or those who assert now that only social utility, progress, and the exercise of mutual benefits are the intention of these dark associations. Explain to them often and fix deeper in their minds the pontifical decrees on this matter. Teach them that these decrees refer not only to Masonic groups in Europe, but also those in America and in other regions of the world.

31. As for the rest since we have fallen on these evil times let us take care first and foremost, as good soldiers of Christ, not to lose heart. Indeed, in the very storms in which we are tossed, there is a certain hope of achieving future tranquility and greater serenity in the Church. So let us arouse ourselves and the toiling clergy and laity, propped up by divine help and inspired by that most noble statement of Chrysostom: "Many waves and dire storms, press on but we do not fear lest we be submerged, for we stand on a rock. Let the sea rage, it cannot dissolve the rock. Let the waves rise, they cannot sink the bark of Christ. Nothing is stronger than the Church. The Church is stronger than the heavens. Heaven and earth shall pass away, but my words will not pass away. What words? Thou art Peter and upon this rock I will build my Church and the gates of Hell will not prevail against it. If you do not trust the words, trust the deeds. How many tyrants have tried to oppress the Church! How many cauldrons, furnaces, teeth of beasts, sharp swords! They have accomplished

nothing. Where are those enemies? They are handed over to silence and forgetfulness. Where is the Church? It shines brighter than the sun. Their deeds are extinct, its deeds are immortal. If when they were few, the Christians were not conquered, how can you conquer them when the whole world is full of this holy religion? Heaven and earth will pass, my words will not pass away."[57] Therefore not moved by any danger and not hesitating at all, let us persevere in prayer. Let us all strive to placate the celestial anger provoked by the sins of mankind so that the Almighty will rise up and command the winds and bring about tranquility.

32. In the meantime, We lovingly grant the apostolic blessing as a testimony of the special benevolence We have to you all, venerable brothers, and the clergy and the entire people committed to the care of each of you.

Given in Rome at St. Peter's, 21 November 1873, in the 28th year of Our Pontificate.

Paragraph 28:
In this section, Pope Pius IX points to Masonic sects and other sects, whose intentions inveigh against the spiritual or temporal interests of the Catholic Church, as the source of why the war against the Church *"extends so widely."* He believes these borderless secret societies have exported and imported persecution against the Catholic Church. Pius IX says we can know if this is true by comparing what these groups profess with the *"nature, purpose, and amplitude of the conflict"* being waged. Through this comparison, Pius offers there can be no *"doubt but that the*

---

[57] Homily, *ante exil.*, nos. 1 and 2.

present calamity must be attributed to their deceits and machinations for the most part."

Etsi Multa is the first instance of a Pope referring to Freemasonry and secret sects like them as a *"Synagogue of Satan,"* which makes its usage a striking escalation of the Church's understanding of the danger and threat that these groups pose to God's People. In the book of *Revelation* (vv. 2:9 and 3:9) and throughout the early tradition of pious Catholic writing, the term *"Synagogue of Satan"* was a term reserved exclusively for groups that teach heresy but pretend to be orthodox so that they can steal Christ's flock.

Paragraph 29:

Here, Pope Pius IX recalls the prohibitions found in *In Eminenti, Providas Romanorum, Quo Graviora, Traditi Humiltati, Qui Pluribus,* and *Ecclesiam a Jesu Christ* as a reminder of the work of his predecessors, who *"struck out again and again with their condemnations"* against Freemasonry and sects like them. He then blames these groups' pervasive growth and infiltration partly on the disloyalty of pastors in the Church. Pius IX believes that if these pastors had not been disobedient to Church teaching, this *"pernicious plague"* could have been adverted.

In the second part, Pope Pius IX explains how the Church arrived at this position of being hated. It is due to the laxity and apathy of those under whose charge it is to enforce what the Church teaches, and that is why the Church is now being persecuted. Paying no heed to these synagogues of Satan has allowed them to achieve their goal of subjecting the Catholic Church *"to a most harsh servitude, to tear up the supports on which it rests, and to attempt to distort the marks by which it stands out gloriously."* If it were possible, though it is not, these groups would completely wipe out the Catholic Church *"from the world after they had shaken it with frequent blows, ruined it, and overturned it."*

Paragraph 30:

This is a critical paragraph in the history of Papal pronouncements against Freemasonry because it not only charges bishops to apply all their efforts to protect those under their care against *"the snares and contagions of these sects"* and to bring back those who have *"unhappily joined,"* but it offers, most succinctly, the perfect roadmap on how to accomplish these things. According to Pope Pius IX, these are the three steps to prevent Catholics from falling into Freemasonry and how to bring those who have fallen into its error back in the faith:

1. To expose them to the error of thinking, Freemasonry is just an organization engaged in polite socializing, progressive civic engagement, charity work, or mutual benefits. We saw this, perhaps, with Haydn, whose petition for membership expressed that he thought Freemasonry was just a social organization. Today, Freemasons and appendant Masonic bodies like the Shriners aggressively push this idea out into the public that charity work is a central emphasis of their organization. Still today, people join Freemasonry due to this clever marketing scheme and pretentious displays.
2. To explain to them the dogmatic teaching on this matter that the Supreme Pontiffs have promulgated. As I stated in the Preface of this catechism, arguing that Catholics cannot be Freemasons based on what Freemasonry teaches about itself is ineffective. The most effective method, according to Blessed Pope Pius IX, is to argue that Catholics cannot be Freemasons based upon what the Catholic Church teaches about Freemasonry and

3. To teach them that the prohibition against Freemasonry and sects like them is global; it is not just for Europe, but also for all continents *"and in other regions of the world."* This is a vital point because, in the coming decades and centuries, there will be efforts made by Catholics to argue that the Anglo and Prince Hall Masonic sects are acceptable for Catholics to join. This will cause the Catholic Church to revisit the topic and affirm, once again, that no matter the region where Freemasonry is being practiced, or the race of people practicing it, the principles of Freemasonry remain in them and, thereby, the Church makes no distinctions or gives dispensations for the various sects of Freemasonry.

Paragraphs 31 - 32:

Before concluding this encyclical with his Apostolic blessing, Pope Pius IX offers a word of encouragement to preserve the faith, regardless of the turbulence we encounter. Pressing deep into this theme, he inserts a quote from a homily given by Saint John Chrysostom, stating that nothing in the world can conqueror or destroy the holy religion because, quoting from the sixteenth chapter of the *Gospel of Matthew*, Christ Jesus established the Catholic Church on Peter and promised that the gates of Hell would not prevail against it.

The importance of *Etsi Multa* is that it was the first time in over a century that the prohibition against Freemasonry had been revisited as an individual topic and not a part of the broader subject of secret societies or Masonic philosophes, such as indifferentism. By name, Pius IX cites how *Etsi Multa* belongs to the body of previous Papal pronouncements on this issue and states that the Catholic Church maintains the exact prohibitions against Freemasonry that his predecessors set forth.

Uniquely important to *Etsi Multa* is that this was the first time that it was clarified that there are no global distinctions with Freemasonry and that the prohibition against Freemasonry is global and not specific just to Europe. Also unique is the three-step action to prevent Catholics from falling into the error of Freemasonry and how to bring those who have fallen into its error back into the faith. Pope Leo XIII's encyclical Humanum Genus will include a similar action plan.

Chapter VII | Humanum Genus

The Pope who wrote most prolifically against Freemasonry is Pope Leo XIII. From the date he was elected to the Throne of Peter on February 20, 1878, until his death on July 20, 1903, Leo XIII wrote six Papal documents about the dangers of Freemasonry and secret societies like it: *Officio Sanctissimo* (1887), *Dall'alto dell'Apostolicio Seggio* (1890), *Custodi Di Quella Fede* (1892), *Inimica Vis* (1892), *Praeclara Gratulationis Pune fois encoreublicae* (1894), and *Vehementer Nos* (1906). The latter document of this group primarily concerned the broader subject of secret societies rather than focusing almost exclusively on Freemasonry as the former writings did.

Pope Leo XIII was born Gioacchino Pecci on March 2, 1810, in Carpineto Romano, Italy. He was the sixth of seven sons of Count Ludovico Pecci. One of his brothers, Giuseppe Pecci, became a notable Jesuit (i.e., a religious brother of the Society of Jesus) and specialized in the philosophy of Saint Thomas Aquinas. Gioacchino was ordained a priest in the Catholic Church six years after graduating with a doctorate in civil and Canon Law from the Pontifical Academy of Ecclesiastical Nobles. He was elevated to the College of Cardinals in 1853. He attended the First

Vatican Council, which his brother, now a Cardinal, helped organize.

The uniqueness of Leo XIII's papacy is that it was the first in many centuries that did not have trouble with the dealings of monarchial rule and all that which came along with having to protect and turn revenue from the Papal States. Being that he was the first Pope in a very long time who had the freedom to focus on the spiritual health of his flock simply, it presented him with an opportunity to shape who the Church would be in the world and what relationship She ought to have with State governments. With a twenty-five-year Pontificate that took him to the age of ninety-three, thereby making him the oldest person ever to serve as Pope, Leo XIII was given many years to reflect on this new dynamism in Catholic history.

Leo XIII found that the world's borders were just as fluid as they had been for many of his predecessors. However, the moving borders were not primarily in Europe any longer. Instead, the wealthiest European nations began focusing their energies on expanding their empires across the expanse of the world. Leo XIII's response to the exploitation of human beings that accompanied the European colonization model was to send missionaries to spread the faith in new lands and protect the local communities from material harm.

The demands for goods and services brought about by empire expansion began to shed new light on the depths to which corporate greed can cause significant harm to society. In his 1891 encyclical *Rerum Novarum*, Leo XIII pointed out the intrinsic flaws in capitalism and communism. He introduced the idea of *subsidiarity* to argue that local problems are best solved by the local people closest to the problem rather than by distant central authorities far removed from the people's needs and concerns.

Even more prolific than his writings against Freemasonry, Leo XIII wrote about the Rosary. The Holy Father wrote eleven encyclicals, earning him the title, 'Rosary Pope.' His devotion to the Blessed Mother Mary extended to him being the first Pope to ever refer to her as the Mediatrix and Co-Redemptrix in his encyclical on the Rosary, entitled *Fidentem piumque animum*. He also approved two new Marian scapulars.

The un-relationship between the Catholic Church and Freemasonry during the Pontificate of Leo XIII cannot be rightly told without inserting into here the curious case of Marie Joseph Gabriel Antoine Jogand-Pagès, who is most famously known by his pen name, Léo Taxil. Never before has anyone made such financial gain by mocking Catholicism to the applause of Freemasons and then mocking Freemasonry to the applause of Catholics in two separate breaths as Léo Taxil did at the end of the nineteenth century.

Born in Marseille, France, in 1854 and educated in a Jesuit seminary since the age of five, Léo Taxil left his faith and, in 1881, became an Entered Apprentice in a lodge belonging to the Grand Orient of France. He was eventually expelled from his lodge because the Grand Orient thought he was bringing too much negative attention. Starting in 1879 with his pamphlet *A Bas la Calotte* ("*Down with the Cloth*") that led to him being persecuted and acquitted on the charge of attacking a recognized religion, Léo Taxil went on to pen several more anti-Catholic and anti-Clerical pieces. After such salacious titles as *The Amusing Bible, The Life of Jesus, The Debaucheries of a Confessor, The Holy Pornographers Confession and Confessors, The Pope's Mistress,* and *The Secret Life of Pope Pius IX,* Léo Taxil decided to repent and convert back to the Catholic Church; the news of which led him to be kicked out the Anti-Clerical League.

After writing a retraction letter denouncing everything he had written against the Church, Léo Taxil went to a Jesuit house for a retreat. It was there, after engaging in the Spiritual Exercises of Saint Ignatius, that he confessed to killing someone. He had not, but he just wanted to test the secrecy of confession. After going to the Vatican to be absolved of the grave sin of murder, Taxil moved on to phase two of his prank to win acclaim from Catholics by slandering Freemasonry. After publishing such works as *Are There Women Freemasons, The Three-Pointed Brothers, The Anti-Christ and the Origin of Masonry, Masonic France: New Revelations, Memoirs of an Ex-Pallanist by Miss Diana Vaughan,*[58] and *The Masonic Murders*, he went to the Vatican to have an audience with Leo XIII. According to Taxil, Cardinal Rampolia and Pope Leo XIII told him they had also been initiated into Freemasonry as Entered Apprentices during their youth.[59] He also said that Leo XIII told him that he had read all his books on Freemasonry and was convinced, both after being initiated himself and after reading his books, that the devil is truly in the Masonic lodge. Taxil had been writing that Freemasons use the name 'Grand Architect of the Universe' as a clever way to conceal Satan.

According to Ridley, Taxil's budding hoax led to an Anti-Masonic Congress held in Trent (Austria/Hungary) in September of 1896, attended by seven hundred delegates, including thirty-six

---

[58] This was a twenty-four part series by Léo Taxil about a secret organization called the Palladium founded by Albert Pike – a very notable American Freemason.
[59] Bernheim, Alan, Samii, A. William, Serejski, Eric. *The Confession of Leo Taxil.* Heredom: The Transactions of the Scottish Rite Research Society. Scottish Rite Research Society. 1996. Vol. 5, 137 -168.

bishops.⁶⁰ This congress produced a fresh round of persecution against Freemasonry in the Austrian empire.

Finally, on April 19, 1897, Taxil used his fame to attract a large audience ready to meet Diana Vaughan, whom he had claimed was the real person behind his *Memoirs of an Ex-Pallanist* series. Rather, they heard, *"The Palladium exists no more. I created it, and I have destroyed it. You have nothing more to fear form I sinister influence."* Léo Taxil stood on stage at the Geographical Society and unraveled his nearly twenty-year-old hoax against Freemasonry and the Catholic Church. His honest confession was met with laughter and jeering from the audience. He had profited and won fame from those who feared the Catholic Church and from Catholics who feared Freemasons by making up stories that exaggerated the worst fears of both groups: that Lucifer himself appears in Masonic lodge meetings and that Catholic clerics are all sexual deviants.

Pope Leo XIII also granted a private audience to a more credible person on the threat of Freemasonry. On December 3, 1878, Leo XIII met with Sister Mary of the Cross (Mélanie Calva), a French Catholic nun, who along with Maximin Giraud on September 19, 1846, saw a *"beautiful lady"* on Mount Sous-Les Baisses dressed in white with a crucifix around her neck that was surrounded by hammer and pincers. She was carrying a heavy chain and roses on her shoulders, and her head was surrounded with roses.

Maximin and Mélanie were just children, eleven and fourteen, respectively. They said that when they first saw the beautiful lady, she sat down with her elbows resting on her knees as she bitterly wept. She then arose to speak to them in French and their

---

⁶⁰ Ridley, Jasper. *The Freemasons: A History of the World's Most Powerful Secret Society.* Arcade Publishing. New York. 2011. 225. See also Winterburgh. *Prague: A Centre of Freemasonry.* Ars Quatuor Coronatorum. LXXVII. 70.

local Occitan dialect about "her Son," while offering examples of their own life. The Lady appears to be weeping because people are not keeping the Lord's Day holy and cursing with the Lord's name. *"These are the two things that weigh so heavily on my Son's arm,"* the Lady says. She then prophesized a potato famine due to people's failure to revere God's name and His Holy day. This apparition transpired right before the potato famine occurred in France and Ireland during the winter of 1846 – 1847.

On September 19, 1851, after five years of investigation, the apparition was approved by Philibert de Brouillard, Bishop of Grenoble, and was given the name 'Our Lady of La Salette,' writing:

> *"The apparition of the Blessed Virgin to two shepherds on the mountain of La Salette [...] carries within itself all the characters of truth and that the faithful are justified in believing it unmistakable and certain."*

That December 1878 meeting with Sister Mary of the Cross must have left some lasting impression on Pope Leo XIII because, on August 21, 1879, he granted a canonical coronation to the image of Our Lady of La Salette that resides today in the Basilica named in her honor in La Salette, France.

Our Lady of La Salette also individually shared with Maximin and Mélanie several secrets,[61] which, given the contents of *Etsi Multa* (1873) and *Humanum Genus* (1884), show that these secrets must have been known to both Pope Pius IX and Leo XIII because both of these encyclicals point to the persecutions that Our Lady of La Salette says that the Catholic Church will have to endure. However, it is the Freemasons and their philosophy that His Holiness largely blames for the spread of anti-Catholicism.

---

[61] See: http://www.catholicplanet.com/future/lasalette-maximin.htm and http://www.catholicplanet.com/future/lasalette-melanie.htm (retrieved 12/03/2019).

A year prior to his meeting with Sister Mary of the Cross, the Grand Orient of France had rejected the 1813 constitution of the United Grand Lodge of England that required Freemasons to accept belief in 'The Grand Architect of the Universe (GAOTU),' and began accepting Atheists as members. Also, in 1877, the Grand Orient of Italy chartered Propaganda Massonica (also known today as P2), a subordinate lodge purposed to ensure the complete privacy of membership for notable and notorious men, both within and without the organization. In 1976, the Grand Orient of Italy formally seized the charter of P2. It expelled its Worshipful Master, Licio Gelli (a Fascist), who continued to operate P2 as an unaffiliated lodge in Italy until 1984.

At its height, P2's list of known scandals included the 1977 takeover of the *Corriere Della Sera* - a leading print newspaper in Italy, interference in the 1980 Bologna massacre and the 1982 collapse of the Vatican Bank. The prominence of the members of P2 is what allowed it to exercise tremendous amounts of influence throughout the world. Freemasons belonging to P2 included parliament members, notable journalists, military leaders, prominent businessmen, Italian mafia members, Italian Catholic cardinals, bishops, priests, and laity. Gelli also exported P2 to Argentina, where several high-ranking officials in government and military also joined.

On September 12, 1978, months before his death in March 1979, Italian journalist and lodge member of P2 and the Grand Orient of Italy, Carmine Pecorelli, purportedly published a list of one hundred and twenty Freemasons who belonged to P2 and who were notable Catholics; including cardinals, bishops, priests, and members of the laity. The Vatican has never corroborated this list, but the name Carmine Pecorelli is found on the 1981 list of nine hundred and twenty-six P2 members discovered during a police raid on the home of Licio Gelli. Over a decade later,

Gelli's nomination for the Nobel Prize in Literature was supported by Mother Teresa of Calcutta and others.[62]

It was here in the waning hours of the nineteenth century, where global borders were being challenged, where communism and Marxism were trying to replace capitalism, and where Freemasonry was silently continuing to take root and grow stronger wherever the English and French had landed that Pope Leo XIII wrote the lengthiest, most precise, and most authoritative argument against Freemasonry in the history of the Catholic Church.

In the sixth year of his Pontificate, Leo XIII promulgated his encyclical *Humanum Genus*, where he exposes Freemasonry as being created by Satan to use it to destroy the world by freeing countries and state governments from the influence of Catholic teaching and replacing it with naturalism.

---

[62] *Death of the Puppet Master.* la Repubblica. (http://the-view-from-rome.blogautore.repubblica.it/2015/12/16/death-of-the-puppetmaster/ - retrieved 1/1/2020).

Humanum Genus
(The Human Race)
Pope Leo XIII - 1884

To the Patriarchs, Primates, Archbishops, and Bishops of the Catholic World in Grace and Communion with the Apostolic See.

The race of man, after its miserable fall from God, the Creator and the Giver of heavenly gifts, "through the envy of the devil," separated into two diverse and opposite parts, of which the one steadfastly contends for truth and virtue, the other of those things which are contrary to virtue and to truth. The one is the kingdom of God on earth, namely, the true Church of Jesus Christ; and those who desire from their heart to be united with it, so as to gain salvation, must of necessity serve God and His only-begotten Son with their whole mind and with an entire will. The other is the kingdom of Satan, in whose possession and control are all whosoever follow the fatal example of their leader and of our first parents, those who refuse to obey the divine and eternal law, and who have many aims of their own in contempt of God, and many aims also against God.

2. This twofold kingdom St. Augustine keenly discerned and described after the manner of two cities, contrary in their laws because striving for contrary objects; and with a subtle brevity he expressed the efficient cause of each in these words: "Two loves formed two cities: the love of self, reaching even to contempt of God, an earthly city; and the love of God, reaching to contempt of self, a heavenly one."[63] At every period of time each has been

---
[63] De civ. Dei, 14, 28 (PL 41, 436).

in conflict with the other, with a variety and multiplicity of weapons and of warfare, although not always with equal ardor and assault. At this period, however, the partisans of evil seem to be combining together, and to be struggling with united vehemence, led on or assisted by that strongly organized and widespread association called the Freemasons. No longer making any secret of their purposes, they are now boldly rising up against God Himself. They are planning the destruction of holy Church publicly and openly, and this with the set purpose of utterly despoiling the nations of Christendom, if it were possible, of the blessings obtained for us through Jesus Christ our Savior. Lamenting these evils, We are constrained by the charity which urges Our heart to cry out often to God: "For lo, Thy enemies have made a noise; and they that hate Thee have lifted up the head. They have taken a malicious counsel against Thy people, and they have consulted against Thy saints. They have said, 'come, and let us destroy them, so that they be not a nation.'[64]

3. At so urgent a crisis, when so fierce and so pressing an onslaught is made upon the Christian name, it is Our office to point out the danger, to mark who are the adversaries, and to the best of Our power to make head against their plans and devices, that those may not perish whose salvation is committed to Us, and that the kingdom of Jesus Christ entrusted to Our charge may not stand and remain whole, but may be enlarged by an ever-increasing growth throughout the world.

4. The Roman Pontiffs Our predecessors, in their incessant watchfulness over the safety of the Christian people, were prompt in detecting the presence and the purpose of this capital enemy immediately it sprang into the light instead of hiding as a

---

[64] *Psalms* 82:24.

dark conspiracy; and, moreover, they took occasion with true foresight to give, as it were on their guard, and not allow themselves to be caught by the devices and snares laid out to deceive them.

5. The first warning of the danger was given by Clement XII in the year 1738,[65] and his constitution was confirmed and renewed by Benedict XIV[66] Pius VII followed the same path;[67] and Leo XII, by his apostolic constitution, *Quo Graviora*,[68] put together the acts and decrees of former Pontiffs on this subject, and ratified and confirmed them forever. In the same sense spoke Pius VIII,[69] Gregory XVI,[70] and, many times over, Pius IX.[71]

6. For as soon as the constitution and the spirit of the masonic sect were clearly discovered by manifest signs of its actions, by the investigation of its causes, by publication of its laws, and of its rites and commentaries, with the addition often of the personal testimony of those who were in the secret, this apostolic see denounced the sect of the Freemasons, and publicly declared its constitution, as contrary to law and right, to be pernicious no less to Christendom than to the State; and it forbade any one to enter the society, under the penalties which the Church is wont to inflict upon exceptionally guilty persons. The sectaries, indignant at this, thinking to elude or to weaken the force of these decrees, partly by contempt of them, and partly by calumny, ac-

---

[65] Const. *In Eminenti,* April 24, 1738.
[66] Const. *Providas,* May 18, 1751.
[67] Const. *Ecclesiam* a Jesu Christo, Sept. 13, 1821.
[68] Const. given March 13, 1825.
[69] Encyc. *Traditi,* May 21, 1829.
[70] Encyc. *Mirari,* August 15, 1832.
[71] Encyc. *Qui Pluribus,* November 9, 1846; address *Multiplices inter,* September 25, 1865, etc.

cused the sovereign Pontiffs who had passed them either of exceeding the bounds of moderation in their decrees or of decreeing what was not just. This was the manner in which they endeavored to elude the authority and the weight of the apostolic constitutions of Clement XII and Benedict XIV, as well as of Pius VII and Pius IX.[72] Yet, in the very society itself, there were to be found men who unwillingly acknowledged that the Roman Pontiffs had acted within their right, according to the Catholic doctrine and discipline. The Pontiffs received the same assent, and in strong terms, from many princes and heads of governments, who made it their business either to denounce the masonic society to the apostolic see, or of their own accord by special enactments to brand it as pernicious, as, for example, in Holland, Austria, Switzerland, Spain, Bavaria, Savoy, and other parts of Italy.

7. But, what is of highest importance, the course of events has demonstrated the prudence of Our predecessors. For their provident and paternal solicitude had not always and everywhere the result desired; and this, either because of the simulation and cunning of some who were active agents in the mischief, or else of the thoughtless levity of the rest who ought, in their own interest, to have given to the matter their diligent attention. In consequence, the sect of Freemasons grew with a rapidity beyond conception in the course of a century and a half, until it came to be able, by means of fraud or of audacity, to gain such entrance into every rank of the State as to seem to be almost its ruling power. This swift and formidable advance has brought upon the Church, upon the power of princes, upon the public well-being, precisely that grievous harm which Our predecessors had long

---

[72] Clement XII (1730-40); Benedict XIV (1740-58); Pius VII (1800-23); Pius IX (1846-78).

before foreseen. Such a condition has been reached that henceforth there will be grave reason to fear, not indeed for the Church - for her foundation is much too firm to be overturned by the effort of men - but for those States in which prevails the power, either of the sect of which we are speaking or of other sects not dissimilar which lend themselves to it as disciples and subordinates.

8. For these reasons We no sooner came to the helm of the Church than We clearly saw and felt it to be Our duty to use Our authority to the very utmost against so vast an evil. We have several times already, as occasion served, attacked certain chief points of teaching which showed in a special manner the perverse influence of Masonic opinions. Thus, in Our encyclical letter, *Quod Apostolici Muneris*, We endeavored to refute the monstrous doctrines of the socialists and communists; afterwards, in another beginning *Arcanum*, We took pains to defend and explain the true and genuine idea of domestic life, of which marriage is the spring and origin; and again, in that which begins *Diuturnum*,[73] We described the ideal of political government conformed to the principles of Christian wisdom, which is marvelously in harmony, on the one hand, with the natural order of things, and, in the other, with the well-being of both sovereign princes and of nations. It is now Our intention, following the example of Our predecessors, directly to treat of the masonic society itself, of its whole teaching, of its aims, and of its manner of thinking and acting, in order to bring more and more into the light its power for evil, and to do what We can to arrest the contagion of this fatal plague.

9. There are several organized bodies which, though differing in name, in ceremonial, in form and origin, are nevertheless so

---

[73] See nos. 79, 81, 84.

bound together by community of purpose and by the similarity of their main opinions, as to make in fact one thing with the sect of the Freemasons, which is a kind of center whence they all go forth, and whither they all return. Now, these no longer show a desire to remain concealed; for they hold their meetings in the daylight and before the public eye, and publish their own newspaper organs; and yet, when thoroughly understood, they are found still to retain the nature and the habits of secret societies. There are many things like mysteries which it is the fixed rule to hide with extreme care, not only from strangers, but from very many members, also; such as their secret and final designs, the names of the chief leaders, and certain secret and inner meetings, as well as their decisions, and the ways and means of carrying them out. This is, no doubt, the object of the manifold difference among the members as to right, office, and privilege, of the received distinction of orders and grades, and of that severe discipline which is maintained.

Candidates are generally commanded to promise - nay, with a special oath, to swear - that they will never, to any person, at any time or in any way, make known the members, the passes, or the subjects discussed. Thus, with a fraudulent external appearance, and with a style of simulation which is always the same, the Freemasons, like the Manichees of old, strive, as far as possible, to conceal themselves, and to admit no witnesses but their own members. As a convenient manner of concealment, they assume the character of literary men and scholars associated for purposes of learning. They speak of their zeal for a more cultured refinement, and of their love for the poor; and they declare their one wish to be the amelioration of the condition of the masses, and to share with the largest possible number all the benefits of civil life. Were these purposes aimed at in real truth, they are by no means the whole of their object. Moreover, to be enrolled, it is necessary that the candidates promise and undertake to be thenceforward strictly obedient to their leaders and masters with the utmost submission and fidelity, and to be in readiness to do their bidding upon the slightest expression of their will; or, if disobedient, to submit to the direst penalties and death itself. As a fact, if any are judged to have betrayed the doings of the sect or to have resisted commands given, punishment is inflicted on them not infrequently, and with so much audacity and dexterity that the assassin very often escapes the detection and penalty of his crime.

10. But to simulate and wish to lie hid; to bind men like slaves in the very tightest bonds, and without giving any sufficient reason; to make use of men enslaved to the will of another for any arbitrary act; to arm men's right hands for bloodshed after securing impunity for the crime - all this is an enormity from which nature recoils. Wherefore, reason and truth itself make it plain that the society of which we are speaking is in antagonism with justice and natural uprightness. And this becomes still plainer, inasmuch as other arguments, also, and those very manifest, prove that it is essentially opposed to natural virtue. For, no matter how great may be men's cleverness in concealing and their experience in lying, it is impossible to prevent the effects of any cause from showing, in some way, the intrinsic nature of the cause whence they come. "A good tree cannot produce bad fruit, nor a bad tree produce good fruit."[74] Now, the masonic sect produces fruits that are pernicious and of the bitterest savior. For, from what We have above most clearly shown, that which is their ultimate purpose forces itself into view - namely, the utter overthrow of that whole religious and political order of the world which the

---

[74] *Matthew* 7:18.

Christian teaching has produced, and the substitution of a new state of things in accordance with their ideas, of which the foundations and laws shall be drawn from mere naturalism.

11. What We have said, and are about to say, must be understood of the sect of the Freemasons taken generically, and in so far as it comprises the associations kindred to it and confederated with it, but not of the individual members of them. There may be persons amongst these, and not a few who, although not free from the guilt of having entangled themselves in such associations, yet are neither themselves partners in their criminal acts nor aware of the ultimate object which they are endeavoring to attain. In the same way, some of the affiliated societies, perhaps, by no means approve of the extreme conclusions which they would, if consistent, embrace as necessarily following from their common principles, did not their very foulness strike them with horror. Some of these, again, are led by circumstances of times and places either to aim at smaller things than the others usually attempt or than they themselves would wish to attempt. They are not, however, for this reason, to be reckoned as alien to the masonic federation; for the masonic federation is to be judged not so much by the things which it has done, or brought to completion, as by the sum of its pronounced opinions.

12. Now, the fundamental doctrine of the naturalists, which they sufficiently make known by their very name, is that human nature and human reason ought in all things to be mistress and guide. Laying this down, they care little for duties to God, or pervert them by erroneous and vague opinions. For they deny that anything has been taught by God; they allow no dogma of religion or truth which cannot be understood by the human intelligence, nor any teacher who ought to be believed by reason of his authority.

And since it is the special and exclusive duty of the Catholic Church fully to set forth in words truths divinely received, to teach, besides other divine helps to salvation, the authority of its office, and to defend the same with perfect purity, it is against the Church that the rage and attack of the enemies are principally directed.

13. In those matters which regard religion let it be seen how the sect of the Freemasons acts, especially where it is more "free to act without restraint, and then let any one judge whether in fact it does not wish to carry out the policy of the naturalists. By a long and persevering labor, they endeavor to bring about this result - namely, that the teaching office and authority of the Church may become of no account in the civil State; and for this same reason they declare to the people and contend that Church and State ought to be altogether disunited. By this means they reject from the laws and from the commonwealth the wholesome influence of the Catholic religion; and they consequently imagine that States ought to be constituted without any regard for the laws and precepts of the Church.

14. Nor do they think it enough to disregard the Church - the best of guides - unless they also injure it by their hostility. Indeed, with them it is lawful to attack with impunity the very foundations of the Catholic religion, in speech, in writing, and in teaching; and even the rights of the Church are not spared, and the offices with which it is divinely invested are not safe. The least possible liberty to manage affairs is left to the Church; and this is done by laws not apparently very hostile, but in reality framed and fitted to hinder freedom of action. Moreover, We see exceptional and onerous laws imposed upon the clergy, to the end that they may be continually diminished in number and in necessary

means. We see also the remnants of the possessions of the Church fettered by the strictest conditions, and subjected to the power and arbitrary will of the administrators of the State, and the religious orders rooted up and scattered.

15. But against the apostolic see and the Roman Pontiff the contention of these enemies has been for a long time directed. The Pontiff was first, for specious reasons, thrust out from the bulwark of his liberty and of his right, the civil princedom; soon, he was unjustly driven into a condition which was unbearable because of the difficulties raised on all sides; and now the time has come when the partisans of the sects openly declare, what in secret among themselves they have for a long time plotted, that the sacred power of the Pontiffs must be abolished, and that the papacy itself, founded by divine right, must be utterly destroyed. If other proofs were wanting, this fact would be sufficiently disclosed by the testimony of men well informed, of whom some at other times, and others again recently, have declared it to be true of the Freemasons that they especially desire to assail the Church with irreconcilable hostility, and that they will never rest until they have destroyed whatever the Holy Pontiffs have established for the sake of religion.

16. If those who are admitted as members are not commanded to abjure by any form of words the Catholic doctrines, this omission, so far from being adverse to the designs of the Freemasons, is more useful for their purposes. First, in this way they easily deceive the simple-minded and the heedless, and can induce a far greater number to become members. Again, as all who offer themselves are received whatever may be their form of religion, they thereby teach the great error of this age-that a regard for

religion should be held as an indifferent matter, and that all religions are alike. This manner of reasoning is calculated to bring about the ruin of all forms of religion, and especially of the Catholic religion, which, as it is the only one that is true, cannot, without great injustice, be regarded as merely equal to other religions.

17. But the naturalists go much further; for, having, in the highest things, entered upon a wholly erroneous course, they are carried headlong to extremes, either by reason of the weakness of human nature, or because God inflicts upon them the just punishment of their pride. Hence it happens that they no longer consider as certain and permanent those things which are fully understood by the natural light of reason, such as certainly are - the existence of God, the immaterial nature of the human soul, and its immortality. The sect of the Freemasons, by a similar course of error, is exposed to these same dangers; for, although in a general way they may profess the existence of God, they themselves are witnesses that they do not all maintain this truth with the full assent of the mind or with a firm conviction. Neither do they conceal that this question about God is the greatest source and cause of discords among them; in fact, it is certain that a considerable contention about this same subject has existed among them very lately. But, indeed, the sect allows great liberty to its votaries, so that to each side is given the right to defend its own opinion, either that there is a God, or that there is none; and those who obstinately contend that there is no God are as easily initiated as those who contend that God exists, though, like the pantheists, they have false notions concerning Him: all which is nothing else than taking away the reality, while retaining some absurd representation of the divine nature.

18. When this greatest fundamental truth has been overturned or weakened, it follows that those truths, also, which are known by the teaching of nature must begin to fall - namely, that all things were made by the free will of God the Creator; that the world is governed by Providence; that souls do not die; that to this life of men upon the earth there will succeed another and an everlasting life.

19. When these truths are done away with, which are as the principles of nature and important for knowledge and for practical use, it is easy to see what will become of both public and private morality. We say nothing of those more heavenly virtues, which no one can exercise or even acquire without a special gift and grace of God; of which necessarily no trace can be found in those who reject as unknown the redemption of mankind, the grace of God, the sacraments, and the happiness to be obtained in heaven. We speak now of the duties which have their origin in natural probity. That God is the Creator of the world and its provident Ruler; that the eternal law commands the natural order to be maintained, and forbids that it be disturbed; that the last end of men is a destiny far above human things and beyond this sojourning upon the earth: these are the sources and these the principles of all justice and morality. If these be taken away, as the naturalists and Freemasons desire, there will immediately be no knowledge as to what constitutes justice and injustice, or upon what principle morality is founded. And, in truth, the teaching of morality which alone finds favor with the sect of Freemasons, and in which they contend that youth should be instructed, is that which they call "civil," and "independent," and "free," namely, that which does not contain any religious belief. But, how insufficient such teaching is, how wanting in soundness, and how easily moved by every impulse of passion, is sufficiently proved by

its sad fruits, which have already begun to appear. For, wherever, by removing Christian education, this teaching has begun more completely to rule, there goodness and integrity of morals have begun quickly to perish, monstrous and shameful opinions have grown up, and the audacity of evil deeds has risen to a high degree. All this is commonly complained of and deplored; and not a few of those who by no means wish to do so are compelled by abundant evidence to give not infrequently the same testimony.

20. Moreover, human nature was stained by original sin, and is therefore more disposed to vice than to virtue. For a virtuous life it is absolutely necessary to restrain the disorderly movements of the soul, and to make the passions obedient to reason. In this conflict human things must very often be despised, and the greatest labors and hardships must be undergone, in order that reason may always hold its sway. But the naturalists and Freemasons, having no faith in those things which we have learned by the revelation of God, deny that our first parents sinned, and consequently think that free will is not at all weakened and inclined to evil.[75] On the contrary, exaggerating rather the power and the excellence of nature, and placing therein alone the principle and rule of justice, they cannot even imagine that there is any need at all of a constant struggle and a perfect steadfastness to overcome the violence and rule of our passions.

Wherefore we see that men are publicly tempted by the many allurements of pleasure; that there are journals and pamphlets with neither moderation nor shame; that stage-plays are remarkable for license; that designs for works of art are shamelessly sought in the laws of a so called verism; that the contrivances of

---

[75] Trid., sess. vi, De justif., c. 1. Text of the Council of Trent: "tametsi in eis (sc. Judaeis) liberum arbitrium minime extinctum esset, viribus licet attenuatum et inclinatum".

a soft and delicate life are most carefully devised; and that all the blandishments of pleasure are diligently sought out by which virtue may be lulled to sleep. Wickedly, also, but at the same time quite consistently, do those act who do away with the expectation of the joys of heaven, and bring down all happiness to the level of mortality, and, as it were, sink it in the earth. Of what We have said the following fact, astonishing not so much in itself as in its open expression, may serve as a confirmation. For, since generally no one is accustomed to obey crafty and clever men so submissively as those whose soul is weakened and broken down by the domination of the passions, there have been in the sect of the Freemasons some who have plainly determined and proposed that, artfully and of set purpose, the multitude should be satiated with a boundless license of vice, as, when this had been done, it would easily come under their power and authority for any acts of daring.

21. What refers to domestic life in the teaching of the naturalists is almost all contained in the following declarations: that marriage belongs to the genus of commercial contracts, which can rightly be revoked by the will of those who made them, and that the civil rulers of the State have power over the matrimonial bond; that in the education of youth nothing is to be taught in the matter of religion as of certain and fixed opinion; and each one must be left at liberty to follow, when he comes of age, whatever he may prefer. To these things the Freemasons fully assent; and not only assent, but have long endeavored to make them into a law and institution. For in many countries, and those nominally Catholic, it is enacted that no marriages shall be considered lawful except those contracted by the civil rite; in other places the law permits divorce; and in others every effort is used to make it lawful as soon as may be. Thus, the time is quickly coming when

marriages will be turned into another kind of contract - that is into changeable and uncertain unions which fancy may join together, and which the same when changed may disunite.

With the greatest unanimity the sect of the Freemasons also endeavors to take to itself the education of youth. They think that they can easily mold to their opinions that soft and pliant age, and bend it whither they will; and that nothing can be more fitted than this to enable them to bring up the youth of the State after their own plan. Therefore, in the education and instruction of children they allow no share, either of teaching or of discipline, to the ministers of the Church; and in many places they have procured that the education of youth shall be exclusively in the hands of laymen, and that nothing which treats of the most important and most holy duties of men to God shall be introduced into the instructions on morals.

22. Then come their doctrines of politics, in which the naturalists lay down that all men have the same right, and are in every respect of equal and like condition; that each one is naturally free; that no one has the right to command another; that it is an act of violence to require men to obey any authority other than that which is obtained from themselves. According to this, therefore, all things belong to the free people; power is held by the command or permission of the people, so that, when the popular will changes, rulers may lawfully be deposed and the source of all rights and civil duties is either in the multitude or in the governing authority when this is constituted according to the latest doctrines. It is held also that the State should be without God; that in the various forms of religion there is no reason why one should have precedence of another; and that they are all to occupy the same place.

23. That these doctrines are equally acceptable to the Freemasons, and that they would wish to constitute States according to this example and model, is too well known to require proof. For some time past they have openly endeavored to bring this about with all their strength and resources; and in this they prepare the way for not a few bolder men who are hurrying on even to worse things, in their endeavor to obtain equality and community of all goods by the destruction of every distinction of rank and property.

24. What, therefore, sect of the Freemasons is, and what course it pursues, appears sufficiently from the summary We have briefly given. Their chief dogmas are so greatly and manifestly at variance with reason that nothing can be more perverse. To wish to destroy the religion and the Church which God Himself has established, and whose perpetuity He insures by His protection, and to bring back after a lapse of eighteen centuries the manners and customs of the pagans, is signal folly and audacious impiety. Neither is it less horrible nor more tolerable that they should repudiate the benefits which Jesus Christ so mercifully obtained, not only for individuals, but also for the family and for civil society, benefits which, even according to the judgment and testimony of enemies of Christianity, are very great. In this insane and wicked endeavor we may almost see the implacable hatred and spirit of revenge with which Satan himself is inflamed against Jesus Christ. So also the studious endeavor of the Freemasons to destroy the chief foundations of justice and honesty, and to cooperate with those who would wish, as if they were mere animals, to do what they please, tends only to the ignominious and disgraceful ruin of the human race.

The evil, too, is increased by the dangers which threaten both domestic and civil society. As We have elsewhere shown,[76] in marriage, according to the belief of almost every nation, there is something sacred and religious; and the law of God has determined that marriages shall not be dissolved. If they are deprived of their sacred character, and made dissoluble, trouble and confusion in the family will be the result, the wife being deprived of her dignity and the children left without protection as to their interests and wellbeing. To have in public matters no care for religion, and in the arrangement and administration of civil affairs to have no more regard for God than if He did not exist, is a rashness unknown to the very pagans; for in their heart and soul the notion of a divinity and the need of public religion were so firmly fixed that they would have thought it easier to have city without foundation than a city without God. Human society, indeed for which by nature we are formed, has been constituted by God the Author of nature; and from Him, as from their principle and source, flow in all their strength and permanence the countless benefits with which society abounds. As we are each of us admonished by the very voice of nature to worship God in piety and holiness, as the Giver unto us of life and of all that is good therein, so also and for the same reason, nations and States are bound to worship Him; and therefore it is clear that those who would absolve society from all religious duty act not only unjustly but also with ignorance and folly.

25. As men are by the will of God born for civil union and society, and as the power to rule is so necessary a bond of society that, if it be taken away, society must at once be broken up, it follows that from Him who is the Author of society has come also the authority to rule; so that whosoever rules, he is the minister

---

[76] See *Arcanum*, no. 81.

of God. Wherefore, as the end and nature of human society so requires, it is right to obey the just commands of lawful authority, as it is right to obey God who rules all things; and it is most untrue that the people have it in their power to cast aside their obedience whenever they please.

26. In like manner, no one doubts that all men are equal one to another, so far as regards their common origin and nature, or the last end which each one has to attain, or the rights and duties which are thence derived. But, as the abilities of all are not equal, as one differs from another in the powers of mind or body, and as there are very many dissimilarities of manner, disposition, and character, it is most repugnant to reason to endeavor to confine all within the same measure, and to extend complete equality to the institutions of civic life. Just as a perfect condition of the body results from the conjunction and composition of its various members, which, though differing in form and purpose, make, by their union and the distribution of each one to its proper place, a combination beautiful to behold, firm in strength, and necessary for use; so, in the commonwealth, there is an almost infinite dissimilarity of men, as parts of the whole. If they are to be all equal, and each is to follow his own will, the State will appear most deformed; but if, with a distinction of degrees of dignity, of pursuits and employments, all aptly conspire for the common good, they will present the image of a State both well constituted and conformable to nature.

27. Now, from the disturbing errors which We have described the greatest dangers to States are to be feared. For, the fear of God and reverence for divine laws being taken away, the authority of rulers despised, sedition permitted and approved, and the popular passions urged on to lawlessness, with no restraint save

that of punishment, a change and overthrow of all things will necessarily follow. Yea, this change and overthrow is deliberately planned and put forward by many associations of communists and socialists; and to their undertakings the sect of Freemasons is not hostile, but greatly favors their designs, and holds in common with them their chief opinions. And if these men do not at once and everywhere endeavor to carry out their extreme views, it is not to be attributed to their teaching and their will, but to the virtue of that divine religion which cannot be destroyed; and also because the sounder part of men, refusing to be enslaved to secret societies, vigorously resist their insane attempts.

28. Would that all men would judge of the tree by its fruit, and would acknowledge the seed and origin of the evils which press upon us, and of the dangers that are impending! We have to deal with a deceitful and crafty enemy, who, gratifying the ears of people and of princes, has ensnared them by smooth speeches and by adulation. Ingratiating themselves with rulers under a pretense of friendship, the Freemasons have endeavored to make them their allies and powerful helpers for the destruction of the Christian name; and that they might more strongly urge them on, they have, with determined calumny, accused the Church of invidiously contending with rulers in matters that affect their authority and sovereign power. Having, by these artifices, insured their own safety and audacity, they have begun to exercise great weight in the government of States; but nevertheless they are prepared to shake the foundations of empires, to harass the rulers of the State, to accuse, and to cast them out, as often as they appear to govern otherwise than they themselves could have wished. In like manner, they have by flattery deluded the people. Proclaiming with a loud voice liberty and public prosperity, and saying that it was owing to the Church and to sovereigns that the

multitude were not drawn out of their unjust servitude and poverty, they have imposed upon the people, and, exciting them by a thirst for novelty, they have urged them to assail both the Church and the civil power. Nevertheless, the expectation of the benefits which was hoped for is greater than the reality; indeed, the common people, more oppressed than they were before, are deprived in their misery of that solace which, if things had been arranged in a Christian manner, they would have had with ease and in abundance. But, whoever strive against the order which Divine Providence has constituted pay usually the penalty of their pride, and meet with affliction and misery where they rashly hoped to find all things prosperous and in conformity with their desires.

29. The Church, if she directs men to render obedience chiefly and above all to God the sovereign Lord, is wrongly and falsely believed either to be envious of the civil power or to arrogate to herself something of the rights of sovereigns. On the contrary, she teaches that what is rightly due to the civil power must be rendered to it with a conviction and consciousness of duty. In teaching that from God Himself comes the right of ruling, she adds a great dignity to civil authority, and on small help towards obtaining the obedience and good will of the citizens. The friend of peace and sustainer of concord, she embraces all with maternal love, and, intent only upon giving help to mortal man, she teaches that to justice must be joined clemency, equity to authority, and moderation to lawgiving; that no one's right must be violated; that order and public tranquility are to be maintained; and that the poverty of those are in need is, as far as possible, to be relieved by public and private charity. "But for this reason," to use the words of St. Augustine, "men think, or would have it believed, that Christian teaching is not suited to the good of the

State; for they wish the State to be founded not on solid virtue, but on the impunity of vice."[77] Knowing these things, both princes and people would act with political wisdom, and according to the needs of general safety, if, instead of joining with Freemasons to destroy the Church, they joined with the Church in repelling their attacks.

30. Whatever the future may be, in this grave and widespread evil it is Our duty, venerable brethren, to endeavor to find a remedy. And because We know that Our best and firmest hope of a remedy is in the power of that divine religion which the Freemasons hate in proportion to their fear of it, We think it to be of chief importance to call that most saving power to Our aid against the common enemy. Therefore, whatsoever the Roman Pontiffs Our predecessors have decreed for the purpose of opposing the undertakings and endeavors of the masonic sect, and whatsoever they have enacted to enter or withdraw men from societies of this kind, We ratify and confirm it all by our apostolic authority: and trusting greatly to the good will of Christians, We pray and beseech each one, for the sake of his eternal salvation, to be most conscientiously careful not in the least to depart from what the apostolic see has commanded in this matter.

31. We pray and beseech you, venerable brethren, to join your efforts with Ours, and earnestly to strive for the extirpation of this foul plague, which is creeping through the veins of the body politic. You have to defend the glory of God and the salvation of your neighbor; and with the object of your strife before you, neither courage nor strength will be wanting. It will be for your prudence to judge by what means you can best overcome the dif-

---

[77] *Epistola* 137, ad *Volusianum*, c. v, n. 20 (PL 33 525).

ficulties and obstacles you meet with. But, as it befits the authority of Our office that We Ourselves should point out some suitable way of proceeding, We wish it to be your rule first of all to tear away the mask from Freemasonry, and to let it be seen as it really is; and by sermons and pastoral letters to instruct the people as to the artifices used by societies of this kind in seducing men and enticing them into their ranks, and as to the depravity of their opinions and the wickedness of their acts. As Our predecessors have many times repeated, let no man think that he may for any reason whatsoever join the masonic sect, if he values his Catholic name and his eternal salvation as he ought to value them. Let no one be deceived by a pretense of honesty. It may seem to some that Freemasons demand nothing that is openly contrary to religion and morality; but, as the whole principle and object of the sect lies in what is vicious and criminal, to join with these men or in any way to help them cannot be lawful.

32. Further, by assiduous teaching and exhortation, the multitude must be drawn to learn diligently the precepts of religion; for which purpose we earnestly advise that by opportune writings and sermons they be taught the elements of those sacred truths in which Christian philosophy is contained. The result of this will be that the minds of men will be made sound by instruction, and will be protected against many forms of error and inducements to wickedness, especially in the present unbounded freedom of writing and insatiable eagerness for learning.

33. Great, indeed, is the work; but in it the clergy will share your labors, if, through your care, they are fitted for it by learning and a well-turned life. This good and great work requires to be helped also by the industry of those amongst the laity in whom a love of religion and of country is joined to learning and goodness

of life. By uniting the efforts of both clergy and laity, strive, venerable brethren, to make men thoroughly know and love the Church; for, the greater their knowledge and love of the Church, the more will they be turned away from clandestine societies.

34. Wherefore, not without cause do We use this occasion to state again what We have stated elsewhere, namely, that the Third Order of St. Francis, whose discipline We a little while ago prudently mitigated,[78] should be studiously promoted and sustained; for the whole object of this Order, as constituted by its founder, is to invite men to an imitation of Jesus Christ, to a love of the Church, and to the observance of all Christian virtues; and therefore it ought to be of great influence in suppressing the contagion of wicked societies. Let, therefore, this holy sodality be strengthened by a daily increase. Amongst the many benefits to be expected from it will be the great benefit of drawing the minds of men to liberty, fraternity, and equality of right; not such as the Freemasons absurdly imagine, but such as Jesus Christ obtained for the human race and St. Francis aspired to: the liberty, We mean, of sons of God, through which we may be free from slavery to Satan or to our passions, both of them most wicked masters; the fraternity whose origin is in God, the common Creator and Father of all; the equality which, founded on justice and charity, does not take away all distinctions among men, but, out of the varieties of life, of duties, and of pursuits, forms that union

---

[78] The text here refers to the encyclical letter *Auspicato Concessum* (Sept. 17, 1882), in which Pope Leo XIII had recently glorified St. Francis of Assisi on the occasion of the seventh centenary of his birch. In this encyclical, the Pope had presented the Third Order of St. Francis as a Christian answer to the social problems of the times. The constitution *Misericors Dei Filius* (June 23, 1883) expressly recalled that the neglect in which Christian virtues are held is the main cause of the evils that threaten societies. In confirming the rule of the Third Order and adapting it to the needs of modern times, Pope Leo XIII had intended to bring back the largest possible number of souls to the practice of these virtues.

and that harmony which naturally tend to the benefit and dignity of society.

35. In the third place, there is a matter wisely instituted by our forefathers, but in course of time laid aside, which may now be used as a pattern and form of something similar. We mean the associations of guilds of workmen, for the protection, under the guidance of religion, both of their temporal interests and of their morality. If our ancestors, by long use and experience, felt the benefit of these guilds, our age perhaps will feel it the more by reason of the opportunity which they will give of crushing the power of the sects. Those who support themselves by the labor of their hands, besides being, by their very condition, most worthy above all others of charity and consolation, are also especially exposed to the allurements of men whose ways lie in fraud and deceit. Therefore, they ought to be helped with the greatest possible kindness, and to be invited to join associations that are good, lest they be drawn away to others that are evil. For this reason, We greatly wish, for the salvation of the people, that, under the auspices and patronage of the bishops, and at convenient times, these gilds may be generally restored. To Our great delight, sodalities of this kind and also associations of masters have in many places already been established, having, each class of them, for their object to help the honest workman, to protect and guard his children and family, and to promote in them piety, Christian knowledge, and a moral life. And in this matter We cannot omit mentioning that exemplary society, named after its founder, St. Vincent, which has deserved so well of the lower classes. Its acts and its aims are well known. Its whole object is to give relief to the poor and miserable. This it does with singular prudence and modesty; and the less it wishes to be seen, the better is it fitted

for the exercise of Christian charity, and for the relief of suffering.

36. In the fourth place, in order more easily to attain what We wish, to your fidelity and watchfulness We commend in a special manner the young, as being the hope of human society. Devote the greatest part of your care to their instruction; and do not think that any precaution can be great enough in keeping them from masters and schools whence the pestilent breath of the sects is to be feared. Under your guidance, let parents, religious instructors, and priests having the cure of souls use every opportunity, in their Christian teaching, of warning their children and pupils of the infamous nature of these societies, so that they may learn in good time to beware of the various and fraudulent artifices by which their promoters are accustomed to ensnare people. And those who instruct the young in religious knowledge will act wisely if they induce all of them to resolve and to undertake never to bind themselves to any society without the knowledge of their parents, or the advice of their parish priest or director.

37. We well know, however, that our united labors will by no means suffice to pluck up these pernicious seeds from the Lord's field, unless the Heavenly Master of the vineyard shall mercifully help us in our endeavors. We must, therefore, with great and anxious care, implore of Him the help which the greatness of the danger and of the need requires. The sect of the Freemasons shows itself insolent and proud of its success, and seems as if it would put no bounds to its pertinacity. Its followers, joined together by a wicked compact and by secret counsels, give help one to another, and excite one another to an audacity for evil things. So vehement an attack demands an equal defense-namely, that all

good men should form the widest possible association of action and of prayer. We beseech them, therefore, with united hearts, to stand together and unmoved against the advancing force of the sects; and in mourning and supplication to stretch out their hands to God, praying that the Christian name may flourish and prosper, that the Church may enjoy its needed liberty, that those who have gone astray may return to a right mind, that error at length may give place to truth, and vice to virtue. Let us take our helper and intercessor the Virgin Mary, Mother of God, so that she, who from the moment of her conception overcame Satan may show her power over these evil sects, in which is revived the contumacious spirit of the demon, together with his unsubdued perfidy and deceit. Let us beseech Michael, the prince of the heavenly angels, who drove out the infernal foe; and Joseph, the spouse of the most holy Virgin, and heavenly patron of the Catholic Church; and the great Apostles, Peter and Paul, the fathers and victorious champions of the Christian faith. By their patronage, and by perseverance in united prayer, we hope that God will mercifully and opportunely succor the human race, which is encompassed by so many dangers.

38. As a pledge of heavenly gifts and of Our benevolence, We lovingly grant in the Lord, to you, venerable brethren, and to the clergy and all the people committed to your watchful care, Our apostolic benediction.

Given at St. Peter's in Rome, the twentieth day of April, 1884, the sixth year of Our pontificate.

LEO XIII

Paragraphs 1 - 2:

In his opening preamble to *Humanum Genus*, Pope Leo XIII delineates the ontological terms on which war is now being waged against the Catholic Church. Due to the consequences of the fall from God (i.e., humanity's original sin), man is now pitted against each other in two kingdoms. One kingdom is the Kingdom of God, which Leo XIII calls the Church of Jesus Christ (i.e., the One, Holy, Catholic, and Apostolic Church), whose citizens cling to it for salvation. The other is the kingdom of Satan, whose citizens are those who *"follow the fatal example of their leader and of our first parents, those who refuse to obey the divine and eternal law, and who have many aims of their own in contempt of God, and many aims also against God."*

Quoting from Saint Augustine's *City of God*, Leo XIII describes how these two kingdoms came to be, *"Two loves formed two cities: the love of self, reaching even to the contempt of God, an earthly city; and the love of God, reaching to con-tempt of self, a heavenly one."* Since there has never been a time when these two cities were not at war, through whatever passions and devices were available at the time, in this present age, the kingdom of Satan is being *"assisted by that strongly organized and widespread association called the Freemasons,"* who Leo XIII says have openly and publicly declared their intentions to destroy the Catholic Church.

Paragraphs 3 - 5:

In these paragraphs, Pope Leo XIII explains why this issue falls under the purview of the Apostolic duty to guard and defend the sheep whose salvation was committed unto their care by Christ Jesus. On the dangers of Freemasonry, the Catholic Church was not slow in detecting and warning the world how

Satan was using Freemasonry, even though the enemy had cleverly tried to conceal himself and his intentions.

Leo XIII then recounts all the constitutions, acts, and decrees that his predecessors had promulgated against Freemasonry, secret societies, and the Masonic principals, beginning with Pope Clement XII's *In Eminenti* in 1738, which was confirmed and renewed by Benedict XIV in his *Providas Romanorum* in 1751 and by Pius VII in his *Ecclesiam a Jesu Christo* in 1821. Now, with *Humanum Genus*, that gives this dogmatic prohibition against Freemasonry a nearly one hundred and fifty-year legacy.

Paragraphs 6 - 7:

This section notes that it was through the investigation of what was publicly known about Freemasonry, such as the exposé rituals and *Anderson's Constitution,* that have been previously discussed here in *The Catholic Catechism on Freemasonry* and through *"the personal testimony of those who were in the secret, this apostolic see denounced the sect of the Freemasons, and publicly declared its constitution, as contrary to law and right, to be pernicious no less to Christendom than to the State; and it forbade any one to enter the society, under the penalties which the Church is wont to inflict upon exceptionally guilty persons."* That is, the penalties attached to disobeying the laws of the Church on this matter belong to the category of penalties reserved for the gravest of sins.

Despite the continuity and consistency of Papal pronouncements on this issue, there were those in the Church who sought to undermine this teaching by arguing that a Pope could not regulate one's membership in Freemasonry, that this aspect of their private life was not under the purview of the Apostolic see. However, there were also those who were obedient to Church teaching and many princes and heads of governments who either enforced the Church teaching on Masonic sects or denounced Freemasonry according to their laws.

Similar to Pope Pius IX's statement in paragraph twenty-nine of *Etsi Multa*, in paragraph seven here, Leo XIII states that since his predecessors acted prudently, the world did not heed their warning. *"In consequence, the sect of Freemasons grew with a rapidity beyond conception in the course of a century and a half, until it came to be able, by means of fraud or of audacity, to gain such entrance into every rank of the State as to seem to be almost its ruling power."* Indeed, Masonic colonization throughout the world is something to fear; not for the Church to fear, because *"her foundation is much too firm to be overturned by the effort of men – but for those States in which prevails the power, either of the sect of which we are speaking or of other sects not dissimilar which lend themselves to it as disciples and subordinates."*

Paragraph 8:

In this final section, before Leo XIII launches into his complete treatment on Freemasonry, he returns to explaining why it belongs to his Apostolic duties as the Supreme Pontiff to *"arrest the contagion of this fatal plague."* He states that while in previous documents he attacked Masonic philosophy indirectly by demonstrating how it is related to other false teachings, such as socialism, communism, nihilism, and divorce, now here in *Humanum Genus*, he will offer a direct and frontal attack against Freemasonry and sects like it.

Paragraphs 9 – 10:

Leo XIII opens up his treatment of Freemasonry through what Pope Clement XII found *in In Eminenti Apostolatus specula* to be that institution's third error: its secrecy and lack of transparency. Leo XIII finds that Freemasonry and its many appendant Masonic bodies use this secrecy to create a fraudulent pretense. On the one hand, Freemasonry attempts to create a public face through its publications, newspapers, love for people experiencing poverty, desire for cultural refinement, learning, and scholarship. Then, there are the inner workings of Freemasonry that he compares to the pseudo-Christian and gnostic religion called Manichaeism from the third-century.[79] By selecting its own members and binding them to secrecy and obedience under pain of fatal penalties, Freemasonry can hide its deepest mysteries and designs from the public and its members of lower grades. Leo XIII calls this obligated promise to assassinate their members if they reveal their secrets a form of enslavement and contrary to natural virtue and uprightness.

Drawing from *Matthew* 7:18, Leo XIII finds that Freemasonry is corrupt with evil at its core, and no wrong tree can produce bad fruit; thereby, *"the masonic sect produces fruits that are pernicious and of the bitterest savor."*

This section closes with Leo XIII stating that as proof already provided, the true objective of Freemasonry is to supplant the Catholic Church by installing a new world order of religion and politics that is inspired by naturalism and which completely diverges from the divinely inspired order of religion and politics that has been brought and nurtured through Christian teaching.

---

[79] Founded by the Iranian prophet Mani, Manichaeism, at its core, was just Zoroastrianism (sixth-century B.C.) revisited with the import of some elements of Christianity. Both of these religions use the concept of good struggling against evil to create a dualistic cosmology.

Paragraph 11:

Before Pope Leo XIII begins his treatise on the relationship between Freemasonry and naturalism, he moves in this paragraph to define how he uses the term 'Freemasonry.' First, he states that using the term 'Freemasonry' is to encompass all of the appendant Masonic bodies broadly. Second, he admits that every person associated with Freemasonry, *"although not free from the guilt of having entangled themselves in such associations,"* may not be fully aware of the evil they are partaking in. Similarly, it is the case with some of the appendant Masonic bodies that may differ in some aspects from what is appropriately called 'Freemasonry' but are not entirely alien from what they have attached themselves to. Therefore, they, too, can be judged according to the philosophy of their parent body.

Paragraphs 12 – 15

In these paragraphs, Pope Leo XIII explains how Freemasonry promotes naturalism and how it is exporting that philosophy around the world to supplant divine revelation as the source of all that is good. Leo XIII's very generic working definition of naturalism is simply a philosophy that denies the intentional intercession of God through revelation, grace, and supernatural works; rather, it is through natural laws that things come to be what they are. That is, *"human nature and human reason ought to be in all things to be mistress and guide."*

The Freemason is indeed taught that through his intellect and reason, he comes to know how to apply the liberal arts and sciences (e.g., rhetoric, logic, and geometry) and the working tools of an operative mason to his own life for the benefit of self-improvement. As a naturalistic philosophy, Freemasonry promotes autonomy on several levels, such as freedom from authority and freedom from religious dogma by choosing how one's intellect and reason will guide them to build their own life, as long as it remains within the circumscribed bounds of Masonic law.

Freemasonry intends to build into its initiates a Masonic conscience, which, from the Catholic perspective, is a deformed conscience because it rejects divine revelation as the basis of its life. Denying supernatural faith and the efficacy of God's grace and relying only on reason, logic, and things that are perceptible to the senses, the Masonic conscience is the crowning height of naturalism par excellence.

Leo XIII understood that the religious naturalism found in Freemasonry inveighs against what he views as the two duties of the Catholic Church, which are to proclaim, defend, and teach the Gospel and to administer the sacraments (i.e., offer divine help to salvation). That is, as was stated previously in the chapter on the religion of Freemasonry, through its sacraments, Freemasonry offers its initiates an autosoteric method of deliverance from immorality through personal freedom and due attention to moral discipline, which is the opposite of the Christian hetrosoteric delivery method that demands that man must be saved by another (namely, Jesus Christ).

Leo XIII believes that it is this idea of being autonomous from divine revelation and religious dogma that Freemasonry is importing into governments throughout the world. Through this exercise, not only are laws designed apart from divine revelation and Church teaching, but laws are being designed to allow religious institutions and religious people to be attacked. Indeed, notice how, in one breath, the First Amendment of the *Constitution of the United States* enshrines religious autonomy, and in the next breath, enshrines religious persecution through the exercise of freedom of speech. In this way, the inevitable outcome of naturalism is that state laws become pervasively more and more detached from divine revelation and, thereby, more and more hostile to the teachings of the Catholic Church.

Paragraphs 16 – 21:

In these sections, Pope Leo XIII connects naturalism with indifferentism. Freemasonry is clever in not refusing initiates based on their religion. There are subordinate lodges that will far sooner refuse a candidate on the grounds of their race, their profession, their reputation, or their physical condition than they would refuse them based upon their religion. Leo XIII states that it is more beneficial for Freemasonry to be indifferent towards their initiate's religion because it creates the pretense that one's religion is to be subject to the universal religion they are being initiated into. Once made an Entered Apprentice, the initiate learns that all religions are equal and unexceptional, and the name of their personal God is to be subordinated to the Grand Architect of the Universe. The great theophany of Freemasonry is that God is disinterested in humanity.

The seed of indifferentism towards religion that Freemasonry has exported throughout the world ruins "all forms of religion," especially Catholicism, which posits that it proclaims with authority the fullness of truth. There is no reconciliation between Catholicism, which teaches that there is no religion equal to it because it proclaims the fullness of God's truth and the teaching of Freemasonry that Catholicism is just one of many mere opinions of man.

Nevertheless, when indifferentism is married with naturalism, the fruit of Freemasonry wields something far graver. While the initiate first learns to subjugate the name of his personal God into a pantheistic collection of other gods, his advancement in learning how to apply the liberal arts and sciences and the working tools of an operative mason is teaching him that he does not need God at all. It is through this light of reason alone that either convinces the Freemason that there is no personal God interested in assisting him or that the existence of God needs to be questioned altogether.

Leo XII finds it a joke that Freemasons may profess the existence of God, but *"they are witnesses that they do not all maintain this truth with the full assent of the mind or with a firm conviction."* How can they profess God's existence but simultaneously confess that God is not exceptional, all true and without equal? How can they profess the existence of God but simultaneously bind themselves to an organization in which they cannot discuss God or even mention the personal name of their God during open lodge meetings?

The acceptance of indifferentism engrains the rejection of divine revelation. By importing this idea into society, Freemasonry comes closer to making naturalism its rule and guide. Leo XIII finds that we will know that naturalism has taken root when Christian education is removed and when there is *"no knowledge as to what constitutes justice and injustice, or upon what principle morality is founded."* His Holiness saw a world in which state governments, influenced by Freemasonry, would take charge of education. However, he did not see a world in which even Catholic schools and universities would be corrupted with these same principles of Freemasonry.

Paragraphs 20 – 23:

Pope Leo XIII narrates the relationship between naturalism and representative government in these paragraphs. Four years previous to *Humanum Genus*, Leo XIII promulgated his encyclical *Arcaum* on the topic of Christian Marriage in which he pushed back, in the strongest terms, against states determining who is married according to civil contracts rather than being determined by the Sacrament of the Church. He also wrote about the evils of divorce. Here, Leo XIII returns to those topics found in *Arcaum* and ties them to naturalism. He is not against representative government but finds that its major flaw is that it is susceptible to being more easily swayed by popular opinion than unchanging divine revelation. Here again, the Pontiff proved prophetic in his assessment of what type of laws come to life in governments that abandon divine revelation as the basis of all law.

Picking up from all of the anti-clerical reforms and persecution of the Catholic Church that his predecessor Pope Pius IX outlined in *Etsi Multi*, Leo XIII points to the Freemasons being intimately involved with the movement to secularize education, *"and in many places, they have procured that the education of youth shall be exclusively in the hands of laymen, and that nothing which treats of the most important and most holy duties of men to God shall be introduced into the instructions on morals."* Leo XIII argues that once schools become free from divine revelation and religious dogma, all they have to teach is indifferentism and naturalism. Indeed, this is why schools today have no recourse but to teach homosexualism because their curriculum cannot be grounded in truth.

A central argument of this section is that all of these demonic attacks on government, family, and children have the full endorsement of Freemasonry and, through them, have been exported to every country where the false promises of Protestantism and indifferentism have taken hold.

Paragraphs 24 – 28:

Having demonstrated that Freemasonry is using its chief dogma of naturalism to deconstruct the very foundations of society, in these paragraphs, Pope Leo XIII makes six succinct points about the mission and outcome of its effort:

1. Freemasonry wishes to replace Catholicism with the customs of paganism. *"In this insane and wicked endeavor, we may almost see the implacable hatred and spirit of revenge with which Satan himself is inflamed against Jesus Christ."* This endeavor of Freemasonry *"tends only to the ignominious and disgraceful ruin of the human race."*

2. Men were created for the society which Christ, through His Church, has inspired to be just and civil through the authority of His rule. In contrast, Freemasonry attempts to replace the rule of justice and civility with a society ruled by autonomy.

3. The teaching that all men are equal should not be determined to mean that they are autonomous and free to follow their own will. *"If they are to be all equal, and each is to follow his own will, the State will appear most deformed..."* Men are equal in origin and nature. However, different in abilities, dignity, physical characteristics, disposition, and mannerisms, their common pursuit should not be individual happiness but a mutual conspiring for the common good, which will conform the state with the nature that God intended.

4. Through deliberate planning, Freemasons are working with socialists and communists to overthrow society's fear of God and reverence for divine laws and replace it with human worship. However, if their plots do not come to fruition, it is not because they have not committed to

their effort; instead, it is because the divine religion cannot be destroyed and because men who refuse to be enslaved to secret societies *"vigorously resist their insane attempts."*

5. Freemasons have ingratiated themselves with rulers *"under the pretense of friendship"* and have convinced many that the Catholic Church is their enemy and a threat to their authority and sovereignty. Through this campaign of whispering into the ears of rulers, Freemasonry secured its security and began exercising significant influence in governments.

6. Freemasons have also deluded the masses by charging that the Church and their ruler's relationship with the Church are why they are not as accessible and rich as they deserve. This campaign of whispering into the ears of the common people has *"urged them to assail both the Church and the civil power."* Leo XIII believed that these attacks were an attack on the order that Divine Providence had instituted, and such rash attacks usually result in the penalty of their pride, which is more affliction and misery.

Paragraphs 29:

Pope Leo XIII argues against the separation of Church and state in this paragraph. He makes the case of how society benefits when the state listens to the teaching authority of the Church on matters that affect the wellbeing of its citizens. It is wrong to believe that the Church is attempting to usurp the state of its rights and sovereignty when She directs men to obey God's laws. Rather, what She is doing is guiding and reminding the state that all it ought to be brought into conformity with God's will for his people so that justice will be joined to clemency, *"equity to authority, and moderation to lawgiving; that no one's right must be violated; that order and public tranquility are to be maintained; and that the poverty of those are in need is, as far as possible, to be relieved by public and private charity."* In the instant case, both princes and people would be wise to heed the warnings of the Church about the dangers of Freemasonry and to cooperate with the Church in repelling their attacks.

Paragraphs 30 - 38:

Similar to what his predecessor, Bl. Pope Pius IX did at the end of his encyclical *Etsi Multa.* Here, Leo XIII, having explained precisely how the principles of Freemasonry plot against the Church and undermine society, now begins his transition to offering key tactics that bishops, priests, and laypeople can adopt to remedy the world of the Masonic plague.

The first thing that Leo XIII does in this section is to ratify and confirm the dogmatic prohibitions against Freemasonry that his predecessors set forth. For one's salvation, Leo XIII warns each person to be conscientious and *"careful not in the least to depart from what the apostolic see has commanded in this matter."* That is, there is no allowance for those in the present or future to deviate from this dogmatic teaching against Freemasonry.

Second, he beeches his brother bishops to make it their priority to uproot and destroy *"this foul plague"* through unremitting and persistent sermons and pastoral letters to instruct people about the sacred truths of the Church and also the clever strategies used by Freemasonry and societies like it to seduce unwitting men into their ranks.

Leo XIII comments on the pretense that Freemasonry presents as not contrary to religion and morality. However, once their principles are examined, we see that they are a vicious and criminal sect. The bishops are admonished not to let men think they may join any Masonic sect for any reason *"if he values his Catholic name and his eternal salvation as he ought to value them."* Suppose the bishops persist in teaching the faith and warning against the dangers of Freemasonry. In that case, Leo XIII believes that the outcome will *"be that the minds of men will be made sound by instruction, and will be protected against many forms of error and inducements to wickedness, especially in the present unbounded freedom of writing and insatiable eagerness for learning."*

Third, Leo XIII called upon the bishops to engage the clergy and laity in this battle so that their love and knowledge of the Church would grow. They will be less likely to fall into the snares of secret societies. In addition, the bishops should support and encourage the laity in seeking membership into the Third Order of Saint Francis and associations of guilds for workers like Saint Vincent's Society. Such Christian-oriented organizations can suppress interest in Freemasonry by giving men and women fraternity and the opportunity to labor for the common good and to be detached from the contagion of evil.

Fourth, Leo XIII states that the bishops should devote the most significant part of their care to the instruction of the youth. They should keep them away from schools under the influence of Freemasonry and, under their guidance, let parents, religious teachers, and priests warn children about the danger and nature of Freemasonry so that they will not become ensnared.

Lastly, Pope Leo XIII asks all Christians to pray to beg for God's help. As Freemasons are united in secret councils and are bound to assist one another toward their evil ends, so too should Christians *"form the widest possible association of action and prayer."* Christians must seek out the intercession of the Virgin

Mary, Saint Michael, the prince of the Heavenly Angels, Saint Joseph, the spouse of the most holy Virgin and heavenly patron of the Catholic Church, and Ss. Peter and Paul are the fathers and victorious champions of the Christian faith. *"By their patronage and perseverance in united prayer, we hope that God will mercifully and opportunely succor the human race, which is encompassed by so many dangers."*

Due to its exhaustive precision, incisiveness, and prophetic content, Leo XIII's *Humanum Genus* is the most well-known and cited Papal document on Freemasonry. Its place in the Church as an encyclical teaching tool lies in its examination of Freemasonry as a naturalistic philosophy and its societal impacts.

Chapter VIII — Officio Sanctissimo

In 1887, the Kingdom of Bavaria was a federal state belonging to the unified German Empire. There had long been tensions with the Kingdom of Prussia to the north of it due to the persecution of Catholics and other political issues. In 1850, following the 1848 revolution, relations were looking better after the new Prussian constitution allowed for freedom of religion. However, from about 1872 to 1878, a fresh wave of Catholic persecution swept across the Kingdom of Prussia in what was called *Kulturkampf* (i.e., culture struggle). These new laws were primarily targeted at taking education out of the hands of the Catholic Church, putting it into the hands of the government, and putting the state in control of ecclesial appointments and determining the qualifications of clerics.

In *Officio Sanctissimo*, Leo XIII expressed his gratitude to the people of Bavaria for their resistance against *Kulturkampf*. Bl. Pope Pius IX's 1873 encyclical *Etsi Multa* was the first response of the Catholic Church to this persecution in Germany and other countries. The belief of Bl. Pius IX's immediate predecessor was that the Freemasons and the philosophy of Freemasonry were generally responsible for this spreading *"contagion."* To be sure, *Kulturkampf* was just a lighter version of the demonic hostility that the Catholic Church had experienced during the Reign of

Terror in France (1789 – 1799) and the hostility that would still endure there until a separation between Church and State would be established in 1905.

Bavaria, as well, had in recent history persecuted Protestants. However, now, during the Regency of Prince-Regent Luitpold, Pope Leo XIII notes in this encyclical that due to the affairs of the Catholic Church in Prussia being *"somewhat improved,"* the relationship between the Churches in these two kingdoms should begin to flourish.

Altogether, this encyclical is Papal walk through how he views the history of Catholicism in the Kingdom of Bavaria, its current state, and a warm offering of words of guidance, admonishment, and encouragement to the Church of Bavaria to persevere in defending the faith and to stand firm in the authority of the Church that Christ established on earth.

Since Pope Clement XII's *In Eminenti*, the formal objection to Freemasonry has been both theological and temporal; that is, Freemasonry plots against the Church and the State. Pope Leo XIII's central contribution to the theological threat of Freemasonry was expressed in *Humanum Genus,* where he expanded the charge of indifferentism against Freemasonry to include naturalism. Here in *Officio Sanctissimo* and his later encyclicals, Leo XIII will detail precisely how it is that Freemasons have used the principles of Freemasonry to infiltrate and plot against the State so that it can be manipulated and used as a tool to supplant the Catholic Church.

Officio Sanctissimo
(Most Sacred Duty)
Pope Leo XIII - 1887

12. It is likewise a matter of extreme importance, Venerable Brethren, that you should warn and guard your flocks against the dangers arising from the contagion of Freemasonry. We have in a special Encyclical Letter shown how full of evil and danger to the State is this sect of darkness, and We have pointed out means to contract and destroy its influence. The faithful can never be sufficiently warned against this wicked faction, for although from the very beginning it conceived a deep hatred against the Catholic Church, and has ever since increased and inflamed it, its enmity is not always openly displayed, but more often exercises itself in an underhand and hypocritical way, especially among the young, who inexperienced and wanting in wisdom, are sadly ensnared by its deceits often concealed by appearances of piety and charity. As to being cautious in regard to those outside the Catholic faith, keep to what the Church prescribes, so that intercourse with them or the depravity of their doctrines may not become a source of danger to a Christian people.

We know and regret, as you do, that Our power to ward off such dangers does not equal Our zeal and Our desire to do so; nevertheless We do not think it useless to excite your pastoral solicitude and to stimulate at the same time the activity of Catholics, so that our united efforts may turn aside, or at least lessen obstacles set in the way of Our common desires. And We exhort you in the words of Our predecessor Leo the Great: "Be full of pious zeal for religion, and let the anxiety of all the faithful be aroused against the most cruel enemies of souls." (Serm. xv. c. 6). Therefore throwing off their torpid neglect let all good persons embrace the cause of religion and of the Church as their own, and let them fight faithfully and constantly on her behalf.

Too often the wicked are confirmed in their wickedness and their power for evil, and win the day by the sluggishness and timidity of good persons. The efforts and zeal of Catholics have not indeed always the effect intended and to be expected; but at heart they serve to restrain the enemy and at the same time to encourage the feeble and timid, even without counting the advantages gained from the satisfaction of having fulfilled a duty. Moreover, We are not ready to admit that the zeal and activity of Catholics cannot attain their end if properly guided and with perseverance. For it ever has chanced and will happen that enterprises most surrounded with difficulties end happily, provided, as We have said they are carried out with courageous energy, guided and aided by Christian prudence. And indeed truth, naturally desired by all men, will sooner or later win men's minds. Truth may be tried and oppressed by intellectual troubles and diseases, but it can never be destroyed.

All that has gone before seems to apply in a special way to Bavaria. For by God's grace, since it ranks among Catholic kingdoms, it must keep and nourish rather than accept that Divine faith which it received from its forefather. Moreover, they who in the people's name make laws to govern the kingdom are mostly Catholics, as are also many of its citizens and inhabitants, and therefore We doubt not they will aid with their utmost strength the Church, their mother, in her many trials. If all unite their efforts as energetically and actively as they ought, there will, by God's grace, be reason to rejoice at the happy results of their zeal. We recommend to all such union, for as there is nothing so baneful as discord, there is concord of spirit, when in united force they are brought to bear for some common purpose. Effectively the laws give Catholics an easy way of seeking to amend the condition and order of the State and to desire and will a constitution which, if not favorable and well-intentioned towards the Church, shall at least, as justice requires, be not harshly hostile. It would be unjust to accuse or blame anyone amongst us who has recourse to such means, for those means, used by the enemies of Catholicity to obtain and to extort, as it were, from rulers laws inimical to civil and religious freedom, may surely be used by Catholics in an honorable manner for the interests of religion and in defense of the property, privileges, and right divinely granted to the Catholic Church, and that ought to be respected with all honor by rulers and subjects alike.

Paragraph 12:

After Leo XIII again rails against the spiritual harm inflicted when the State is separated from the authority of the Church and warns the Church of Bavaria about the dangers of a state-run educational system that is devoid of religious and moral formation, he offers them a second warning; this one against *"the dangers arising from the contagion of Freemasonry."*

Unless they are unaware of *Humanum Genus*, which he promulgated three years ago, he informs them that in that encyclical, he explained the full scope of evil and danger that *"this sect of darkness"* poses to the State and the steps that can be taken to destroy its influence. Unlike the Church today, in which one will rarely, if ever, hear a bishop or priest speak about the wickedness of Freemasonry, Leo XIII believes that *"the faithful can never be sufficiently warned against [it]."* He then turns to the topic of the youth, which he also addressed in *Humanum*

Genus. They are the ones who especially need to be warned early on about the dangers of Freemasonry so that they do not get ensnared by its pretense of piety in their search for wisdom.

Pope Leo XIII regrets that the influence of the Catholic Church in the world cannot match the zeal of Catholics regarding this topic. However, he believes that the zeal of the faithful is enough to win the battle *"if properly guided and with perseverance. . . . If all unite their efforts as energetically and actively as they ought, there will, by God's grace, be reason to rejoice at the happy results of their zeal."*

The importance of *Officio Sanctissimo* is not that anything about Freemasonry was said here that was not already elucidated upon in *Humanum Genus*, but simply in the continuity of Papal prohibitions against Freemasonry that it continues. Freemasonry was active in Bavaria, and given that the country was where the Illuminati was founded, the Bavarians know well the history of infiltration and subversion of secret societies like these. In this way, Pope Leo XIII's simple message is a timeless message for the Church; that is, the Catholic Church needs to stay awake and alert to the clear and present dangers, as well as those that are more subtle and pretentious.

Chapter IX | Dall'alto dell'Apostolicio Seggio

As was addressed in the chapter on *Etsi Multa*, with the French forces withdrawn to join the Franco-Prussian War, King Victor Emmanuel II used that open opportunity to seize what was left of the Republic of Saint Peter in September of 1870 and made Rome the capital of Italy; leaving Pope Pius IX confined to the Vatican.

The Catholic Church refused to recognize the Kingdom of Italy until the signing of the Lateran Pacts in 1929. Italy began an earlier version of *Kulturkampf* after the 1848 revolutions under the Pontificate of Pius IX when the government established its form of state-sponsored education. Under King Victor Emmanuel II, *Kulturkampf* followed the French and German constructs where Church tithes were abolished, access to religious education in schools became limited, and Church funds were confiscated for state use.[80]

The upcoming general elections in Italy on November 23 of this year would have also been on the mind of Pope Leo XIII. The Historic Left had won control of parliament in 1876. It had been

---

[80] Pollard, John. *Catholicism in Modern Italy: Religion, Society and Politics Since 1861 (Christianity and Society in the Modern World)*. Routledge. London. 2008. 41.

led by Freemason Agostino Depretis, until 1887 when Francesco Crispi, a Freemason and a Deist, succeeded him as Prime Minister. Crispi had distinguished himself as a reformist, authoritarian, and anti-cleric. In the following years, Crispi believed better relations with the Vatican were good for Italy. However, such notions won him the threat of being excommunicated by the Grand Orient of Italy in 1894 for *"Masonic apostasy."*[81]

This encyclical and the two to follow, concerning the threat of Freemasonry in Italy, are particularly noteworthy concerning the time they were written. From 1831 until the revolutions of 1848, the influence of the Catholic Church suppressed Freemasonry on the peninsula to the point that there was not even one active Masonic lodge. Italy still had Freemasons during this period, but they would have been initiated abroad in foreign lodges. Freemasonry appeared to have become active again in Italy after 1848 but did not develop a clear mission, doctrine, and formal agenda until 1870 – 1872.[82]

By 1904, the revolutionary socialists in Italy demanded that Freemasons be expelled from their party. This petition would finally be granted by Benito Mussolini in 1914, and Freemasonry was outright banned from the country in 1923. Due to the heavy persecution of Freemasons under Fascism, in 1925, the two grand lodges of Italy, the Grand Orient of Italy and the Grand Lodge of Italy decided to force their lodges into darkness (i.e.,

---

[81] *Crispi to be Expelled by Freemasons* - https://www.nytimes.com/1894/10/10/archives/crispi-to-be-expelled-by-freemasons.html (retrieved 12/28/2019). See also Rao, John C. *Secular Italy and Catholicism: 1848 – 1915: Liberalism, Nationalism, Socialism and the Romantic Idealist Temptation.* Models and Images of Catholicism in Italian and Italian American Life Forum Italicum of thnole Center for Italian Studies at S.U.N.Y. Stony Brook. 2004. 195-230

[82] Mola, Aldo Alessandro. *Masons in Italy: The Borderland Between Fanaticism and Liberty.* REHMLAC ISSN 1659-4223. Special Issue UCLA - Grand Lodge of California. 2013. 230.

closure).[83] Freemasonry would not return to Italy until Fascism fell towards the end of the Second World War.

Into this brief window of Masonic influence in Italy and the fear of it becoming as strong as Freemasonry was in France at the time enters Pope Leo XIII with three encyclicals to the Italians concerning the plot of Freemasonry against the Catholic Church, beginning with *Dall'alto dell'Apostolicio Seggio*.

As with *Officio Sanctissimo*, here in *Dall'alto dell'Apostolicio Seggio*, Leo XIII continues to explain how the principles of Freemasonry have inspired Freemasons to infiltrate and plot against the State so that it can be easily manipulated and used as a tool to supplant the Catholic Church. Leo XIII would follow his plea to Italy two years later with *Custodi Di Quella Fede* and *Inimica Vis*.

---

[83] Ibid.

Dall'alto dell'Apostolicio Seggio
(From the Apostolic Throne)
Pope Leo XIII - 1890

To the Bishops, the Clergy, and the People of Italy.

Venerable Brethren and Beloved Children, Health and Apostolic Benediction.

From the height of the Apostolic Throne, where Divine Providence has placed Us to watch over the salvation of all nations, We look upon Italy in whose bosom, by an act of singular predilection, God has established the See of His Vicar, and from which come to Us at the present time many and most bitter sorrows. — It is not any personal offense that saddens Us, nor the privations and sacrifices imposed upon Us by the present condition of things, nor the outrages and scoffs which an insolent press has full power to hurl every day against Us. If only Our person were concerned, and not the ruin to which Italy threatened in its faith is hastening, We should bear these offenses without complaint, rejoicing even to repeat what one of Our most illustrious Predecessors said of himself: "If the captivity of my country did not every moment for each day increase, as to the contempt and scorn of myself I should joyfully be silent."[84] — But, besides the independence and dignity of the Holy See, the religion itself and the salvation of a whole nation are concerned, of a nation which from the earliest times opened its bosom to the Catholic Faith and has ever jealously preserved it. Incredible it seems, but it is true; to such a pass have we come, that we have to fear for this Italy of ours the loss even of the faith. — Many times have We sounded the alarm, to give warning of the danger; but We do not

---

[84] St. Gregory the Great: Letter to the Emperor Maurice, Reg.

therefore think that We have done enough. In face of the continued and fiercer assaults that are made, We hear the voice of duty calling upon Us more powerfully than before to speak to you again, Venerable Brethren, to your Clergy, and to the whole Italian people. As the enemy makes no truce, so neither you nor We must remain silent or inert. By the Divine mercy We have been constituted guardians and defenders of the religion of the people entrusted to Our care, Pastors and watchful sentinels of the flock of Christ; and for this flock We must be ready, if need be, to sacrifice everything, even life itself.

2. We shall not say anything new; for facts have not changed from what they were, and We have had at other times to speak of them when occasion was given. — But We now intend to recapitulate these facts in some way, and to group them into one picture, so as to draw out for general instruction the consequences which flow from them. The facts are incontestable which have happened in the clear light of day; not separated one from another, but so connected together as in their series to reveal with fullest evidence a system of which they are the actual operation and development. The system is not new; but the audacity, the fury, and the rapidity with which it is now carried out, are new. It is the plan of the sects that is now unfolding itself in Italy, especially in what relates to the Catholic religion and the Church, with the final and avowed purpose, if it were possible, of reducing it to nothing. — It is needless now to put the Masonic sects upon their trial. They are already judged; their ends, their means, their doctrines, and their action, are all known with indisputable certainty. Possessed by the spirit of Satan, whose instrument they are, they burn like him with a deadly and implacable hatred of Jesus Christ and of His work; and they endeavor by every means to overthrow and fetter it. This war is at present waged more

than elsewhere in Italy, in which the Catholic religion has taken deeper root; and above all in Rome, the center of Catholic unity, and the See of the Universal Pastor and Teacher of the Church.

3. It is well to trace from the beginning the different phases of this warfare.

4. The war began by the overthrow of the civil power of the Popes, the downfall of which, according to the secret intentions of the real leaders, afterwards openly avowed, was, under a political pretext, to be the means of enslaving at least, if not of destroying the supreme spiritual power of the Roman Pontiffs. — That no doubt might remain as to the true object of this warfare, there followed quickly the suppression of the Religious Orders; and thereby a great reduction in the number of evangelical laborers for the propagation of the faith amongst the heathens, and for the sacred ministry and religious service of Catholic countries. — Later, the obligation of military service was extended to ecclesiastics, with the necessary result that many and grave obstacles were put to the recruiting and due formation even of the secular Clergy. Hands were laid upon ecclesiastical property, partly by absolute confiscation, and partly by charging it with enormous burdens, so as to impoverish the Clergy and the Church, and to deprive the Church of what is necessary for its temporal support and for carrying on institutions and works in aid of its divine apostolate. This the sectaries themselves have openly declared. To lessen the influence of the Clergy and of clerical bodies, one only efficacious means must be employed: to strip them all their goods, and to reduce them to absolute poverty. So also the action of the State is of itself all directed to efface from the nation its religious and Christian character. From the

laws, and from the whole of official life, every religious inspiration and idea is systematically banished, when not directly assailed. Every public manifestation of faith and of Catholic piety is either forbidden or, under vain pretenses, in a thousand ways impeded.-From the family are taken away its foundation and religious constitution by the proclaiming of civil marriage, as it is called; and also by the entirely lay education which is now demanded, from the first elements to the higher teaching of the universities, so that the rising generations, as far as this can be effected by the State, have to grow up without any idea of religion, and without the first essential notions of their duties towards God. This is to put the ax to the root. No more universal and efficacious means could be imagined of withdrawing society, and families, and individuals, from the influence of the Church and of the faith. To lay Clericalism (or Catholicism) waste in its foundations and in its very sources of life, namely, in the school and in the family: such is the authentic declaration of Masonic writers.

5. It will be said that this does not happen in Italy only, but is a system of government which States generally follow. — We answer, that this does not refute, but confirms what We are saying as to the designs and action of Freemasonry in Italy. Yes, this system is adopted and carried out wherever Freemasonry uses its impious and wicked action; and, as its action is widespread, so is this anti-Christian system widely applied. But the application becomes more speedy and general, and is pushed more to extremes, in countries where the government is more under the control of the sect and better promotes its interest.-Unfortunately, at the present time the new Italy is of the number of these countries. Not today only has it become subject to the wicked and evil influence of the sects; but for some time past they have

tyrannized over it as they liked, with absolute dominion and power. Here the direction of public affairs, in what concerns religion, is wholly in conformity with the aspirations of the sects; and for accomplishing their aspirations, they find avowed supporters and ready instruments in those who hold the public power. Laws adverse to the Church and measures hostile to it are first proposed, decided, and resolved, in the secret meetings of the sect; and if anything presents even the least appearance of hostility or harm to the Church, it is at once received with favor and put forward. — Amongst the most recent facts We may mention the approval of the new penal code, in which what was most obstinately demanded, in spite of all reasons to the contrary, were the articles against the Clergy, which form for them an exceptional law, and even condemn as criminal certain actions which are sacred duties of their ministry. — The law as to pious works, by which all charitable property, accumulated by the piety and religion of our ancestors under the protection and guardianship of the Church, was withdrawn altogether from the Church's action and control, had been for some years put forward in the meetings of the sect, precisely because it would inflict a new outrage on the Church, lessen its social influence, and suppress at once a great number of bequests made for divine worship. — Then came that eminently sectarian work, the erection of the monument to the renowned apostate of Nola, which, with the aid and favor of the government, was promoted, determined, and carried out by means of Freemasonry, whose most authorized spokesmen were not ashamed to acknowledge its purpose and to declare its meaning. Its purpose was to insult the Papacy; its meaning that, instead of the Catholic Faith, must now be substituted the most absolute freedom of examination, of criticism, of thought, and of conscience: and what is meant by such language in the mouth of the sects is well known. — The seal was put by the most explicit declarations made by the head of the government, which were to the following effect: — That the true and real conflict, which the government has the merit of understanding, is the conflict between faith and the Church on one side and free examination and reason on the other. That the Church may try to act as it has done before, to enchain anew reason and free-thought, and to prevail; but the government in this conflict declares itself openly in favor of reason as against faith, and takes upon itself the task of making the Italian State the evident expression of this reason and liberty: a sad task, which has just now been boldly reaffirmed on a like occasion.

6. In the light of such facts and such declarations as these, it is more than ever clear that the ruling idea which, as far as religion is concerned, controls the course of public affairs in Italy, is the realization of the Masonic program. We see how much has already been realized; we know how much still remains to be done; and we can foresee with certainty that, so long as the destinies of Italy are in the hands of sectarian rulers or of men subject to the sects, the realization of the program will be pressed on, more or less rapidly according to circumstances, unto its complete development. — The action of the sects is at present directed to attain the following objects, according to the votes and resolutions passed in their most important assemblies, — votes and resolutions inspired throughout by a deadly hatred of the Church. The abolition in the schools of every kind of religious instruction, and the founding of institutions in which even girls are to be withdrawn from all clerical influence whatever it may be; because the State, which ought to be absolutely atheistic, has the inalienable right and duty to form the heart and the spirit of its citizens, and no school should exist apart from its inspiration and control. — The rigorous application of all laws now in force, which aim at

securing the absolute independence of civil society from clerical influence. — The strict observance of laws suppressing religious corporations, and the employment of means to make them effectual. — The regulation of all ecclesiastical property, starting from the principle that its ownership belongs to the State, and its administration to the civil power. — The exclusion of every Catholic or clerical element from all public administrations, from pious works, hospitals, and schools, from the councils which govern the destinies of the country, from academicals and other unions, from companies, committees, and families, — an exclusion from everything, everywhere, and forever. Instead, the Masonic influence is to make itself felt in all the circumstances of social life, and to become master and controller of everything. — Hereby the way will be smoothed towards the abolition of the Papacy; Italy will thus be free from its implacable and deadly enemy; and Rome, which in the past was the center of universal Theocracy will in the future be the center of universal secularization, whence the Magna Charta of human liberty is to be proclaimed in the face of the whole world. Such are the authentic declarations, aspirations, and resolutions, of Freemasons or of their assemblies.

7. Without exaggeration, this is the present condition and the future prospect of religion in Italy. To shrink from seeing the gravity of this would be a fatal error. To recognize it as it is, to confront it with evangelical prudence and fortitude, to infer the duties which it imposes on all Catholics, and upon us especially who as Pastors have to watch over them and guide them to salvation, is to enter into the views of Providence, to do a work of wisdom and pastoral zeal. — As far as We are concerned, the Apostolic office lays upon Us the duty of protesting loudly once more against all that has been done, is doing, or is attempted in

Italy to the harm of religion. Defending and guarding the sacred rights of the Church and of the Pontificate, We openly repel and denounce to the whole Catholic world the outrages which the Church and the Pontificate are continually receiving, especially in Rome, and which hamper Us in the government of the Catholic Church, and add difficulty and indignity to Our condition. We are determined not to omit anything on Our part which can serve to maintain the faith lively and vigorous amidst the Italian people, and to protect it against the assaults of its enemies. We, therefore, make appeal, Venerable Brethren, to your zeal and your great love for souls, in order that, possessed with a sense of the gravity of the danger which they incur, you may apply the proper remedies and do all you can to dispel this danger.

8. No means must be neglected that are in your power. All the resources of speech, every expedient in action, all the immense treasures of help and grace which the Church places in your hands, must be made use of, for the formation of a Clergy learned and full of the spirit of Jesus Christ, for the Christian education of youth, for the extirpation of evil doctrines, for the defense of Catholic truths, and for the maintenance of the Christian character and spirit of family life.

9. As to the Catholic people, before everything else it is necessary that they should be instructed as to the true state of things in Italy with regard to religion, the essentially religious character of the conflict in Italy against the Pontiff, and the real object constantly aimed at, so that they may see by the evidence of facts the many ways in which their religion is conspired against, and may be convinced of the risk they run of being robbed and spoiled of the inestimable treasure of the faith. — With this conviction in their minds, and having at the same time a certainty that without faith

it is impossible to please God and to be saved, they will understand that what is now at stake is the greatest, not to say the only interest, which every one on earth is bound before all things, at the cost of any sacrifice, to put out of danger, under penalty of everlasting misery. They will, moreover, easily understand that, in this time of open and raging conflict, it would be disgraceful for them to desert the field and hide themselves. Their duty is to remain at their post, and openly to show themselves to be true Catholics by their belief and by actions in conformity with their faith. This they must do for the honor of their faith, and the glory of the Sovereign Leader whose banner they follow; and that they may escape that great misfortune of being disowned at the last day, and of not being recognized as His by the Supreme Judge who has declared that whosoever is not with Him is against Him. — Without ostentation or timidity, let them give proof of that true courage which arises from the consciousness of fulfilling a sacred duty before God and men. To this frank profession of faith Catholics must unite a perfect docility and filial love towards the Church, a sincere respect for their Bishops, and an absolute devotion and obedience to the Roman Pontiff. In a word, they will recognize how necessary it is to cease from everything that is the work of the sects, or that receives impulse or favor from them, as being undoubtedly infected by the anti-Christian spirit; and they will, on the contrary, devote themselves with activity, courage and constancy, to Catholic works, and to the associations and institutions which the Church has blessed, and which the Bishops and the Roman Pontiff encourage and sustain.-Moreover, seeing that the chief instrument employed by our enemies is the press, which in great part receives from them its inspiration and support, it is important that Catholics should oppose the evil press by a press that is good, for the defense of truth, out of love for religion, and to uphold the rights of the Church. While the Catholic press is occupied in laying bare the perfidious designs of the sects, in helping and seconding the action of the sacred Pastors, and in defending and promoting Catholic works, it is the duty of the faithful efficaciously to support this press,-both by refusing or ceasing to favor in any way the evil press; and also directly, by concurring, as far as each one can, in helping it to live and thrive: and in this matter We think that hitherto enough has not been done in Italy.-Lastly, the teaching addressed by Us to all Catholics, especially in the Encyclicals "Humanum genus" and "Sapientiae Christianae," should be particularly applied to the Catholics of Italy, and be impressed upon them. If they have anything to suffer or to sacrifice through remaining faithful to these duties, let them take courage in the thought that the Kingdom of Heaven suffereth violence and is gained only by doing violence to ourselves; and that he who loves himself and what is his own more than Jesus Christ, is not worthy of Him. The example of the many invincible champions who, throughout all time, have generously sacrificed everything for the faith, and the special helps of grace which make the yoke of Jesus Christ sweet and His burden light, ought to animate powerfully their courage and to sustain them in the glorious contest.

10. So far We have considered only the religious side of the present state of things in Italy, inasmuch as this is for Us the most essential, and the subject which eminently concerns Us by reason of the Apostolic office which We hold. But it is worthwhile to consider also the social and political side, so that Italians may see that not only the love of religion, but also the noblest and sincerest love of country should stir them to resist the impious attempts of the sects. — As a convincing proof of this, it suffices to take note of the kind of future, in the social and political order,

which is being prepared for Italy by men whose object is — and they make no secret of it — to wage an unrelenting war against Catholicism and the Papacy.

11. Already the test of the past speaks eloquently for itself. — What Italy has become in this first Period of its new life. as to public and private morality, internal safety, order and peace, national wealth and prosperity, all this is known to you by facts, Venerable Brethren, better than We could describe it in words. The very men whose interest it would be to hide all this, are constrained by truth to admit it. We will only say that, under present conditions, though a sad but real necessity, things could not be otherwise: the Masonic sect, with all its boast of a spirit of beneficence and philanthropy, can only exercise an evil influence — an influence which is evil because it attacks and endeavors to destroy the religion of Christ, the true benefactress of mankind.

12. All know with what salutary effect and in how many ways the influence of religion penetrates society. It is beyond dispute that sound public and private morality gives honor and strength to States. But it is equally certain that, without religion there is no true morality, either public or private. — From the family, solidly based on its natural foundations, comes the life, the growth, and the energy of society. But without religion, and without morality, the domestic partnership has no stability, and the family bonds grow weak and waste away. — The prosperity of peoples and of nations comes from God and from His blessings. If a people does not attribute its prosperity to Him, but rises up against Him, and in the pride of its heart tacitly tells Him that it has no need of Him, its prosperity is but a semblance, certain to disappear so soon as it shall please the Lord to confound the proud insolence of His enemies. — It is religion which, penetrating to

the depth of each one's conscience, makes him feel the force of duty and urges him to fulfill it. It is religion which gives to rulers feelings of justice and love towards their subjects; which makes subjects faithful and sincerely devoted to their rulers; which makes upright and good legislators, just and incorruptible magistrates, brave and heroic soldiers, conscientious and diligent administrators. It is religion which produces concord and affection between husband and wife, love and reverence between parents and their children; which makes the poor respect the property of others, and causes the rich to make a right use of their wealth. From this fidelity to duty, and this respect for the rights of others come the order, the tranquillity, and the peace, which form so large a part of the prosperity of a people and of a State. Take away religion, and with it all these immensely precious benefits would disappear from society.

13. For Italy, moreover, the loss would be insensible. — All its glories and greatness, which for a long time gave to it the first place among the most cultured nations, are inseparable from religion, which has either produced or inspired them, or certainly has given to them favor, help, and increase. Its communes tell us of its public liberties: of its military glories we read in its many memorable enterprises against the enemies of the Christian name. Its sciences are seen in its universities which, founded, fostered, and privileged by the Church, have been their home and theater. Its arts are shown in the numberless monuments of every kind with which Italy is profusely covered. Of its institutions for the relief of suffering, for the destitute, and the working-classes we have evidence in its many foundations of Christian charity, in the many asylums established for every kind of need and misfortune, and in the associations and corporations which have grown up under the protection of religion. The virtue and the strength

of religion are immortal because religion is from God. It has treasures of help and most efficacious remedies, which can be wonderfully adapted to the needs of every time and epoch. What religion has known how to do and has done in former times, it can do also now with a virtue ever fresh and vigorous. To take away religion from Italy, is to dry up at once the most abundant source of inestimable help and benefits.

14. Moreover, one of the greatest and most formidable dangers of society at the present day, is the agitation of the Socialists, who threaten to uplift it from its foundations. From this great danger Italy is not free; and although other nations may be more infested than Italy by this spirit of subversion and disorder, it is not therefore less true that even here this spirit is widely spreading and increasing every day in strength. So criminal is its nature, so great the power of its organization and the audacity of its designs, that there is need of uniting all conservative forces, if we are to arrest its progress and successfully to prevent its triumph. Of these forces the first, and above all the chief one, is that which can be supplied by religion and the Church: without this, the strictest laws, the severest tribunals, and even the force of arms, will prove useless or insufficient. As, in old times, material force was of no avail against the hordes of barbarians, but only the power of the Christian religion, which entering into their souls quenched their ferocity, civilized their manners, and made them docile to the voice of truth and to the law of the gospel; so against the fury of lawless multitudes there will be no effectual defense without the salutary power of religion. It is only this power which, casting into their minds the light of truth, and instilling into their hearts the holy moral precepts of Jesus Christ, can make them listen to the voice of conscience and of duty, and, before restraining their hand, restrain their minds and allay the

violence of passion. — To assail religion, is therefore to deprive Italy of its most powerful ally against an enemy that becomes every day more formidable.

15. But this is not all. — As, in the social order, the war against religion is becoming most disastrous and destructive to Italy, so, in the political order, the enmity against the Holy See and the Roman Pontiff is for Italy a source of the greatest evils. Even as to this, demonstration is not needed; it is enough, for the full expression of our thought, to state in few words its conclusions. The war against the Pope is for Italy, internally, a cause of profound division between official Italy and the great part of Italians who are truly Catholic: and every division is a weakness. This war deprives our country of the support and co-operation of the party which is the most frankly conservative; it keeps up in the bosom of the nation a religious conflict which has never yet brought any public good, but ever bears within itself the fatal germs of evil and of most heavy chastisement.-Externally, the conflict with the Holy See, besides depriving Italy of the prestige and splendor which it would most certainly have by living in peace with the Pontificate, draws upon it the hostility of the Catholics of the whole world, is a cause of immense sacrifices, and may on any occasion furnish its enemies with a weapon to be used against it.

16. Such is the so-called welfare and greatness prepared for Italy by those who, having its destinies in their hands, do all they can, in accordance with the impious aspiration of the sects, to overthrow the Catholic religion and the Papacy.

17. Suppose, instead of this, that all connection and connivance with the sects were given up; that religion and the Church, as the

greatest social power, were allowed real liberty and full exercise of their rights. — What a happy change would come over the destinies of Italy! The evils and the dangers which we have lamented, as the result of the war against religion and the Church, would cease with the termination of the conflict; and further, we should see once more flourish on the chosen soil of Catholic Italy the greatness and glory which religion and the Church have ever abundantly produced. From their divine power would spring up spontaneously a reformation of public and private morality; family ties would be strengthened; and under religious influences, the feeling of duty and of fidelity in its fulfillment would be awakened in all ranks of the people to a new life. — The social questions which now so greatly occupy men's minds would find their way to the best and most complete solution, by the practical application of the gospel precepts of charity and justice. Popular liberty, not allowed to degenerate into license, would be directed only to good ends, and would become truly worthy of man. The sciences, through that truth of which the Church is mistress, would rise speedily to a higher excellence; and so also would the arts, through the powerful inspiration which religion derives from above, and which it knows how to transfuse into the minds of men. — Peace being made with the Church, religious unity and civil concord would be greatly strengthened; the separation between Italy and Catholics faithful to the Church would cease, and Italy would thus acquire a powerful element of order and stability. The just demands of the Roman Pontiff being satisfied, and his sovereign rights acknowledged, he would be restored to a condition of true and effective independence; and Catholics of other parts of the world, who, not through external influence of ignorance of what they want, but through a feeling of faith and sense of duty, all raise their voice in defense of the dignity and liberty of the supreme Pastor of their souls, would no longer have reason to regard Italy as the enemy of the Pontiff. — On the contrary, Italy would gain greater respect and esteem from other nations by living in harmony with the Apostolic See; for not only has this See conferred special benefits on Italians by its presence in the midst of them, but also, by the constant diffusion of the treasures of faith from this center of benediction and salvation, it has made the Italian name great and respected among all nations. Italy reconciled with the Pontiff, and faithful to its religion, would be able worthily to emulate the glory of its early times; and from whatever real progress there is in the present age it would receive a new impulse to advance in its glorious path. Rome, preeminently the Catholic city, destined by God to be the center of the religion of Christ and the See of His Vicar, has had in this the cause of its stability and greatness throughout the eventful changes of the many ages that are past. Placed again under the peaceful and paternal scepter of the Roman Pontiff, it would again become what Providence and the course of ages made it — not dwarfed to the condition of a capital of one kingdom, nor divided between two different and sovereign powers in a dualism contrary to its whole history; but the worthy capital of the Catholic world, great with all the majesty of Religion and of the supreme Priesthood, a teacher and an example to the nations of morality and of civilization.

18. These are not vain illusions, Venerable Brethren, but hopes resting upon the most solid and true foundation. The assertion which for some time has been commonly repeated, that Catholics and the Pontiff are the enemies of Italy, and in alliance, so to speak, with those who would overturn everything, is a gratuitous insult and a shameless calumny, artfully spread abroad by the sects to disguise their wicked designs, and to enable them to continue without obstacle their hateful work of stripping Italy of its

Catholic character. The truth which is seen most clearly from what we have thus far said, is that Catholics are Italy's best friends. By keeping altogether aloof from the sects, by renouncing their spirit and their works, by striving in every way that Italy may not lose the faith, but preserve it in all its vigor-may not fight against the Church, but be its faithful daughter, — may not assail the Pontificate, but be reconciled to it, — Catholics give proof by all this of their strong and real love for the religion of their ancestors and for their country. — Do all that you can, Venerable Brethren, to spread the light of truth among the people so that they may come at last to understand where their welfare and their true interest are to be found; and may be convinced that only from fidelity to religion and from peace with the Church and with the Roman Pontiff, can they hope to obtain for Italy a future worthy of its glorious past. — To this We would call the attention, not of those affiliated to the sects, whose deliberate purpose it is to establish the new settlement of the Italian Peninsula upon the ruins of the Catholic Religion; but of others who, without welcoming such malevolent designs, help these men in their work by supporting their policy; and especially of young men, who are so liable to go astray through inexperience and the predominance of mere sentiment. We would that everyone should become convinced that the course which is now followed cannot be otherwise than fatal to Italy; and, in once more making known this danger, We are moved only by a consciousness of duty and by love of our country.

19. But, for the enlightening of men's minds, we must above all ask for special help from heaven. Therefore, to our united action, Venerable Brethren, we must join prayer; and let it be a prayer that is general, constant, and fervent: a prayer that will offer gentle violence to the heart of God. and render Him merciful to Italy

our country, so that He may avert from it every calamity, especially that which would be the most terrible — the loss of faith. — Let us take as our mediatrix with God the most glorious VIRGIN MARY, the invincible Queen of the Rosary, Who has such great power over the forces of hell, and has so many times made Italy feel the effects of Her maternal love. — Let us also with confidence have recourse to the holy Apostles PETER and PAUL, who subjected this blessed land to the faith, sanctified it by their labors, and bathed it in their blood.

20. As a pledge meanwhile of the help which We ask, and in token of Our most special affection, receive the Apostolic Benediction, which from the depth of Our heart We grant to you, Venerable Brethren, to your Clergy, and to the Italian people.

Given in Rome, at St. Peter's, on the 15th of October, 1890, the thirteenth year of Our Pontificate.

Paragraph 1 - 2:
Being alone in a world hostile to the faith was not a new position for a Pontiff to find the Catholic Church, for such had been the case for Christ Himself and the vast majority of its history. Nor was it the personal offense taken that caused Leo XIII sleepless nights, for even Pope Gregory the Great (590 – 604) wrote to Byzantine Emperor Maurice, *"If the captivity of my country did not every moment for each day increase, as to the contempt and scorn of myself I should joyfully be silent."* Instead, what was new was the consequences of the freedom of an *"insolent"* press that was relentlessly attacking the Church, coupled with *Kulturkampf* that was causing the incredible situation of Italy losing its faith. This country in the earliest times had *"jealously preserved"* their faith.

Over a century later, Pope Francis would come along and opine that because many countries are no longer under a Christian regime and because our beliefs are *"denied, derided, marginalized, and ridiculed,"* the Church needs to adapt and change the way that it evangelizes by finding a necessary balance with the world and move away from being ridged with our beliefs, which causes imbalance.[85]

Here in *Dall'alto Dell'Apostolico Seggio*, the approach of Leo XIII was vastly different than that of Francis. From this Pontiff, there is no call to adapt to secularism, change the way the Church evangelizes, or be less ridged with the faith. On the contrary, Pope Leo XIII calls it the duty of the bishops and the clergy to teach even more powerfully than before in warning about the dangers of Freemasonry, to be defenders of the religion, to be watchful sentinels of the flock of Christ, and be ready *"to sacrifice everything, even life itself."*

Although there is nothing new in this encyclical by way of facts or methods of evangelization, the reason for the encyclical is that Leo XIII truly believes that enough has not been done to warn the people about the dangers of Freemasonry, which he calls *"possessed by the Spirit of Satan, whose instrument they are,"* and whom they will burn with. *"The system is not new, but the audacity, the fury, and the rapidity with which it is now carried out, are new It is the plan of the sects that is new unfolding itself in Italy, especially in what relates to the Catholic religion and the Church, with the final and avowed purpose, if it were possible, of reducing it to nothing."*

---

[85] Audience of the Holy Father to the Roman Curia on the occasion of the presentation of Christmas wishes. December 21, 2019.

Paragraph 3 – 4:

In this section, Pope Leo XIII delineates the various stages of the war with Freemasonry:

1. The war began through a political pretext, which led to the overthrow of the civil powers of the Pope. That is the stripping away of the Republic of Peter and, thereby, the end of the Papal monarchy.
2. The suppression of Religious Orders led to a decline in their vocations and, thereby, their ability to evangelize the people.
3. The obligation to military service extended to clerics.
4. The confiscation of Church property money and placing taxes and other financial burdens upon religious institutions forced some into poverty.
5. Separating Church and State in law and public manifestation, including annexing control of the instruction of marriage and education away from the Church, was an attack on the family.

Paragraph 5:

Leo XIII states that, at the moment, Italy has become just like other countries whose governments have fallen under the control of Freemasons. As proof that these anti-Catholic and evil machinations were first *"proposed, decided, and resolved in the secret meetings of the sect,"* he offers the example of the monument of *"the renowned apostate of Nola."*

On June 9, 1889, five years after the promulgation of *Humanum Genus*, a statue of Giordano Bruno was erected at Campo de' Fiori in Rome, Italy, where the Dominican friar, philosopher, mathematician, poet, and Hermetic occultist was burned at stake on February 17, 1600. Bruno was born in Nola, Italy, and had been found guilty of heresy by the Congregation of Inquisition due to his denials of eternal damnation, the Trinity, the divinity of Christ Jesus, the virginity of Mary, and transubstantiation. Freemason Ettore Ferrari sculpted the bronze statue of him. At its reveal, the Freemason and politician Giovanni Bovio gave its dedication speech in the presence of about one hundred Masonic flags.

Given that it was a known fact that the Grand Orient of Italy Freemasons colluded with the government of Rome to erect a statue of Giordano Bruno in response to *Humanum Genus*, it was easy for Leo XIII to conclude that the purpose of this monument was to promote the religion of genuine human autonomy where man is given to think and to be who he will himself to be; that is, apart from the strictures that the Christian religion and dogma attempt to force upon him. The Freemasons intended the statue to disgrace the Catholic Church for its persecution and murder of a person who was a 'free-thinker' who dared to think outside of the dogma that was forced upon the people. Today, this statue of Giordano Bruno still stands in the same place in Rome, and another like it was created by Alexander Polzin and placed at Potsdamer Platz in Berlin, Germany, on March 2, 2008.

Paragraph 6:

Whereas Pope Leo XIII had in previous sections delineated the various stages in the *Kulturkampf* or war with Freemasonry, here, he calls Freemasonry a religion and lists its three goals under what he labels as a Masonic program. This is a borrowed term from Freemasonry that Leo XIII has decided to clarify according to what he believes the program is. According to Mola, the Masonic programs of Grand Orient of Italy Grand Masters Ludoico Frapolli and Giuseppe Maria Garibaldi in the late nineteenth century were clear departures from the Masonic orthodoxy found in *Anderson's Constitution:*

> "In 1864 and then again in 1872, Garibaldi wrote his Masonic program. For him, Freemasonry was a philanthropic association committed to social reforms, an organization that was the "mother of democracy" and open to women. In order to confirm such a claim, he initiated his daughter, Teresita, and many other women. He even celebrated Masonic baptisms and weddings according to a ritual that thereafter became widespread and which in some way recalled Catholic ceremonies. In his last years he ordered his body to be burnt in the open air, but his wish wasn't accomplished as in his funeral a member of royalty was present and the crown wanted to avoid any conflict with the Catholic Church, which condemned cremation as an act of positivistic naturalism and contrary to Catholic faith. However the Homeric pyre referenced by Garibaldi was not really of a Masonic nature, because Freemasonry did not consider cremation as a major, bounding rule, because due to health and hygiene reasons it was impossible to execute in the cities of that time, which lacked proper sanitation. Some Freemasons proposed to build cremation chambers."[86]

Pope Leo XIII's understanding of these Masonic programs, even evident from Garibaldi's, was that Freemasonry attempted to replace the Catholic Church with itself. Therefore, according to Leo XIII, the first goal of the Masonic program was to abolish all religious schools and replace them with atheistic state-controlled schools. The second goal is to craft laws and public policy in a way that achieves the separation of Church and State and the separation of Church and social life so that the state and the people will be independent and free from clerical influence or

---

[86] Mola, Aldo Alessandro. *Masons in Italy: The Borderland Between Fanaticism and Liberty*. REHMLAC ISSN 1659-4223. Special Issue UCLA - Grand Lodge of California. 2013. 231.

elements in any manner, and to replace it with Masonic influences so that Freemasonry will be the *"master and controller of everything."* The third goal is to strip all ecclesiastical bodies of their property ownership, thereby stripping the Church of its own freedom and independence.

According to Pope Leo XIII, the Masonic program's ultimate aim is to craft the state into being a type of theocratic Masonic lodge at work. The language that he uses here about the Freemason's desire to create a society in which universal secularism will be the center of union and where divine revelation is rejected sounds very similar to the language found in *Anderson's Constitution* of 1728, which points to the system Freemasonry, supplanting men's religions and, thereby, becoming the center of union through which all men can agree.

Paragraphs 7 – 11:

In this section, it is clear how deeply His Holiness truly loves Italy and her people. He is heartbroken that they have turned away from their Catholic roots. Due to these constant attacks on the Church and the Pope, they have been hampered in performing their duties. The solution to this problem is to fight back and not surrender Italy to the Masonic program. Leo XIII implores the bishops to use every resource at their disposal to fight for their clergy's Christ-centered formation, Catholic education, the orthodoxy of the faith, and the *"Christian character and spirit of family life."* Along with the clergy, the Catholic press supported this war as an instrument to reiterate the faith and defend and promote Catholic works.

Leo XIII wanted Italy to understand how Freemasonry plotted against the Church and how those attacks intended to affect Italy's social and political space. It is through understanding the true intentions of Freemasonry that the pretense of it being merely a fraternity of *"beneficence and philanthropy"* is exposed, and its true evil nature is evident to all.

Again, the idea of Freemasonry being an innocent beneficence and philanthropic fraternity was a concept lifted from Garibaldi's Masonic program that Leo XIII decided to rip the mask off of. Garibaldi would have borrowed this concept from the revised Grand Orient of France constitution from 1839, which states that *"Masonry is a universal philanthropic association,"* with one of the objectives being *"the examination and discussion of all social and economic questions which concern the happiness of humanity."*[87]

Paragraphs 12 – 16:

In this section, Pope Leo XIII builds upon this argument on Italy losing its religion to explain the benefits of religion (i.e., the one true religion – Catholicism) and why society needs it. According to Leo XIII, there is no true justice or public or private morality without religion; religion is the basis of true morality. Religion is the thread that binds family, and without religion, *"the family bonds grow weak and waste away."* Religion is why rulers and citizens seek the common good of all. Without religion, peace will be a fading attribute in society.

The loss of the Catholic Church for Italy would be insensible because everything that Italy is springs from its intimate relationship with the Church and the Pope. Out of this relationship, Italy reached such heights amongst the nations. Its culture, its military glories, its advancements in the arts and sciences at its universities, its work of charity for the suffering, destitute, and working class, and its associations and corporations are all indebted to

---

[87] Ridley, Jasper. *The Freemasons: A History of the World's Most Powerful Secret Society.* Arcade Publishing. New York. 2011. 208.

the strength and virtue it received from religion, *"because religion is from God."*

Leo XIII believes that religion is what Italy needs most right now. If religion were taken away, it would leave them very vulnerable to the dangers of the Masonic program and Socialism, which he views as the *"most formidable danger"* to religion today. Seven months from the date of this encyclical, Pope Leo XIII will offer his complete treatment of the dangers of socialism and communism in his encyclical *Rerum Novarum*. For now, he says that Socialism threatens to uproot the foundations of society; while other nations are more infested by this ideology, Italy is not free from it. Socialism is criminal, and Christianity is the only force to repel it.

Unfortunately, the Church today is silent in telling the faithful how to vote or which political parties to support. Their preferred modus operandi is the mere exercise of political indifference. They prefer to lay before the faithful a list of the pros and cons of each political party and politician but never publicly favor any, even if it is a political party bent on committing acts of anti-Catholicism, genocide, and infanticide. Rather than guide and form the conscience of the faithful, they prefer to let them form their conscience and allow them to determine their path to Heaven or Hell. To that, I say, what a complete waste and ruin of Apostolic authority!

Such was not the path of indifference with Pope Leo XIII, who saw that in Italy, there was a war afoot that was using the political order to suppress the authority of the Church and the Pope. Rather than issue an apathetic voter's guide, Leo XIII sides with one political party in Italy, writing, *"This war deprives our country of the support and co-operation of the party which is the most frankly conservative...*" It was most likely the so-called 'Historical Right' party that Leo XIII was unapologetically referring to here.

Paragraphs 17 – 20:
Pope Leo XIII would close this encyclical to Italy with a vision of hope and a promise if they gave up all the sects seeking to destroy the Catholic Church. He imagines for his readers a beautiful Catholic utopia where the Church is free to exercise her full rights from God. He imagines an Italy in harmony with the Pope would *"emulate the glory of its early times"* and be a majestic capital of the Catholic world. He believes such a vision is possible if men's minds are enlightened, but that will only be possible with exceptional help from Heaven. To fulfill this hope, Leo XIII asked his brother bishops to be united in constant and fervent prayer for God to have mercy on Italy. He asks them to petition for the intercession of the Virgin Mary, whom he calls the mediatrix and the invincible Queen of the Rosary, and *"the holy Apostles Peter and Paul, who subjected this blessed land to the faith, sanctified it by their labors, and bathed it in their blood."*

The lasting impact of *Dall'alto dell'Apostolicio Seggio* is found in the immensity of love that Leo XIII pours out for Italy. Other Popes have fought for Italy with an army, and some have paid the price of imprisonment and death for their love of Italy. However, of the Popes whose only power was mere words, none were more significant than Pope Leo XIII. Indeed, his heart is in deep pain over his country's loss of faith. He is clinging to Italy as a husband clings to his wife as she walks out the door and into the arms of another suitor. This other man is an adulterer who has lied to her about her husband being oppressive and how she can be free to be whoever she wants to be if she leaves her husband for him. Leo XIII pleads with his beloved to understand that what this man is promising will only lead to her ruin and turn her into a whore. He desperately asks her to imagine how perfect of a life they would have together if she were to return home and be faithful to him again. Like every man who loves his wife and finds himself in this desperate situation, he promises that if she comes home, things will be like they used to be back when they first got together. This hope is so vital to him that he does not leave it to his efforts; instead, he implores the intercessory prayer of his brothers and their Heavenly Mother.

Pope Leo XIII is not done fighting for Italy. He loves her far too much to surrender her to the adulterous forces of evil. Two years later, he will pen *Custodi Di Quella Fede* and *Inimica Vis* in one final effort to bring his beloved back home.

Chapter X
Custodi De Quella Fede

It may have been partly due to Pope Leo XIII openly advocating in his encyclical *Dall'alto dell'Apostolicio Seggio* for people to vote for the most conservative party. This is why in the 1892 General Election on November 6, the Historical Right party picked up forty-five seats in parliament and the Historical Left party lost fifty-nine. It may have also been partly due to Giovanni Giolitti taking responsibility for Italy's banking scandals during his first term as Prime Minister.

However, the gains occurred; one month after the election, Pope Leo XIII seized upon the small victory to publish two encyclicals on the same day that repeated his similar themes. Whereas *Dall'alto dell'Apostolicio Seggio* was written *"To the Bishops, the Clergy, and the People of Italy," Custodi Di Quella Fede* was addressed *"To the Italian People." Inimica Vis* was addressed *"To the Bishops of Italy."*

Custodi Di Quella Fede
(Guardians of the Faith)
Pope Leo XIII - 1892

To the Italian People.

Guardians of that faith to which the Christian nations owe their morality and civil redemption, We must dutifully discharge each one of Our supreme tasks. Therefore We must raise Our voice in loud protestations against the impious war which tries to take such a precious treasure away from you, beloved children. Already taught by long and sorrowful experience, you know well the terrible trials of this war, you who deplore it in your hearts as Catholics and as Italians. Can one be Italian in name and sentiment and not resent these continual offenses against divine beliefs? These beliefs are the most beautiful of our glories, for they gave to Italy its primacy over the other nations and to Rome the spiritual scepter of the world. They likewise made the wonderful edifice of Christian civilization rise over the ruins of paganism and barbarism.

Can we be Catholic in mind and heart and gaze with dry eyes on that land where our wondrous Redeemer deigned to establish the seat of His kingdom? Now We see His teachings attacked and His reverence outraged, His Church embattled and His Vicar opposed. So many souls redeemed by His blood are now lost, the choicest portion of His flock, a people faithful to Him for nineteen centuries. How can We bear to look upon His chosen people exposed to a constant and ever-present danger of apostasy, pushed toward error and vice, material miseries, and moral degradation?

2. This war is directed at the same time against the heavenly and the earthly kingdoms, against the faith of our ancestors and the culture which they handed on to us. It is thus doubly evil, being guilty of a divine offense no less than a human one. Is its chief source not that very masonic sect which We discussed at length in the encyclical "*Humanum Genus*" of April 20, 1884, and in the more recent one of October 15, 1890, addressed to the bishops, the clergy and the Italian people? With these two letters We tore from the face of masonry the mask which it used to hide itself and We showed it in its crude deformity and dark fatal activity.

3. We shall restrict Ourselves now to its deplorable effects on Italy. For a long time now it has bored its way under the deceitful guise of a philanthropic society and redeemer of the Italian people. By way of conspiracies, corruptions, and violence, it has finally come to dominate Italy and even Rome. To what troubles, to what calamities has it opened the way in a little more than thirty years?

4. Our country has seen and suffered great evils in such a short span of time, for the faith of our fathers has been made a sign for persecutions of every sort. The satanic intent of the persecutors has been to substitute naturalism for Christianity, the worship of reason for the worship of faith, so-called independent morality for Catholic morality, and material progress for spiritual progress. To the holy maxims and laws of the Gospel, they have opposed laws and maxims which can be called the code of revolution. They have also opposed an atheistic doctrine and a vile realism to school, science, and the Christian arts. Having invaded the temple of the Lord, they have squandered the booty of the Church's goods, the greatest part of the inheritance necessary for

the ministers, and reduced the number of priests by the conscription of clerics beyond the limits of extreme need. If the administration of the sacraments could not be impeded, they sought nonetheless to introduce and promote civil marriages and funerals. If they have not yet succeeded in seizing control of education and the direction of charitable institutions, they always aim with perseverance to laicize everything, which is to remove the mark of Christianity from it. If they could not silence the voice of the Catholic press, they made every effort to discredit and revile it.

5. In this battle against the Catholic religion, what partiality and contradictions there are! They closed monasteries and convents, but they let multiply at will masonic lodges and sectarian dens. They proclaimed the right of association, while the legal rights which all kinds of organizations use and abuse are denied to religious societies. They proclaim freedom of religion and reserve odious intolerance and vexations precisely for the religion of the Italians — which, for that reason, should be assured respect and a special protection. They made protests and great promises for the protection of the dignity and independence of the pope, but you see their daily contempt of Our person. All kinds of public shows find an open field; yet this or that Catholic demonstration is either prohibited or disturbed. They encourage schisms, apostasies, and revolts against legitimate superiors in the Church. Religious vows and especially religious obedience are rebuked as contrary to human dignity and freedom, while impious associations which bind their followers by wicked oaths and demand blind, absolute obedience in crime are allowed to flourish with impunity.

6. We do not wish to exaggerate the masonic power by attributing to its direct and immediate action all the evils which presently preoccupy Us. However, you can clearly see its spirit in the facts which We have just recorded and in many others which We could recall. That spirit, which is the implacable enemy of Christ and of the Church, tries all ways, uses all arts, and prevails upon all means. It seizes from the Church its first-born daughter and seizes from Christ His favored nation, the seat of His Vicar on earth and the center of Catholic unity. To see the evil and efficacious influence of this spirit on our affairs, We have more than a few fleeting indications and the series of facts which have succeeded themselves for thirty years. Proud of its successes, the sect herself has spoken out and told us all its past accomplishments and future goals. It regards the public powers as its instruments, witting or not, which is to say that the impious sect boasts as one of its principal works the religious persecution which has troubled and is troubling our Italy. Though often executed by other hands, this persecution is inspired and promoted by masonry, in an immediate or mediate, direct or indirect manner, by flattery or threats, seduction or revolution.

7. The road is very short from religious to social ruin. The heart of man is no longer raised to heavenly hopes and loves; capable and needing the infinite, it throws itself insatiably on the goods of this earth. Inevitably there is a perpetual struggle of avid passions to enjoy, become rich, and rise. Then we encounter a large and inexhaustible source of grudges, discords, corruptions, and crimes. In our Italy there was no lack of moral and social disorders before the present events — but what a sorrowful spectacle we see in our days! That loving respect which forms domestic harmony is substantially diminished; paternal authority is too often unrecognized by children and parents alike. Disagreements

are frequent, divorce common. Civil discords and resentful anger between the various orders increase every day in the cities. New generations which grew up in a spirit of misunderstood freedom are unleashed in the cities, generations which do not respect anything from above or below. The cities teem with incitements to vice, precocious crimes, and public scandals. The state should be content with the high and noble office of recognizing, protecting, and helping divine and human rights in their harmonious universality. Now, however, the state believes itself almost a judge and disowns these rights or restricts them at will. Finally, the general social order is undermined at its foundations. Books and journals, schools and universities, clubs and theaters, monuments and political discourse, photographs and the fine arts, everything conspires to pervert minds and corrupt hearts. Meanwhile the oppressed and suffering people tremble and the anarchic sects arouse themselves. The working classes raise their heads and go to swell the ranks of socialism, communism, and anarchy. Characters exhaust themselves and many souls, no longer knowing how to suffer nobly nor how to redeem themselves manfully, take their lives with cowardly suicide.

8. Such are the fruits which the masonic sect has borne to us Italians. And after that it yearns to come before you, extolling its merits towards Italy. It likewise yearns to give Us and all those who, heeding Our words, remain faithful to Jesus Christ, the calumnious title of enemies of the state. The facts reveal the merits of this guilty sect toward our peninsula, "merits" which bear repeating. The facts say that masonic patriotism is no less than sectarian egotism which yearns to dominate everything, particularly the modern states which unite and concentrate everything in their hands. The facts say that in the plans of masonry, the names of political independence, equality, civilization, and progress

aimed to facilitate the independence of man from God in our country. From them, license of error and vice and union of faction at the expense of other citizens have grown. The easy and delicious enjoyment of life by the world's fortunate is nurtured in the same source. A people redeemed by divine blood have thus returned to divisions, corruptions, and the shames of paganism.

9. That does not surprise Us. — After nineteen centuries of Christian civilization, this sect tries to overthrow the Catholic Church and to cut off its divine sources. It absolutely denies the supernatural, repudiating every revelation and all the means of salvation which revelation shows us. Through its plans and works, it bases itself solely and entirely on such a weak and corrupt nature as ours. Such a sect cannot be anything other than the height of pride, greed, and sensuality. Now, pride oppresses, greed plunders, and sensuality corrupts. When these three concupiscences are brought to the extreme, the oppressions, greed, and seductive corruptions spread slowly. They take on boundless dimensions and become the oppression, plundering and source of corruption of an entire people.

10. Let Us then show you masonry as an enemy of God, Church, and country. Recognize it as such once and for all, and with all the weapons which reason, conscience, and faith put in your hands, defend yourselves from such a proud foe. Let no one be taken in by its attractive appearance or allured by its promises; do not be seduced by its enticements or frightened by its threats. Remember that Christianity and masonry are essentially irreconcilable, such that to join one is to divorce the other. You can no longer ignore such incompatibility between Catholic and mason, beloved children: you have been warned openly by Our predecessors, and We have loudly repeated the warning.

11. Those who, by some supreme misfortune, have given their name to one of these societies of perdition should know that they are strictly bound to separate themselves from it. Otherwise they must remain separated from Christian communion and lose their soul now and for eternity. Parents, teachers, godparents, and whoever has care of others should also know that a rigorous duty binds them to keep their wards from this guilty sect or to draw them from it if they have already entered.

12. In a matter of such importance and where the seduction is so easy in these times, it is urgent that the Christian watch himself from the beginning. He should fear the least danger, avoid every occasion, and take the greatest precautions. Use all the prudence of the serpent, while keeping in your heart the simplicity of the dove, according to the evangelical counsel. Fathers and mothers should be wary of inviting strangers into their homes or admitting them to domestic intimacy, at least insofar as their faith is not sufficiently known. They should try to first ascertain that an astute recruiter of the sect does not hide himself in the guise of a friend, teacher, doctor or other benefactor. Oh, in how many families has the wolf penetrated in sheep's clothing!

13. It is beautiful to see the varied groups which arise everywhere today in every order of social life: worker groups, groups of mutual aid and social security, organizations to promote science, arts, letters, and other similar things. When they are inspired by a good moral and religious spirit, these groups certainly prove to be useful and proper. But because the masonic poison has penetrated and continues to penetrate here also, especially here, any groups that remove themselves from religious influence should be generally suspect. They can easily be directed and more or less

dominated by masons, becoming the sowing ground and the apprenticeship of the sect in addition to providing assistance to it.

14. Women should not join philanthropic societies whose nature and purpose are not well-known without first seeking advice from wise and experienced people. That talkative philanthropy which is opposed to Christian charity with such pomp is often the passport for masonic business.

15. Everyone should avoid familiarity or friendship with anyone suspected of belonging to masonry or to affiliated groups. Know them by their fruits and avoid them. Every familiarity should be avoided, not only with those impious libertines who openly promote the character of the sect, but also with those who hide under the mask of universal tolerance, respect for all religions, and the craving to reconcile the maxims of the Gospel with those of the revolution. These men seek to reconcile Christ and Belial, the Church of God and the state without God.

16. Every Christian should shun books and journals which distill the poison of impiety and which stir up the fire of unrestrained desires or sensual passions. Groups and reading clubs where the masonic spirit stalks its prey should be likewise shunned.

17. In addition, since we are dealing with a sect which has pervaded everything, it is not enough to remain on the defensive. We must courageously go out into the battlefield and confront it. That is what you will do, beloved children, opposing press to press, school to school, organization to organization, congress to congress, action to action.

18. Masonry has taken control of the public schools, leaving private schools, paternal schools, and those directed by zealous ecclesiastics and religious of both sexes to compete in the education of Christian youth. Christian parents especially should not entrust the education of their children to uncertain schools. Masonry has confiscated the inheritance of public charity; fill the void, then, with the treasure of private relief. It has placed pious works in the hands of its followers, so you should entrust those that depend on you to Catholic institutions. It opens and maintains houses of vice, leaving you to do what is possible to open and maintain shelters for honesty in danger. An anti-Christian press in religious and secular matters militates at its expense, so that your effort and money are required by the Catholic press. Masonry establishes societies of mutual help and credit unions for its partisans; you should do the same not only for your brothers but for all the indigent. This will show that true and sincere charity is the daughter of the One who makes the sun to rise and the rain to fall on the just man and sinner alike.

19. May this struggle between good and evil extend to everything, and may good prevail. Masonry holds frequent meetings to plan new ways to combat the Church, and you should hold them frequently to better agree on the means and order of defense. It multiplies its lodges, so that you should multiply Catholic clubs and parochial groups, promote charitable associations and prayer organizations, and maintain and increase the splendor of the temple of God. The sect, having nothing to fear, today shows its face to the light of day. You Italian Catholics should also make open profession of your faith and follow the example of your glorious ancestors who confessed their faith bravely before tyrants, torture, and death. What more? Does the sect try to enslave the Church and to put it at the feet of the state as a humble

servant? You must then demand and claim for it the freedom and independence due it before the law. Does masonry seek to tear apart Catholic unity, sowing discord even in the clergy itself, arousing quarrels, fomenting strife, and inciting insubordination, revolt, and schism? By tightening the sacred bond of charity and obedience, you can thwart its plans, bring to naught its efforts, and disappoint its hopes. Be all of one heart and one mind, like the first Christians. Gathered around the See of Peter and united to your pastors, protect the supreme interests of Church and papacy, which are just as much the supreme interests of Italy and of all the Christian world. The Apostolic See has always been the inspirer and jealous guardian of Italian glory. Therefore, be Italians and Catholics, free and non-sectarian, faithful to the nation as well as to Christ and His visible Vicar. An anti-Christian and antipapal Italy would truly be opposed to the divine plan, and thus condemned to perish.

20. Beloved children, faith and state speak to you at this time through Us. Listen to their cry, arise together and fight manfully the battles of the Lord. May the number, boldness, and strength of the enemy not frighten you, because God is stronger than they; if God is for you, who can be against you?

21. Redouble your prayers so that God might be with you in a greater abundance of grace, fighting and triumphing with you. Accompany your prayers with the practice of the Christian virtues, especially charity toward the needy. Seek God's mercies with humility and perseverance, renewing every day the promises of your baptism.

22. As a pledge of these things and as a sign of Our paternal love, We bestow on you Our apostolic blessing, beloved children.

Given in Rome at Saint Peter's, the eighth day of December, 1892, in the fifteenth year of Our pontificate.

Paragraphs 1 – 2:

Pope Leo XIII opens this encyclical by recasting a central theme of his from *Dall'alto dell'Apostolicio Seggio:* being culturally Italian means being faithfully Catholic. In asking, *"Can one be Italian in name and sentiment and not resent these continual offenses against divine beliefs,"* Leo XIII openly confesses that he does not believe there can be a distinction between being Italian and being a faithful Catholic. For him, these two things are the same. These two things are so intertwined that he views the war against the Catholic Church and Italy's historic Catholic culture as *"doubly evil."*

Leo XIII maintains that the Masonic sect is the chief source of this war against the Catholic Church and the historic Catholic culture of Italy. In Humanum Genus and Dall'alto dell'Apostolicio Seggio, he states, *"We tore from the face of masonry the mask which it used to hide, and We showed it in its crude deformity and dark fatal activity."* In the former work, Leo XIII posited that naturalism is a core Masonic principle, which expanded the Church's traditional position since Clement XII that indifferentism was the core principle of Freemasonry. In the latter work, Leo XIII explained how the principles of Freemasonry had been exported worldwide to launch a war against the Catholic Church to supplant it as the source of truth.

Paragraphs 3 - 5:

In this section, Leo XIII repeats his knowledge of the Masonic program's effort to convince people that Freemasonry is a philanthropic society interested in helping people. Yet, all that it has offered Italy is *"conspiracies, corruptions, and violence"* with the intent to dominate it. As for a litany of the evils that have overcome Italy in such a short period, Leo XIII presents:

1. The substitution of Christianity for naturalism.
2. Substituting the worship of faith with the worship of reason.
3. The substitution of Catholic morality for independent morality.
4. Substituting spiritual progress with material progress.
5. The seizing of Church property, money, and goods that have been squandered.
6. The substitution of holy maxims and laws from the Gospel with a code of revolution.
7. The insertion of atheistic doctrines and a vile realism in schools, science, and the Christian arts.
8. Reducing the number of priests by forcing an unnecessary number of clerics to serve in the military.
9. Substituting of the Sacrament of Holy Matrimony and the Funeral Mass with civil marriages and funerals.
10. An overall effort to laicize everything, thereby replacing the Church's role in society.
11. Attempting to silence and discredit the Catholic press.
12. Closed monasteries and convents but allowed Masonic lodges and sectarian dens to multiply.
13. Gave rights of association to all kinds of organizations but denied the same legal rights to religious societies.
14. Proclaimed freedom of religion but exercised intolerance towards Catholicism.
15. Promised the Pope's protection, dignity, and independence, but exercised a daily contempt of him.
16. Allowances for public demonstrations against the Pope, but denied the same rights for Catholic demonstrations.

17. The encouragement of *"schisms, apostasies, and revolts against legitimate superiors in the Church."*
18. Allowed for oaths in impious associations, but vows made for religious obedience are rebuked for being *"contrary to human dignity and freedom."*

Paragraph 6:

Here, Pope Leo XIII notes that he does not want to create a Masonic bogeyman, as if Freemasons deserve all the credit for all the evil in the world. However, given the direct role that Freemasons have played in the revolutions, in *Kulturkampf*, and in infiltrating governments to press for the persecution of the Catholic Church, Leo XIII is confident that the spirit of Freemasonry has been the chief instigator of evil for the past thirty years. Leo XIII does not cite what source he is referring to when he writes, *"Proud of its successes, the sect herself has spoken out and told us all its past accomplishments and future goals."* However, there seems to have been either an article in a Masonic periodical or book or series of lectures where the triumphs and successes of the Masonic program had been exalted.

Paragraphs 7 – 8:

In this section, Leo XIII returns to an argument he first made in *Dall'alto dell'Apostolicio Seggio* about the value and contribution of the Catholic religion and how the loss of it undermines moral and social progress and stability. He writes, *"The road is very short from religious to social ruin."* Without religion, man turns his heart from heaven to earth. He becomes immersed in material and passions, which gives birth to more grudges between citizens, division in families that leads to divorce, corruption in business and government, and crime. Without religion, man turns to socialism, communism, paganism, and crime to fix these issues.

Leo XIII believes that such has been the fate of Italy since she moved away from her Catholic Church. He credits the Masonic sect and Masonic patriotism for this press towards *"political independence, equality, civilization, and progress aimed to facilitate the independence of man from God in our country."*

Paragraphs 9 – 12:

In this section of *Custodi di Quella Fede*, Pope Leo XIII offers his most potent condemnation of Freemasonry by essentially calling it a sick joke. First, he returns to the point that he began making in *Humanum Genus* about how Freemasonry denies the supernatural because it relies solely on reason and logic – denying divine revelation – to fulfill its promise to improve the condition of man. *"Through its plans and works, it bases itself solely and entirely on such a weak and corrupt nature as ours. When these three concupiscences are brought to the extreme, oppression, greed, and seductive corruption spread slowly, they take on boundless dimensions and become the oppression, plundering, and source of corruption of an entire people."*

Next, Leo XIII flatly calls Freemasonry *"an enemy of God, Church, and country."* He charges everyone to see it for what it is and defend themselves from its pretensions, promises, seducements, enticements, and threats. Most clearly, the Supreme Pontiff charges that *"Christianity and masonry are essentially irreconcilable, such that to join one is to divorce the other"* and that ignorance of this incompatibility can no longer be ignored because *"you have been warned openly by Our predecessors, and We have loudly repeated the warning."*

Third, Leo XIII moves onto the consequences reserved for those who have fallen into *"one of these societies of perdition."*

They are to separate themselves from it or remain separated from Christian communion. If they should choose the latter, they lose their soul now and for eternity. He then charges parents, teachers, godparents, and whoever has cared for other persons with the duty to use all prudence to protect those under their care from being seduced into joining these sects *"or to draw them from it if they have already entered."*

Fourth, he illustrates examples of what that care for the soul of others looks like. It means *"should fear the least danger, avoid every occasion, and take the greatest precautions,"* using *"all the prudence of the serpent while keeping in your heart the simplicity of the dove,"* fathers and mothers being cautious of inviting strangers into their homes, especially before their visitor's faith life have sufficiently determined, and to be aware of what friends, teachers, doctors, or other benefactors, are recruiters for these guilty sects. In closing, Leo XIII laments how Freemasons have infiltrated families, penetrating them as wolves in sheep's clothing.

Paragraphs 13 – 22:

Pope Leo XIII opens this section up by praising the realization of the idea he first promoted in Humanum Genus; Catholics push back against Freemasonry by establishing guilds, associations, and mutual aid groups in society. Nevertheless, he says these groups are only worthy if they *"are inspired by a good moral and religious spirit."* Lest they are easily infiltrated and become *"more or less dominated by masons."* Even women's philanthropy societies that are not in harmony with Christian charity can be easily guided into being a front for Masonic enterprise.

Leo XIII shows continuity with Pope Clement XII by repeating his comprehensive prohibition from *In Eminenti* that charged Catholics to avoid all familiarity, friendship, and association with anyone suspected to be a Freemason or belonging to any appendant Masonic body. That restriction includes men already publicly known to be Freemasons and their ideological allies who promote the Masonic principles of indifferentism, secularism, relativism, and naturalism. According to Leo XIII, this guise of universal tolerance, respect for all religions, and celebrating the coexistence between religions are just attempts *"to reconcile Christ and Belial, the Church of God and the state without God."*

The Holy Father closes this section by repeating the same action plan that he set forth in Humanum Genus; Catholics need to push back in every venue that Freemasons have infiltrated, pervaded, and taken control of by offering truth to their lies. Every place they are, Catholics must be, and every hour they are plotting against us, Catholics must be plotting against them. *"That is what you will do, beloved children, opposing press to press, school to school, organization to organization, congress to congress, action to action."* He calls this a battlefield and tells Catholics that being on the defensive will not win this battle. *"We must courageously go out into the battlefield and confront it. . . . Be all of one heart and one mind, like the first Christians."*

Leo XIII truly believes that this war against Freemasonry for the soul of Italy is the duty of every Italian. He invites them under this Apostolic blessing to redouble their prayers to God so that He will be with them in this fight and to unite their prayers with the practice of the Christian virtue, especially toward the needy.

There was no new information about Freemasonry or any new condemnation against the Masonic sects offered in this encyclical that was not already presented in *Humanum Genus* and *Dall'alto dell'Apostolicio Seggio*. In fact, rather than being an encyclical, it presented itself more like an Apostolic Charge or an

Apostolic Exhortation. This document is primarily a letter of encouragement to the Italian people from their Pope to maintain vigilance in the war against Freemasonry and to redouble their efforts because the fate of their country is at risk.

Chapter XI | Inimica Vis

This encyclical was promulgated with *Custodi di Quella Fede*. However, whereas the former was addressed to the Italian People, *Inimic Vis* was addressed to the Italian Bishops. This document was the briefest of all of Pope Leo XIII's works against Freemasonry.

Inimica Vis
(Enemy Forces)
Pope Leo XIII - 1892

To the Bishops of Italy.

The enemy forces, inspired by the evil spirit, ever wage war on the Christian name. They join forces in this endeavor with certain groups of men whose purpose is to subvert divinely revealed truths and to rend the very fabric of Christian society with disastrous dissent. Indeed, how much damage these cohorts, as it were, have inflicted on the Church is well known. And yet, the spirit of all previous groups hostile to Catholic institutions has come to life again in that group called the Masonic sect, which, strong in manpower and resources, is the leader in a war against anything sacred.

2. Our predecessors in the Roman pontificate have in the course of a century and a half outlawed this group not once, but repeatedly. We too, in accordance with Our duty, have condemned it strongly to Christian people, so that they might be aware of its wiles and bravely repel its impious assaults. Moreover, lest cowardice and sloth overtake us imperceptibly, We have deliberately endeavored to reveal the secrets of this pernicious sect and the means by which it labors for the destruction of the Catholic enterprise.

3. Now, though, a certain thoughtless indifference on the part of many Italians has resulted in their not recognizing the magnitude and extent of the peril. And so the faith of our ancestors, the salvation won for mankind by Jesus Christ, and, consequently the great benefits of Christian civilization are endangered. Indeed,

fearing nothing and yielding to no one, the Masonic sect proceeds with greater boldness day by day: with its poisonous infection it pervades entire communities and strives to entangle itself in all the institutions of our country in its conspiracy to forcefully deprive the Italian people of their Catholic faith, the origin and source of their greatest blessings.

4. This is the reason for the endless artifices they employ in their assault on the divinely inspired faith; this is the reason why the legitimate liberty of the Church is treated with contempt and beset with legal oppression. They believe that the Church does not possess the nature and essence of a true society, that the State has priority over it, and that civil authority takes precedence over sacred authority. This false and destructive doctrine has been frequently condemned by the Holy See. Among many other ills, it has been responsible for the usurpation on the part of civil authorities of that to which they have no right and for their unscrupulous appropriation of what they have alienated from the Church. This is clear in the case of ecclesiastical benefices; they usurp the right to give or withhold the revenues of these according to their good pleasure.

5. Likewise, in a manner no less insidious, they plan to soften the opposition of the lower clergy with their promises. Their purpose in this endeavor can easily be detected, especially since the very authors of this undertaking do not take sufficient pains to conceal what they intend. They wish to win over the clergy by cajolery; once the novelties have confused them, they will withdraw their obedience to legitimate authority. And yet in this matter they seem to have underestimated the virtue of our clergy, who for so many years have given manifest examples of their moderation and loyalty. We have every reason to be confident

that, with God's help, they will continue their devotion to duty no matter what circumstances may arise.

6. This summary indicates both the extent of the activity of the Masonic sect and the goal of its endeavors. What compounds this harmful situation, however, and causes Us deep anxiety is that far too many of our compatriots, driven by hope of their personal advantage or by perverse ambition, have given their names or support to the sect. This being so, We commend first and foremost to your efforts the eternal salvation of those whom we have just mentioned: may your zeal never waver in constantly and insistently recalling them from their error and certain destruction. To be sure, the task of extricating those who have fallen into the snares of the Masons is laborious, and its outcome is doubtful, if we consider the cleverness of the sect: still the recovery of no one should ever be despaired of since the force of apostolic charity is truly marvelous.

7. Next, we must heal those who have erred in this respect out of faint-heartedness, that is, those who, not because of a debased nature but because of weakness of spirit and lack of discretion, have allowed themselves to be drawn into supporting the Masonic enterprises. Sufficiently weighty are the words of Our predecessor Felix III in this regard. "An error which is not resisted is approved; a truth which is not defended is suppressed.... He who does not oppose an evident crime is open to the suspicion of secret complicity." By reminding them of the examples of their forefathers, the broken spirits of these men must be reanimated with that courage which is the guardian of duty and dignity alike, so that they may be ashamed and regret their cowardly actions. For surely our whole life is involved in a constant battle in which

our salvation itself is at stake; nothing is more disgraceful for a Christian than cowardice.

8. It is likewise necessary to strengthen those who fall because of ignorance. By this we mean those, not few in number, who, deceived by appearances and allured by various enticements, allow themselves without understanding it to be enrolled in the Masonic order. In these cases We hope that with divine inspiration they will be able someday to repudiate their error and perceive the truth, especially if you try to remove the false outward appearance of the sect and reveal its hidden designs. Indeed these can no longer be considered hidden since their very accomplices have themselves disclosed them in many ways. Why, within the last few months, the designs of the Masons have been publicly proclaimed throughout Italy, even to the point of ostentation! They wish to see the religion founded by God repudiated and all affairs, private as well as public, regulated by the principles of naturalism alone; this is what, in their impiety and stupidity, they call the restoration of civil society. And yet the State will plunge headlong into ruin if Christians are not willing to be vigilant and not willing to labor to support its well-being!

9. But in the presence of such audacious evils, it is not sufficient merely to be aware of the wiles of this vile sect: we must also war against it, using those very arms furnished by the divine faith which once prevailed against paganism. Therefore, it is your task to inflame souls by persuasion, exhortation and example, nourish in the clergy and our people a zeal for religion and salvation which is active, resolute, and intrepid. These qualities frequently distinguish Catholic peoples of other nations in similar situations. It is commonly claimed that the ancient ardor of spirit in protecting their ancestral faith has grown cold among the Italian people.

Nor is this perhaps false; especially since if the dispositions of both sides be inspected, those who wage war on religion seem to show more energy than those who repel it. But for those who seek salvation there can be no middle ground between laborious struggle and destruction. Therefore, in the case of the weak and sluggish, courage must be stirred up through your efforts; in the case of the strong, it must be kept active; with all trace of dissent wiped out, under your leadership and command, the result will be that all alike, with united minds and common discipline, may undertake the battle in a spirited manner.

10. Because of the gravity of the matter and the necessity of repelling the danger, We have decided to address the Italian people in a letter which We are including along with this one; propagate it as widely as possible and, where needed, interpret it to your people. In this manner, with the blessing of God, we can hope that spirits may be aroused through the contemplation of the threatening evils and betake themselves without delay to the remedies which We have pointed out.

11. As a presage of divine gifts and testimony of Our benevolence We affectionately accord to you, Venerable Brethren, and the people entrusted to your care, the apostolic blessing.

Given in Rome at St. Peter's, 8 December 1892, in the 15th year of Our Pontificate.

Paragraphs 1 – 2:

Pope Leo XIII opens his encyclical to the Bishops with a brief recapitulation on the nineteen centuries of warfare against the Catholic Church that was *"inspired by the evil spirit."* The principle aim of the evil spirit is no different than the basis of Eve's conversation with the serpent in the Garden of Eden; that is, it simply desires to subvert divinely revealed truth to destroy humanity. In this present age, the Masonic sect is now the leader in this *"war against anything sacred."*

Leo XIII, without going through the labor again of citing the names of the documents of his predecessors, summarily states that over the past century and a half, the Roman Pontificate has repeatedly outlawed Freemasonry and its appendant bodies. Then, without naming *Humanum Genus*, he states that he has gone even further than his predecessors by revealing the secrets of the Masonic sect. By the term 'secret' here, Leo XIII does not necessarily mean the ceremonial degree work, secret passwords, or secret handshakes, but, rather, the Masonic program; that is, the plot to supplant the Catholic Church in the world and replace it with the dogma of naturalism.

Paragraphs 3 – 9:

In this section, Pope Leo XIII returns to a theme first found in *Dall'alto dell'Apostolicio Seggio* concerning the failure of the Italian people to see Freemasonry for what it is. This indifference on the part of many Italians is costing them their blessed Christian culture. It has emboldened the Masonic sect to attempt to infiltrate every institution in society to seize control of it and then use it to assault the Catholic faith.

Leo XIII also notes the Masonic sect's use of a tactic that every enemy of the Catholic Church has used against her. They attempt to work on local parish priests and those whom Leo XIII calls *"lower clergy"* to persuade them that what the Vatican teaches is distant from reality. Again, this tactic is reminiscent of the serpent's dialogue with Eve. Indeed, the clergy knows what the Church teaches. However, through flattery and concealing their true intentions, the Freemason attempts to persuade the lower clergy that there is nothing harmful about Freemasonry, that it is just a philanthropic organization, that the teachings of the Church are outdated, that Freemasonry is harmless, well-meaning, and not a threat. Nevertheless, despite these attempts, Leo XIII is confident that with God's help, the lower clergy *"will continue their devotion to duty no matter what circumstances may arise."*

Yet, far too many have been misled because they believed Freemasonry would give them some advantage in life. While Leo XIII writes that the Church grieves over their loss and admits how difficult it is to extricate *"those who have fallen in the snares of the Masons,"* he encourages his brother bishops never to lose their zeal in fighting for their eternal salvation.

He also calls the bishops to heal those drawn into supporting the Masonic enterprise because they were fainthearted, weak in spirit, and lacked discretion. Calling it *"sufficiently weighty,"* Leo XIII binds his brother bishops under a quote from a non-referenced document of Pope Felix III (483 – 492) that concerned one of the several heresies that his Pontificate had to defend the Church against, *"An error which is not resisted is approved; a truth which is not defended is suppressed.... He who does not oppose an evident crime is open to the suspicion of secret complicity."*

After treating how the bishops ought to minister to those whose pride led them into Freemasonry and those of weaker spiritual constitutions who have been drawn into supporting it, Leo XIII now advises on how the bishops should minister to those who have been enrolled into the Masonic sects due to their ignorance of it. He says that this group consists of not *"few in number"* of those whom the pretense of Freemasonry has duped; its appearances and enticements. He believes that with the help of divine inspiration and the bishops ripping the masking away from Freemasonry, these fallen souls might once renounce their error. The task of the bishops exposing Freemasonry appears to be much easier now due to an unnamed document in circulation, which proudly boasts of the successes of the Masonic program to supplant Catholicism with naturalism.

While making the faithful aware of the evils of Freemasonry is important, Pope Leo XIII makes a case for the Italian bishops to follow the two simple principles that have strengthened and preserved the Catholic Church in our country's war against Freemasonry, that is: 1) Inflame souls by persuasion, exhortation, and example; and 2) Nourish in the clergy and the people with an undying and active zeal for religion and their salvation. In these two points, Leo XIII again returns to his arguments in *Humanum Genus* and *Custodi di Quella Fede* that Catholics must match them in effort, passion, and enterprise to defeat Freemasonry.

Paragraphs 10 - 11:

In closing, Pope Leo XIII asks the Italian Bishops to disseminate *Custodi di Quella Fede "widely as possible"* so that *"with the blessing of God, we can hope that spirits may be aroused through the contemplation of the threatening evils and betake them-selves without delay to the remedies which We have pointed out."*

Similar to *Custodi di Quella Fede*, there was not any new information added about the Masonic sects or their activities that were not already presented in his early encyclicals on the subject. What is new here is that *Inimica Vis* was addressed to the Italian bishops as more of a letter of exhortation than as an encyclical.

Custodi di Quella Fede and *Inimica Vis* were Pope Leo XIII's final encyclicals that were primarily devoted to the Catholic position on Freemasonry. Together, with the four previous encyclicals on the same subject, Leo XIII established his legacy as the defender of Catholicism and Italy against the Masonic program.

Chapter XII
Praeclara Gratulatiois Pune fois encoreublicae

Appointed Bishop of Perugia, Italy in 1844 by Pope Gregory XVI, Pope Leo XIII found the occasion of his Episcopal Jubilee and what he calls *"the remarkable devotion of the Spanish Nation"* a motivation to write his Apostolic letter *Praeclara Gratulationis Pune fois encoreublicae*, which was a very passionate call for all Christians abandon their divisions with Apostolic See of Rome and to come back into union with the Roman Pontiff. To produce a document on the subject was the intent of the First Vatican Council (1869 – 1870) before it was prematurely closed due to the Franco-Prussian War.

The deep-seated pain that Leo XIII has for the disunity of the Church is evident throughout this lengthy Apostolic letter. While he recognizes the various causes of the divisions between the Eastern Churches and the Protestants, he does not believe those reasons outweigh the call of Jesus' prayer that *"they all may be one, as Thou Father in Me, and I in Thee."*[88] He finds the Divine Mission entrusted to the Catholic Church to be the source of unity for all Christians so that the work of spreading the Gospel to all nations, thereby leaving no one ignorant of Christ Jesus, will be accomplished.

---

[88] Jn.17:21.

In this Apostolic letter, Leo XIII first appeals to the Eastern Churches (Greek and Oriental). He compliments them on their illustrious ancient faith and glorious past and remarks that the Latin Church has borrowed from their teachings, rites, and customs. He admits that their central point of departure is the Primacy of the Roman Pontiff but reminds them that early in their history, it was a point of agreement between them that *"Christ's Divine Utterance, Thou art Peter, and upon this rock I will build My Church, has undoubtedly been realized in the Roman Pontiffs."* To prove this point, he reminds them that from the East, the Church found several of her first Roman Pontiffs, including Saint Anacletus (97), Saint Evaristus (97 – 103), Saint Anicetus (155 – 166), Saint Eleutherius (175 – 189), Saint Zosimus (417 – 418), and Saint Agatho (678 – 681). Even at the beginning of the division, Leo XIII reminds them that Photius sent advocates to Rome *"on matters that concerned him."* Pope Nicolas I sent his Legates to Constantinople, "without the slightest opposition, *"to examine the case of Ignatius the Patriarch with all diligence and bring back to the Apostolic See a full and accurate report."*

Having offered proofs from the history of the Church and dismissing all other theological differences as minor issues, Leo XIII appeals to the Greeks and the Orientals to make the schisms of the Churches cease, assemble those who have been dispersed, bring back those who err and unite them to the One, Holy, Catholic, and Apostolic Church.

Leo XIII then makes a particular appeal to the nations of the Slavonic race. He remarks that the Church is indebted to the merits of Saints Cyril and Methodius and appeals to them based on the *"priceless benefit"* that returning into unity with Rome would give them. He writes, *"The Church is anxious to welcome you also to her arms, that she may give you manifold aids to salvation, prosperity, and grandeur."*

Finally, Leo XIII makes a less affectionate but very strongly worded appeal to other Christian professing religions, who he says were separated due to an *"extraordinary revolution of things and circumstances."* Rightly, he harkens back to the same language he used to speak of Freemasonry when addressing the errors of Protestantism so that he might show the intimate relationship between these two philosophies. He remarks about those who want to uproot every foundation of religion, namely the Divine nature of Jesus Christ, those who deny that God inspires the Scriptures, the denial of the authority of Scripture, the failure of private interpretation, the innovation of the supremacy of individual conscience, the replacement of divine revelation with the doctrines of naturalism and rationalism, and the false nature of a union of brotherly love and bonds of mutual Charity. He calls the Protestants to consider, *"how can hearts be united in perfect Charity where minds do not agree in Faith?"* Such was Leo XIII's opinion of what would pass in the Post-Second Vatican Council Church as ecumenism. Indeed, what passes as ecumenism in the Church today, Leo XIII, Pius IX, and Clement XII would call indifferentism and the spirit of Freemasonry.

A little past halfway into this Apostolic call of unity for Christians, Leo XIII warns his brethren that Freemasonry is a great danger and a threat to their unity.

Praeclara Gratulationis Pune fois encoreublicae
(Splendid Tokens of Public Rejoicing)
Pope Leo XIII - 1894

(numbers (#) added to the paragraphs)

To Our Venerable Brethren, all Patriarchs, Primates, Archbishops and Bishops of the Catholic World
In Grace and Communion with the Apostolic See

Venerable Brethren, Health and Apostolic Benediction,

. . .

(29a) There is likewise a great danger threatening unity on the part of that association which goes by the name of Freemasons, whose fatal influence for a long time past oppresses Catholic nations in particular. Favored by the agitations of the times, and waxing insolent in its power and resources and success, it strains every nerve to consolidate its sway and enlarge its sphere. It has already sallied forth from its hiding-places, where it hatched its plots, into the throng of cities, and as if to defy the Almighty, has set up its throne in this very city of Rome, the Capital of the Catholic world. But what is most disastrous is, that wherever it has set its foot it penetrates into all ranks and departments of the commonwealth, in the hope of obtaining at last supreme control. This is, indeed, a great calamity: for its depraved principles and iniquitous designs are well known.

(29b) Under the pretense of vindicating the rights of man and of reconstituting society, it attacks Christianity; it rejects revealed Doctrine, denounces practices of Piety, the Divine Sacraments, and every Sacred thing as superstition; it strives to eliminate the Christian Character from Marriage and the family and the education of youth, and from every form of instruction, whether public or private, and to root out from the minds of men all respect for Authority, whether human or Divine. On its own part, it preaches the worship of nature, and maintains that by the principles of nature are truth and probity and justice to be measured and regulated. In this way, as is quite evident, man is being driven to adopt customs and habits of life akin to those of the heathen, only more corrupt in proportion as the incentives to sin are more numerous.

(30) Although We have spoken on this subject in the strongest terms before, yet We are led by Our Apostolic watchfulness to urge it once more, and We repeat Our warning again and again, that in face of such an eminent peril, no precaution, howsoever great, can be looked upon as sufficient. May God in His Mercy bring to naught their impious designs; nevertheless, let all Christians know and understand that the shameful yoke of Freemasonry must be shaken off once and for all; and let them be the first to shake it off who are most galled by its oppression—the men of Italy and of France. With what weapons and by what method this may best be done We Ourselves have already pointed out: the victory cannot be doubtful to those who trust in that Leader Whose Divine Words still remain in all their force: I have overcome the world.

. . .

Pope Leo XIII's insertion here into *Praeclara Gratulationis Pune fois encoreublicae* was his final and most concise commentary about the continuity of the Catholic prohibition against Freemasonry, how the Masonic sects plot against the Catholic Church, and why the spirit of Freemasonry is a danger and threat to all Christian people. Altogether, this insertion is merely a recapitulation of things that Leo XIII had written in his previous encyclicals. However, he does note here how the spirit of Freemasonry had essentially taken over France and Italy. According to *Dell'alto dell'Apostolico Seggio, Custodi di Quella Fede*, and *Inimica Vis*, the faithful had been made well aware concerning the attempts of Masonic infiltration in Italy, but in France, where Continental Freemasonry was the strongest and had infiltrated government, society, and the Church most significantly, was not a focus of Leo XIII.

Chapter XIII | The Epoch of Indifferentism

The Twentieth century was one of the most monumental periods for the post-Monarchial Pontificate of the Catholic Church. On the global stage, the Church had to figure out its role during the global wars of World War I and World War II. The long history of animosity, suspicion, and hatred towards the Jewish people, which the Catholic Church had always condemned, had reached its climax during the Holocaust. The age of weapons of mass destruction belonged to this century, and so did the efforts to end the legacy of European colonization. New technologies that revolutionized mass communication and travel also came online, allowing the Church to evangelize like never before.

The usurpation of government control over marriage and divorce, which the Popes had consistently challenged, paved the way for a social disconnect between marriage and sex and children and sex. The so-called 'sexual revolution,' like past revolutions, was just an outright revolt against Catholic morality and Divine revelation. Pope Paul VI's 1968 encyclical *Humanae vitae*, which upheld the dogma on marriage, family, and procreation, came so late in the revolution that it caused massive disappointment among millions of Catholics who took the Church's silent contemplation as acquiescence to the spirit of sexual immorality.

Eventually, the sexual revolution tore down the concept of human sexuality altogether. It disconnected it from sexual gender, creating a distinction between biological sex and psychological gender.

At the opening of this century, the prophetic warnings from Pope Pius IX and Leo XIII about socialism and communism had been realized in Russia after Post-World War I circumstances exasperated preexisting tensions against Tsar Nicholas II. In February of 1917 (per the Julian calendar), revolutionaries began demanding that Nicholas II form a government built on the communistic doctrines of Karl Marx. By March 2, 1917, the revolutionaries seized control of the capital city, Duma, and with no army left to defend him, Nicolas II abdicated his throne, and a provisional government took over. In October of that same year, the Bolsheviks overthrew the provisional government. As their leader, Vladimir Lenin began implementing Lenin's version of Marxism, transforming society into a communist state by first passing through socialism. Communism, according to Marx, is a stateless, classless, and egalitarian society where workers are free from exploitation and alienation and are, thereby, autonomous persons and able to control their destinies.

Freemasonry, which had first come to Russia in 1723 - 1734[89] but was prohibited at several points after that by Catherine the Great, Alexander I, and Nicholas I, and after the Bolshevik revolution in October of 1917, all of the Masonic lodges in Russia went dark.

Just as the birth of Protestantism in 1517 and Freemasonry in 1717 eventually led to the persecution and intolerance of the Catholic Church, so too did the birth of Communism in 1917, which led to an onslaught of persecution against the Catholic

---

[89] MacKillop, Andrew, Murdoc, Steve. *Military Governors and Imperial Frontiers c. 1600 - 1800: A Study of Scotland and Empires.* Brill Academic Publishers. 2003. 103.

Church wherever its poison was spread. Not only do these ideologies agree that Catholicism needs to be destroyed, but they also work independently of the other to replace Catholicism with the sovereignty of autonomous rule, naturalism, indifferentism, and, inevitably, atheism.

The connection between the Masonic program and the efforts of the Communist in Russia in 1917 to destroy both the Catholic Church and Monarchism were made aware to Archbishop Eugenio Pacelli, the Apostolic Nuncio to Germany, in a 1918 letter from Felix von Cardinal Hartmann:[90]

> *"His Majesty the Emperor [German Emperor William II] just has let it be known to me 'that, according to news that came to him yesterday, the Grand Orient has just decided first to depose all Sovereigns – first of all him, the Emperor – then to destroy (?) the Cathol.[olic] Church, to imprison the pope, etc, and, finally, to establish on the ruins of the former bourgeois society a world republic under the leadership of American Big Capital. The German Freemasons are purportedly loyal to the [German] Emperor (which is to be doubted!) and they informed him about it. Also England wants to preserve the current bourgeois order. France and America, however, are said to be under the full influence of the Grand Orient [Masonic Lodge]. Bolshevism is said to be the external tool to establish the desired conditions. In the face of such a great danger which threatens in addition to the Monarchy, also the Catholic Church; it is thus important that the German episcopacy be informed and that also the pope be warned.'*

---

[90] This letter was discovered by German historian, Dr. Michael Hesemann in the Vatican Apostolic Archive (https://insidethevatican.com/news/newsflash/letter-18-2017-fatima-100/ - retrieved – 06/02/2020).

So far the message of His Majesty. I have believed myself to be duty-bound to pass it on to Your Excellency, and I have to leave it up to Your judgment whether You wish to pass this message on to Rome. The stormy demand of the [German] Social Democrats that the Emperor should abdicate gives a certain confirmation to this message. May God protect us and His Holy Church in this terrible turmoil!"

Rightly, the Catholic Church responded to Communism similarly to how she thoughtfully responded to Protestantism and Freemasonry. It began with warnings of the idea itself from Pope Pius IX in *Nostis et Nobiscum* (1849) and Pope Leo XIII in *Rerum Novarum* (1891). Again, with *Quadragesimo Anno* by Pope Pius XI in 1931, after the communist revolutions in Russia, China, and Mexico had been followed by religious persecution, then more harshly by Pius XI in his 1937 *Divini Redemptoris*. Then, the year after Communists swept into Czechoslovakia and began persecuting the Catholic Church in 1948, the Supreme Sacred Congregation of the Holy Office (today the Congregation for the Doctrine of the Faith) issued a Decree Against Communism under the title *Acta Apostolica Sedis* (Done by the Holy See), which answered four questions about Communism and whether Catholics can participate in any part of it:

Decree of the Holy Office
SSC - 1949

Q.1 Whether it is permitted to join the Communist parties to perform the same favor.

R. Negative: Communism is materialistic and Antichristian; Communist leaders, however, although sometimes with professional religion does not oppose itself, however, whether learning or action of God in Christ Church polluted and almost hostile to the show.

Q.2 Whether it is lawful to propagate or to read the books, periodic, diaries, or leaflets, [that support or defend] the action of the Communist, or write on them.
R. Negative: for by the law itself forbidden to exercise.

Q.3 Whether the Christian faithful who are of the act, referred to in the n.1 and 2, both knowing it and they have assigned freely, they may be admitted to the sacraments.
R. Negative, according to ordinary principles also denied to those who are not disposed.

Q.4 Does the faithful of the communist doctrine and materialistic Anti-Christian of their professors, and in the first place, those who defend it or to reproduce the species, by that fact, the Catholic apostates from the faith as upon, run into the excommunication reserved to the Apostolic See, in a special way.
R. Affirmative

By the power of this 1949 decree, which was approved by Pope Pius XII, Communism had joined Freemasonry and Protestantism as ideologies intrinsically irreconcilable to Catholicism. Their unrepentant adherents were unworthy to receive the Sacraments of the Catholic Church. It cannot be said that either of these ideologies ever replaced or paved the way for the other. However, the attention the Catholic Church attributed to each was particular when these ideologies were the most novel and pervasive.

Towards the end of this century, a new ideology called homosexualism would present itself as the most dangerous and pervasive threat the Catholic Church has ever beheld. This ideology posits that individuals are born with the disposition of same-gender attraction and are naturally ordered to God's grace; their inclination towards same-gender sexual relations is natural, unchangeable, and not disordered. The homosexual agenda would become far more successful in infiltrating every aspect of society, government, and the Catholic Church than the Masonic plot could have dreamed of.

For her part, the Catholic Church failed in this century to notice the danger of this error as she had with other heresies. Perhaps it was because homosexualism was not present as an association, religion, or political movement. Instead, the ideology itself was presented as an ontological argument, dealing with human nature and the right and liberty of their sovereign conscience to judge and determine their sexuality. There is an argument that the lack of a strong, clear, and consistent response to the dangers of homosexualism had more to do with the Catholic Church being compromised due to being infiltrated by clerics who had become attached to this heresy.

While it is true that homosexualism does not, by necessity, present its agenda through a formal association, its evident indifference towards the divinely revealed and divinely ordered human sexuality and its appeal to naturalism brings it into full communion with the spirit of Protestantism, Freemasonry, and Communism. To be sure, homosexualism is just one more ideology that intends to replace Catholicism with the sovereignty of autonomous rule, naturalism, indifferentism, and, inevitably, atheism.

The impact of Pope Leo XIII's work to inspire Catholics to defend the faith and the world against the Masonic sects and those like them is questionable. While his efforts and his sincerity are beyond reproach, the memory of his work did not immediately extend beyond the continent of Europe.

Canon Law No. 2335

In 1904, Archbishop Diomede Angelo Raffaele Gennaro Falconio, Apostolic Delegate to the United States, received a letter from Cardinal Girolamo Maria Gotti, Perfect of the Congregation of the Propaganda, commanding him to confer with the other Archbishops of the United States to remedy the humiliating condition of Black Catholics in the country. Gotti noted that he had received information that Black Catholic priests and laity are treated unequally to White Catholics and that such actions are *"not in conformity with the spirit of Christianity, which proclaims the equality of all men before God."*[91]

In response to Gotti's letter, the United States Bishops created an agency in 1907 called the 'Catholic Board of Negro Mission.' They placed Father John E. Burke of New York as its first director. The work of his agency, as Davis notes,[92] was not in any way an effort to truly end the practice of racial segregation in the Catholic Church or the rejection of Blacks from Catholic schools and universities.

One memorable accomplishment that Burke accomplished was issuing a report in 1912 outlining four obstacles that he believed were detrimental to bringing more Blacks into the Catholic Church. Concerning the instant case, one barrier that Burke found preventing more Blacks from becoming Catholic was that too many Blacks belonged to forbidden secret societies like the Freemasons. In response to this obstacle, Burke noted that the ban against such membership should be maintained for Black Catholics. However, permission should be obtained from the

---

[91] Davis, Cyprian. *The History of Black Catholics in the United States.* The Crossroad Publishing Company. New York. 1990. 195.
[92] Ibid. 198.

Holy See, allowing prospective converts to retain their membership in such societies for financial benefits. Burke further stated that Black secret societies did not present the same threat to Catholics as White societies.

Burke found those secret societies correctly; Prince Hall Freemasonry was primarily profoundly entrenched in the Black community. In 1775, Prince Hall, a Black Protestant educator, abolitionist, and revolutionary living in Boston, and fourteen other men were initiated into Freemasonry by a British military regiment, Lodge #411, which was a subordinate lodge working under the authority of the Grand Lodge of Ireland. In 1776, these fifteen men established African Lodge No. 1, according to the permission of a dispensation left to them by Worshipful Master John Batt, giving them the strict ability to meet, celebrate Saint John's Days, and bury their dead.

In 1784, African Lodge No. 1 was granted a charter by the Grand Lodge of England and was renumbered No. 459 (later No. 370). Since then, Freemasonry amongst Blacks in America has spread and become so intimately entangled with its story that it is impossible to accurately tell the history of Blacks in America without explaining the history of Prince Hall Freemasonry. During the epoch of slavery, segregation, and Jim Crow laws in the United States, the Protestant Church and the Prince Hall Masonic Lodge were the two central institutions of stability and leadership in the Black community. Typically, these two institutions share membership and frequently share the same facilities. Molded-in the image of its founder, Prince Hall Freemasonry believed it was not an enemy of Protestantism but indebted to it.

Prince Hall Lodges played an instrumental role in helping enslaved people escape north. Historian Harry E. Davis writes:

"In 1807, there were about 1,500 colored people in Washington, one-third of whom were free. A small group of the men

established a school, and layer became founders of the first Masonic lodge. They also organized a beneficial society, under whose benevolent guise they operated a station of the Underground Railroad. In 1823 a few of these men were initiated in the colored lodges of Philadelphia, and in 1825 they were charted into Social Lodge No. 7."[93]

After the Civil War in the United States, Prince Hall Freemasons served in many roles during the Reconstruction Period, from getting Blacks registered to vote to serving as judges in many local and national offices. Some of the most notable Prince Hall Masons to serve elected office during the Reconstruction Period were: Richard H. Gleaves (Lieutenant Governor of South Carolina, Past Grand Master of Ohio and Past National Grand Master), R. Brown Elliot South Carolina Representative, Past Grand Master of South Carolina), Hiram R. Revels (Mississippi US Senator, Past Grand Chaplain of Ohio), James R. Lynch (Mississippi US Senator, Past Master), O. J. Dunn (Louisiana Lieutenant Governor, Past Grand Master of Louisiana), C. C. Antoine (Louisiana Lieutenant Governor, Master Mason), P. B. S. Pinchback Louisiana Lieutenant Governor, US Senator, Master Mason), Antoine Dubuclet (Louisiana US Senator, Past Master), James H. Burch (Louisiana US Senator, Past Master), George H. White (North Carolina Congressman, Past Grand Master of North Carolina), and W. B. Brown (Superintendent of Education of Louisiana, Master Mason).[94]

In addition, a number of some of the most recognizable Black American men have been Prince Hall Freemasons, including Martin R. Delany (author/activist), Booker T. Washington (educator/author), Richard Allen (founder of the African Methodist

---

[93] Gray, David L. *Inside Prince Hall.* Anchor Communications. Lancaster, Virgina. 2003. 99.
[94] Ibid. 101.

Episcopal Church), W. E. B. Dubois (educator/author), Thurgood Marshall (first Black Supreme Court Justice), Jesse Jackson (activist), Al Green (singer), Sugar Ray Robinson (boxer), Mike Tyson (boxer), Don King (promoter), Scottie Pippen (basketball player), Benjamin L. Hooks (NAACP), Thomas Bradley (Mayor of Los Angeles), Kweisi Mufume (NAACP), Al Sharpton (activist), Louis Stokes (US Congressman), Carol B. Stokes (first Black elected Mayor of Cleveland, Ohio), Wilson Goode (first Black Mayor of Philadelphia), Charles H. Wesley (author), and John H. Johnson (publisher).

While Burke was correct in finding the dependency that the Black community had on the Prince Hall Masonic Lodge for financial benefit, he equally demonstrated a complete ignorance of the philosophical teaching contained in Freemasonry amongst Black Americans and an outright heretical position in positing that there was a distinction between Prince Hall Freemasonry and Anglo Freemasonry, from which it descends, or between it and Continental Freemasonry.

From Clement XII to Leo XIII, no Pope had ever made an allowance for Freemasonry, depending upon where it was practiced or what race of people practiced it. No Pope had ever allowed Freemasonry to continue to be practiced just because of its philanthropic endeavors or its output to the community in which it operated. No Pope had ever permitted anyone to practice Freemasonry just because that particular sect plotted more against Protestantism than it did Catholicism, such as Prince Hall Freemasonry.

Therefore, for Burke to even suggest that candidates for the Sacraments of the Catholic Church be allowed to remain members of the Masonic Order or other secret societies is proof that he was either completely ignorant of the Church's dogmatic teaching against Freemasonry or he was an ideological ally to

Freemasonry, or he was a heretic, or he was pretending to care about the condition of Black Catholics. No faithful Catholic who digested any of the encyclicals or apostolic exhortations about Freemasonry would dare suggest that it be allowed to continue amongst Black Catholics unless they desired the worst for Black Catholics. However, to this day, it is a well-known errant belief among so-called Black Catholic Freemasons that Prince Hall Freemasonry is excluded from the Church's prohibition against Freemasonry.

While the bishops of the United States were figuring out how to do nothing significant about the condition of the Black Catholics in their country, Pope Pius X was working to strengthen the Catholic Church in France, where a new wave of anti-Catholic laws had been put into place, and insinuations that the Vatican was attempting to instigate a religious war were being hurled about. In his 1907 *Une Fois Encore* (Once Again), Pius X responded to this false claim by pointing to Freemasonry and other groups as being the true instigators of a war against the Catholic Church:

> 8. The Church, they said, is seeking to arouse religious war in France and is summoning to her aid the violent persecution which has been the object of her prayers. What a strange accusation! Founded by Him who came to bring peace to the world and to reconcile man with God, a Messenger of peace upon earth, the Church could only seek religious war by repudiating her high mission and belying it before the eyes of all. To this mission of patient sweetness and love she rests and will remain always faithful. Besides, the whole world now knows that if peace of conscience is broken in France, that is not the work of the Church but of her enemies. Fair-minded men, even though not of our faith, recognize that if there is a struggle on the question of religion in your beloved country, it is not because the Church was

the first to unfurl the flag, but because war was declared against her. During the last twenty-five years she has had to undergo this warfare. That is the truth and the proof of it is seen in the declarations made and repeated over and over again in the Press, at meetings, at Masonic congresses, and even in Parliament, as well as in the attacks which have been progressively and systematically directed against her. These facts are undeniable, and no argument can ever make away with them. The Church then does not wish for war and religious war least of all. To affirm the contrary is an outrageous calumny.

As the Catholic Church moved forward into the twentieth century and other threats and dangers began to occupy her time, *Une Fois Encore* would be the final Papal encyclical or apostolic exhortation to mention Freemasonry. From this point forward, the previous prohibitions and penalties would be codified in the Church's Canon Law.

In 1904, after hearing the requests of the fathers of the First Vatican Council, Pope Pius X set to work on a commission to examine and reconcile all the decrees and laws that had been issued by popes, councils, congregations of the Church down through the centuries and to consolidate them into one systematic code of canons. This first official comprehensive codification of Canon Law was completed on May 27, 1917, and promulgated in the following year by Pope Benedict XV, thus earning it the name, 'the Pio-Benedictine Code.'

It was also in 1917, while the young Maximillian Kolbe was studying in Rome when he witnessed the Freemasons loudly celebrating their second centenary anniversary by demonstrating in the streets with black banners depicting the Archangel Saint Michael being trodden underfoot by Satan and people flaunting

Masonic insignia beneath Vatican windows; some of which carried the words, *"Satan will rule on Vatican Hill, and the Pope will serve as his errand boy."*[95] On that day, the future saint fulfilled his promise to the Virgin Mary to fight for her – he established the Knights of the Immaculata.

As evident below, the 1917 *Code of Canon Law* was simply a very concise summation of the prohibitions against Freemasonry first promulgated by Pope Clement XII in his 1738 *In Eminenti:*

(1917) *CANON* No. 2335: Persons joining associations of the Masonic sect or any others of the same kind which plot against the Church and legitimate civil authorities contract excommunication simply reserved to the Apostolic See.

— — —

IN EMINENTI: (1) Now it has come to Our ears, and common gossip has made clear, that certain Societies, Companies, Assemblies, Meetings, Congregations or Conventicles called in the popular tongue Liberi Muratori or Francs Massons or by other names according to the various languages, are spreading far and wide and daily growing in strength; and men of any Religion or sect, satisfied with the appearance of natural virtue, are associated with one another in a union, according to their laws and the statutes laid down for them, by a strict and unbreakable bond which obliges them, both by an oath upon the Holy Bible and by a host of grave penalties, to an inviolable silence about all that they do in secret together. But it is in the nature of crime to betray itself and to show itself by its attendant clamor. Thus these aforesaid Societies or Conventicles have caused in the minds of the faithful the greatest suspicion, and all prudent and upright men have passed the same judgment on them as being depraved and perverted. For if they were not doing evil they would not

---

[95] Madden, Charles. *Freemasonry: Mankind's Hidden Enemy Second Edition.* Tan Books and Publishers, Inc. Rockford, Illinois. 2005. 34.

have so great a hatred of the light. Indeed, this rumor has grown to such proportions that in several countries these societies have been forbidden by the civil authorities as being against the public security, and for some time past have appeared to be prudently eliminated.

(3) Wherefore We command most strictly and in virtue of holy obedience, all the faithful of whatever state, grade, condition, order, dignity or pre-eminence, whether clerical or lay, secular or regular, even those who are entitled to specific and individual mention, that none, under any pretext or for any reason, shall dare or presume to enter, propagate or support these aforesaid societies of Liberi Muratori or Francs Massons, or however else they are called, or to receive them in their houses or dwellings or to hide them, be enrolled among them, joined to them, be present with them, give power or permission for them to meet elsewhere, to help them in any way, to give them in any way advice, encouragement or support either openly or in secret, directly or indirectly, on their own or through others; nor are they to urge others or tell them, incite or persuade them to be enrolled in such societies or to be counted among their number, or to be present or to assist them in any way; but they must stay completely clear of such Societies, Companies, Assemblies, Meetings, Congregations or Conventicles, under pain of excommunication for all the above mentioned people, which is incurred by the very deed without any declaration being required, and from which no one can obtain the benefit of absolution, other than at the hour of death, except through Ourselves or the Roman Pontiff of the time.

The phrase therein contained, *"plot against the Church and legitimate civil authorities..."* is explained in paragraph (1) of *In*

Eminenti as well as throughout *Etsi Multa, Humanum Genus, Officio Sanctissimo,* and *Dell'alto dell'Apostolico Seggio*. These Papal documents clearly explain that the plot of Freemasonry concerns the exportation of its ideologies of indifferentism, secularism, relativism, and naturalism, as well as its role in infiltrating and seducing governments in an attempt to stir revolutions as a means to supplant the authority, role, mission the Catholic Church in the world. Therefore, being well-grounded in the previous Papal encyclicals and apostolic exhortations, Canon No. 2335 is not an innovation but is in continuity with Church dogma and tradition, although weaker, because it only penalizes membership. Canon No. 2335 departs from the discipline of excommunicating those who assist with the Masonic plot and those who ally with Freemasons. The 1983 canon will restore the former.

The Indifferent Post-Conciliar Catholic Church

Canon Law No. 2335 served as the official and unquestionable position on Freemasonry, Masonic sects, and those like them until the liberal revolution finally laid hold of the Catholic Church by installing their own Pope Paul VI and pirating the rollout of the Second Vatican Council.

The First Vatican Council in 1870, which was closed prematurely due to the Franco-Prussian War, which transpired in that same year, left a great deal of unaccomplished work on the table. When Pope John XXII, inspired by the Holy Spirit, opened the Second Vatican Council on October 11, 1962 (closed by Pope Paul VI on December 8, 1965), it was viewed as an opportunity for the council fathers to produce documents that would both guard the sacred deposit of Christian doctrine, as well as teach it more efficaciously. In his opening speech to the council, John XXII's guiding words were:

"In calling this vast assembly of bishops, the latest and humble successor to the Prince of the Apostles who is addressing you intended to assert once again the magisterium (teaching authority), which is unfailing and perdures until the end of time, in order that this magisterium, taking into account the errors, the requirements, and the opportunities of our time, might be presented in exceptional form to all men throughout the world."

It has been the post-Conciliar tendency of some to call the Second Vatican Council a 'pastoral council' rather than a 'dogmatic one.' Although nearly all of this council's documents avoided the tradition of making ridged definitions, closing canons with anathemas, and piling on scholastic or judicial subtleties, there is nothing in the lexicon of the Church that differentiates one ecumenical council from the other along with the terms of 'pastoral' versus 'dogmatic.' On the contrary, according to Pope John XXII's own words, this council fell into line with the intent of all other previous councils, which were to (1) guard the deposit of faith, (2) resolve errors, and (3) evangelize the faith. Moreover, suggesting that the Second Vatican Council lacked the quality of being a 'dogmatic' council ignores the evidence of two dogmatic constitutions accompanied by two non-dogmatic constitutions, nine decrees, and three declarations.

Of the two non-dogmatic constitutions produced by the Second Vatican Council, *Sacrosanctum Concilium*, the Constitution on the Sacred Liturgy, which was approved by 2,147 to 4 votes and promulgated by Pope Paul VI on December 4, 1963, attracts the most attention to those suspicious of Masonic infiltration in the Catholic Church. *Sacrosanctum Concilium* addressed the general principles for the restoration of the Sacred Liturgy (including the participation of the laity during the liturgy and adapting the liturgy to the culture and traditions of the peoples), the most sacred mystery of the Holy Eucharist, the other Sacraments and the sacramentals, the Divine Office, the liturgical year, sacred music, sacred art, and sacred furnishing.

The following month, Paul VI issued his Apostolic letter *Sacram Liturgiam* as an immediate means to implement *Sacrosanctum Concilium*. In this letter, Paul VI states that he is establishing a commission *"whose principle task will be to implement in the best possible way the prescription of the Constitution on Sacred Liturgy itself."* This letter also included eleven decrees that broadly interpreted the written intention of *Sacrosanctum Concilium* and set into motion a broom that would sweep aside Pope Pius V's Apostolic Constitution, *Quo Primum* (July 14, 1570), which established his new liturgical rite as the ordinary form of the Holy Mass and put into its place a different new liturgical rite to be the new ordinary form of the Holy Mass. After that, the liturgy of Pope Pius V would be commonly called the Extraordinary Form of the Mass, and the liturgy of Pope Paul VI would be called the Ordinary Form of the Mass or, more popularly, the New Order Rite (Lat. *Novus Ordo*).

The commission, even more broadly than Paul VI, interpreted *Sacrosanctum Concilium* and took the license given to them to create a whole new liturgy for the Latin Church. According to the diary of Ferdinando Antonelli, very few of the forty-two (later fifty-one) voting members and two hundred consultants even showed up to the first plenary meeting. The intellectual and theological quality of those present ranged from being incompetent to being very liberal. The most dominant force behind the commission was its secretary, Archbishop Annibale Bugnini, who, according to Antonelli, worked at a frantic pace to hurry the completion of the commission's work and conspired behind the scenes to convince Paul VI, whose backing he had, of his ideas prior to the commission discussing them, so that he could overrule any objections by declaring, *"The Pope wills it!"*[96]

Given the vast departures that are evident in the New Order Rite, in form, orientation, and content, as well as the hurriedness of its development, how it was forced upon the laity without sufficient education or explanation, and the confusion surrounding all of the monumental changes taking place in the life and tradition of the Catholic Church, it comes to no surprise that many were very quick to believe the story that Annibale Bugnini was an Italian Freemason. Piers Compton first published Bugnini's purported Masonic membership in his 1983 book *The Broken Cross:*

> *"Bugnini had, in fact, with the approval of Paul VI, put into practice Luther's program, in which it had been recognized that 'when the Mass is destroyed, the Papacy will have been toppled, for the Papacy leans on the Mass as on a rock.' It was true that an orthodox opponent, Dietrich von Hildebrand, had called Bugnini 'the evil spirit of liturgical reform.' But no such consideration figured in the Archbishop's mind as, on a day in 1975, he left a conference room where he had attended a meeting of one of the Commissions where he had a voice, and started to climb a staircase. Suddenly he stopped. His hands, which should have been carrying a briefcase, were empty. The case, containing many of his papers, had been left in the conference room. Never one to hurry, for he was a heavy man and needed exercise; he now fairly ran*

---

[96] Knapman, Hugh Somerville. *The Strange Birth of the Novus Ordo.* The Catholic Herald. (https://catholicherald.co.uk/magazine/the-strange-birth-of-the-novus-ordo/ - retrieved 12/13/2019). See also: Bouyer, Louis. *The decomposition of Catholicism.* Franciscan Herald Press. Chicago. 1969. Giampietro, Nicola. The Development of the Liturgical Reform: As Seen by Cardinal Ferdinando Antonelli from 1948 to 1970. Roman Catholic Books. London. 2010. 191-198.

back and cast his eye over the chairs and tables. The briefcase was nowhere to be seen.

As soon as the meeting broke up, a Dominican friar had gone in to restore the room to order. He soon noticed the brief case, and had opened it in the hope of finding the name of its owner. He put aside the documents relating to the Commission, and had then come upon a folder that contained letters.

Sure enough, there was the name of the person to whom they had been sent, but – and the Dominican gasped – the mode of address was not to His Grace or to the Most Reverend Annibale Bugnini, Archbishop of Dioclentiana, but to Brother Bugnini, while the signatures and place of origin showed that they came from the dignitaries of secret societies in Rome.

Pope Paul VI who was, of course, tarred with the same brush as Bugnini, promptly took steps to prevent the scandal spreading, and to smooth over the dismay of those progressives who, innocent of guile, had no opinion other than that dictated by the media. Bugnini should have been removed, or at least taken to task. But he was, instead, for the sake of appearances, appointed Apostolic Pro Nuncio in Iran, a post where there was little or no call for diplomatic embellishment since the Shah's government had no time for any Western religion, and where the priest who was unfortunate enough *to be banished there, though only for a time, found his function as limited as his surroundings, which consisted of scanty furniture in two rooms in an otherwise empty house."*[97]

Whether Compton's amazing story about the discovery of Bugnini being a Freemason and Paul VI's Machiavellian attempt to cover it up can be trusted, the fact of the matter is that Carmine Pecorelli's 1978/1979 list had already listed Bugnini as a member of the Grand Orient of Italy's Propaganda Massonica (P2). He was initiated on April 23, 1963, under the codename "Buan":

"Bugnini Annibale: 23/4/1963 - Matricola 1365/75 - BUAN (pronunzio [Ambassador] *to Iran)"*

As I previously wrote in the chapter on *Humanum Genus*, the Picorelli list has yet to be verified by the Vatican. Picorelli himself is dead and cannot be questioned. The Grand Orient of Italy has yet to admit that the Archbishop was one of their own. Therefore, we are left only to judge Bugnini by what he said about himself and what other people like Ferdinando Antonelli and Carmine Picorelli wrote about him.

As for any Masonic influence in the New Order Rite, as I presented in my book, *The Divine Symphony: An Exordium on the Theology of the Catholic Mass*, the New Order Rite versus populum orientation around the altar was an evident liturgical innovation. Never before has a monotheistic religion found it suitable to worship in any other direction than the geographic direction of their source of revelation. While orienting the liturgy around the altar of sacrifice can be richly appreciated through Catholic theology, the faithful are not complete lunatics to be suspicious

---

[97] Compton, Piers. *The Broken Cross: The Hidden Hand in the Vatican.* Veritas Publishing. Australia. 1984. 59.

if Bugnini had any amount of influence in this aspect of the liturgical reform. Freemasons also orient their meetings with an altar placed in the center of their gatherings.

The understanding of what it meant to be oriented to Mount Calvary, the disappearance of altar rails, and basic Catholic sanity were not the only things that changed after the Second Vatican Council.

In his May 3, 1966, apostolic constitution *Peculiare*, Pope Paul VI weakened the seriousness and strength of Canon Law No. 2335, which reserved the absolution of Masonic members to the Apostolic see, by extending to local priests during the Jubilee year, the authority to forgive that named grave sin and three others. Previous Popes also had extended years of mercy and given penitents access to remedy their grave condition without appeal to the Supreme Pontiff. However, as I will explain, the timing of *Peculiare* gave it the appearance of being the first sound in an avalanche:

1) absolved of any censures and penalties. The Church Sorry anyone who knowingly teachings schismatics or atheistic matter how outwardly profess their faith, so long as each penitent sincerely regret the errors and confessor to detest and data may be resarturum that causes it; burdens imposed on them are in agreement and of saving penitence, to receive the sacraments frequently, and with the addition of the counsel of the approach;

2) dissolve the church censure and penalties to which the books of apostates, heretics or schismatics, for apostasy, heresy or schism defending minors and the Apostolic Letter expressly prohibited without the knowledge of the reader quarter due either to maintain; compulsory saving penitence, as appropriate, and carefully added the warning about the retention or destruction;

3) dissolve the church censure and penalties those who name to the Masonic sect or other similar associations against the church, or any legitimate civil authorities; Provided completely separate themselves from their school or association, the offense or the loss of their ability to repair themselves and praecauturos to it; burdens imposed on them, according to the measure of guilt, a deep repentance of the Savior;

4) solve modification, given the reasons, the change of one or the other works from all private vows, even reserved, so long as the solution does not injure the rights of others.

In 1967, the Scandinavian Bishop's Conference (consisting of the countries of Sweden, Norway, Finland, Denmark, and Iceland), following a four-year study into Freemasonry in their dioceses that included meeting with Grand Masters from Scandinavian Grand Lodges, investigating their ceremonies, and reading a letter by the late Lutheran King Gustav V of Sweden (1858 - 1950), who was also a Grand Master, in which he explained how Scandinavian Freemasonry is Christian (Protestant-Christian) in character, decided to permit Catholics in their dioceses to retain their Masonic membership, *"but only with the specific permission of that person's bishop."*[98]

The Bishop argued that Scandinavian Freemasonry differed in character from Anglo and Continental Freemasonry and did not 'plot' against the Catholic Church as other Masonic sects did. Moreover, they believed that their decision to interpret Canon Law No. 2335 independently was guided by Pope Paul VI's 1966 post-Conciliar *De Episcoporum Muneribus*, which, drawing from *Lumen Gentium* (n. 27), decentralized some of the authority and

---

[98] The Church in the World. *The Tablet.* March 30, 1968. 25. (https://web.archive.org/web/20150912075547/http://archive.thetablet.co.uk/article/30th-march-1968/25/the-church-in-the-world - Retrieved 9/12/2019).

sacred power previously reserved to the Supreme Pontiff alone, to the bishops. This authority given to bishops to exercise particular care for the flock in their diocese and to dispense with specific laws in individual cases was interpreted by the Scandinavian Bishops to include their right to dispense with Canon Law No. 2335 in individual cases as well.

On March 16, 1968, *The Tablet* reported in their 'The Church in the World' news and noted section:

"Go-ahead for Catholic Masons Vatican sources have recently been quoted as saying that Catholics are now free to join the Masons in the United States, Britain and most other countries of the world. However, the European Grand Orient Lodge of Masons, established primarily in Italy and France, is still considered anti-Catholic or, at least, atheistic.

Pope Clement XII condemned the order in 1738 as atheistic, and his action has been affirmed by seven other popes in sixteen different pronouncements. The Eastern Orthodox Church and some Protestant bodies have also opposed Freemasonry. However, a move to re-evaluate the Catholic Church's position on Masonry began during Vatican II.

Vatican sources said there had been no official revocation of the excommunication law, but the Vatican's Congregation for the Doctrine of the Faith "has let it be known that Catholics joining the Freemasons are no longer automatically excommunicated . . . the Church's new attitude has been in effect for more than a year." The Church's Code of Canon Law drawn up in 1918 and shortly to be reformed, provided for automatic excommunication of Catholics "who enroll in the Masonic sect or in secret societies conspiring against the Church or the legitimate authorities." Vatican sources added that this wording would be changed to modify the Church's position when the new Code of Canon Law was completed.

One of the churchmen who urged a new outlook on Masonry during the Vatican Council was Mgr. Mark Hurley, then chancellor of the diocese of Stockton, California. He urged the fathers of the Church to "make a radical distinction between European Masonry of the Grand Lodge variety and American and British Masonry."

In December of 1965, Pope Paul VI took a first step towards changing Church rules on Masonry by giving confessors the right to lift excommunication from Catholics who joined the Masons and later withdrew. Until then, only the Vatican could lift such excommunications."

Not once, in any document written by any Pope from Clement XII to Pius X, did any of them, at any time whatsoever, permit any bishop to determine whether Freemasonry in their diocese was excluded from the dogmatic prohibition against all Masonic sects around the world. Whoever heard of the Catholic Church has different laws for different Catholics, depending upon where they lived or who their bishop was at the time. The world did not have to wait until the 2019 Amazonian Synod for the Masonic spirit of indifferentism to pollute the dogma of the Church.

Even more, indifferentism was welcomed into the Church on July 19, 1974, when Cardinal Franjo Seper, Prefect of the Sacred Congregation for the Doctrine of the Faith, wrote a letter, which was supposedly intended to be private correspondence, to Cardinal John Krol, the Archbishop of Philadelphia at the time, supporting the Scandinavian interpretation of *De Episcoporum Muneribus* concerning Canon Law No. 2335:

"Many Bishops have asked this Sacred Congregation about the extent and interpretation of Canon 2335 of the Code of Canon Law which prohibits Catholics, under pain of excommunication, to join masonic associations, or similar associations... Taking particular cases into consideration, it is essential to remember that the penal law has to be interpreted in a restrictive sense. For this reason, one can certainly point out, and follow, the opinion of those writers who maintain that Canon 2335 affects only those Catholics who are members of associations which indeed conspire against the Church."

In 1980, the German Bishop's Conference concluded their research into the rituals of Freemasonry and their general practices. It issued twelve points that are in continuity with what every Pope, since Clement XII's *In Eminenti apostolatus specula*, had stated about the principles of Freemasonry:[99]

"1. The Masonic World View. The Masons promote a freedom from dogmatic adherence to any one set of revealed truths. Such a subjective relativism is in direct conflict with the revealed truths of Christianity.

2. The Masonic Notion of Truth. The Masons deny the possibility of an objective truth, placing every truth instead in a relative context.

3. The Masonic Notion of Religion. Again, the Masonic teaching holds a relative notion of religions as all concurrently seeking the truth of the Absolute.

---

[99] The 12 points here are taken from - Jenkins, Ronny E. *The evolution of the Church's prohibition against catholic membership in Freemasonry.* Jurist. Vo. 56. 1996.

4. The Masonic Notion of God. The Masons hold a deistic notion of God which excludes any personal knowledge of the deity.

5. The Masonic Notion of God and Revelation. The deistic notion of God precludes the possibility of God's self-revelation to humankind.

6. Masonic Toleration. The Masons promote a principle of toleration regarding ideas. That is, their relativism teaches them to be tolerant of ideas divergent or contrary to their own. Such a principle not only threatens the Catholic position of objective truth, but it also threatens the respect due to the Church's teaching office.

7. The Masonic Rituals. The rituals of the first three Masonic grades have a clear sacramental character about them, indicating that an actual transformation of some sort is undergone by those who participate in them.

8. The Perfection of Humankind. The Masonic rituals have as an end the perfection of mankind. But Masonry provides all that is necessary to achieve this perfection. Thus, the justification of a person through the work of Christ is not an essential or even necessary aspect of the struggle for perfection.

9. The Spirituality of the Masons. The Masonic Order makes a total claim on the life of the member. True adherence to the Christian faith is thereby jeopardized by the primary loyalty due the Masonic Order.

10. The Diverse Divisions within the Masons. The Masons are comprised of lodges with varying degrees of adherence to Christian teaching. Atheistic lodges are clearly incompatible with Catholicism. But even those lodges comprised of Christian members seek merely to adapt Christianity to the overall Masonic world-view. This is unacceptable.

11. The Masons and the Catholic Church. Even those Catholic-friendly lodges that would welcome the Church's members as its own are not compatible with Catholic teaching, and so closed to Catholic members.

12. The Masons and the Protestant Church. While a 1973 meeting of Protestant Churches determined that individual Protestants could decide whether to be members of both the Christian Church and the Freemasons, it included in its decision the caveat that those Christians must always take care not to lessen the necessity of grace in the justification of the person."

Following the German Bishop's condemnation of Freemasonry, on February 17, 1981, Cardinal Seper, who was well known during the Second Vatican Council for his advocating for religious liberty and the liturgy be prayed in the vernacular, issued what he called a 'clarification' to his, now public, letter to Kroll:

CLARIFICATION CONCERNING STATUS OF CATHOLICS BECOMING FREEMASONS

Congregation for the Doctrine of the Faith

On 19 July 1974, this Congregation wrote to some Episcopal Conferences a private letter concerning the interpretation of can 2335 of the Code of Canon Law which forbids Catholics, under the penalty of excommunication, to enroll in Masonic or other similar associations.

Since the said letter has become public and has given rise to erroneous and tendentious interpretations, this Congregation, without prejudice to the eventual norms of the new Code, issues the following confirmation and clarification:

1) the present canonical discipline remains in full force and has not been modified in any way;

2) consequently, neither the excommunication nor the other penalties envisaged have been abrogated;

3) what was said in the aforesaid letter as regards the interpretation to be given to the canon in question should be understood—as the Congregation intended—merely as a reminder of the general principles of interpretation of penal laws for the solution of the cases of individual persons which may be submitted to the judgment of ordinaries. It was not, however, the intention of the Congregation to permit Episcopal Conferences to issue public pronouncements by way of a judgment of a general character on the nature of Masonic associations, which would imply a derogation from the aforesaid norms.
Rome, from the Office of the S. Congregation for the Doctrine of the Faith, 17 February 1981.

On the vast array of Catholic dogma, Seper was orthodox, especially regarding the traditional teaching on human sexuality, marriage, and the evils of abortion. However, in other areas, such as liturgy and Masonic membership, he leaned into modernism, believing that the Church had been too ridged over the years. His 1974 letter gave an allowance for countless numbers of Catholics to become Freemasons, especially in the United States.

In the instant case, notice in item three (3) how Seper does not move away from the position he issued to Kroll. He still firmly maintains that there can be diverse opinions on which Masonic sect plots against the Church and which sects do not. Seper firmly rejects the teaching of every Pope from Clement XII to Pius X that all Masonic sects are forbidden, no matter their region, racial composition, or any guise or pretense of them being anything other than a *"synagogue of Satan,"* as Pius IX called it in his 1873 *Etsi Multa*. The only thing that Seper is saying in his 'clarification' here is that he did not intend for his 'private' letter to Kroll to be used as a license for bishops to issue sweeping judgments on the character nature of Freemasonry in general. Rather, only in individual cases could a bishop dismiss with Canon Law No. 2335 and allow individuals to maintain their membership in a Masonic sect.

Taking into consideration the Vatican 'sources' of the Tablet, who stated that there would be reform to Church teaching in the upcoming revisions of Canon Law, the condemnations of Freemasonry from the German Bishops, and Seper's 'clarification' seven years after his letter was made public, it is apparent that there was a battle taking place in the Vatican. The Freemasons and their ideological allies in the Catholic Church wanted a watering down of the dogmatic teachings against Freemasonry, to either explicitly name only the Grand Orient Grand Lodges as forbidden or to give bishops the authority to determine which Masonic sects their flock could join. The other wing of the Church was fighting to hold fast to the orthodoxy that every Pope had promulgated until the Second Vatican Council.

After years of debating and backroom negotiations, the outcome of this battle was that the army of Christ compromised with Satan on the dogmatic teaching and created a compromise canon. In the new Canon Law No. 1374, the word 'Masonic' was removed from the original phrase, *"Persons joining associations of the Masonic sect or any others of the same kind which plot against the Church and legitimate civil authorities,"* to now state, *"A person who joins an association which plots against the Church."* In addition, the compromise Canon modified the penalty from *"contract excommunication simply reserved to the Apostolic See,"* to state "[a person who joins] *to be punished with a just penalty; however, a person who promotes or directs an association of this kind is to be punished with an interdict."*

> **(1983) CANON No. 1374:** A person who joins an association which plots against the Church is to be punished with a just penalty; however, a person who promotes or directs an association of this kind is to be punished with an interdict.

> **(1917) CANON No. 2335:** Persons joining associations of the Masonic sect or any others of the same kind which plot against the Church and legitimate civil authorities contract excommunication simply reserved to the Apostolic See.

The *Code of Canons of Oriental Churches* (CCEO), which was codified in 1990 for the twenty-three Eastern Catholic Churches that are union with the Seat of Peter, has a parallel canon to Canon No. 1374 of the 1983 *Code of Canon Law* for the Latins:

(1990) CCEO *CANON No. 1448:* 1. One who uses a public performance or talk or publicly disseminated writing, or other media of communication, to blaspheme, seriously harm good morals, injure religion or the Church, or incite hatred or contempt for religion or the Church, is to be punished with an appropriate penalty. 2. One who joins an organization which plots against the Church, is to be punished with an appropriate penalty.

The 1983 Code of Canon Law, also called the Johanno-Pauline Code, was promulgated by Pope John Paul II on January 25, 1983. The immediate reaction to Canon No. 1374 that year was that its new wording broadened the span of associations that plot against the Church beyond just being the Masonic sects to include such groups as communists and others, but that the determination of which associations Catholics could not belong to was left to the purview of individual bishops. It had seemed that the Masonic lobby of the Catholic Church had won the message despite the compromise.

Then, on November 26, 1983, just one day before the new Code of Canon Law was scheduled to take effect on the First Sunday of Advent, the Congregation of the Doctrine of Faith, under the leadership of Joseph Cardinal Ratzinger, published a *Declaration on Masonic Associations*, which Pope John Paul II approved.

Quaesitum Est
(Query)
Congregation of the Doctrine of the Faith - 1983

Declaration on Masonic Associations:

It has been asked whether there has been any change in the Church's decision in regard to Masonic associations since the new Code of Canon Law does not mention them expressly, unlike the previous Code.

This Sacred Congregation is in a position to reply that this circumstance is due to an editorial criterion which was followed also in the case of other associations likewise unmentioned inasmuch as they are contained in wider categories.

Therefore, the Church's negative judgment in regard to Masonic association remains unchanged since their principles have always been considered irreconcilable with the doctrine of the Church and therefore membership in them remains forbidden. The faithful who enroll in Masonic associations are in a state of grave sin and may not receive Holy Communion.

It is not within the competence of local ecclesiastical authorities to give a judgment on the nature of Masonic associations which would imply a derogation from what has been decided above, and this in line with the Declaration of this Sacred Congregation issued on 17 February 1981 (cf. AAS 73 1981 pp. 240-241; English language edition of L'Osservatore Romano, 9 March 1981).

In an audience granted to the undersigned Cardinal Prefect, the Holy Pontiff John Paul II approved and ordered the publication of this Declaration which had been decided in an ordinary meeting of this Sacred Congregation.

Rome, from the Office of the Sacred Congregation for the Doctrine of the Faith, 26 November 1983.

Joseph Card. RATZINGER
Prefect

+ Fr. Jerome Hamer, O.P.
Titular Archbishop of Lorium
Secretary

Ratzinger's *Quaesitum Est* is important because it connects the general qualifier *"an association which plots against the Church"* with the specific Masonic qualifier *"Masonic association remains unchanged since their principles have always been considered irreconcilable with the doctrine of the Church . . ."* By the term *"principles,"* Ratzinger is bringing his Declaration into continuity with the preexisting dogmatic prohibition against Freemasonry, which has consistently defined the Masonic principles as indifferentism, relativism, secularism, and naturalism. Moreover, this declaration firmly states that it can never be under the purview of individual bishops to deviate from Church teaching and issue independent judgments *"on the nature of Masonic associations."*

Quaesitum Est is also important because it maintains that excommunication is the penalty reserved for those who join Masonic sects. Ratzinger states that the only reason why the word 'Masonic' was not explicitly used in the new Code of Canon Law was due to *"an editorial criterion."* Inasmuch as we might speculate about the intentions of those who lobbied for such an editorial criterion, we cannon speculate whether if the penalty has changed.

On the contrary, *Quaesitum Est* clearly states in three different instances that excommunication is still the penalty reserved for those who join Masonic sects. First, Ratzinger states that *"the Church's negative judgment in regard to Masonic association remains unchanged."* Unchanged, meaning that the 1983 Canon No. 1374 persists in continuity with the 1917 Canon No. 2335 and with every previous Papal Bull and encyclical on this issue. Second, he states that enrolling in Masonic associations is a *"grave sin."* Grave sin, according to Church teaching, *"deprives us of communion with God and therefore makes up incapable of eternal life..."*[100] Third, he states that those who enroll in Masonic associations *"may not receive Holy Communion."* Again, without stating the word 'excommunication,' Ratzinger has, in these three instances, pointed to excommunication as still being the penalty reserved for enrolling in Masonic sects. In this way, *Quaesitum Est* is in line with the Church's teaching on excommunication:

> Catechism of the Catholic Church Para. 1463 Certain particularly grave sins incur excommunication, the most severe ecclesiastical penalty, which impedes the reception of the sacraments and the exercise of certain ecclesiastical acts, and for which absolution consequently cannot be granted, according to canon law, except by the Pope, the bishop of the place or priests authorized by them.[101] In danger of death, any priest, even if deprived of faculties for hearing confessions, can absolve from every sin and excommunication.[102]

---

[100] Catechism of the Catholic Church, paragraph 1472. (2013 printing).
[101] Cf. ⇒ CIC, cann. 1331; ⇒ 1354-1357; CCEO, can. 1431; 1434; 1420.
[102] Cf. ⇒ CIC, can. 976; CCEO, can. 725.

In the instant case, excommunication for enrolling in Masonic sects is proven by *Quaesitum Est*, affirming it is a 'grave sin' and that it impedes the reception of the Sacrament of the Holy Eucharist (communion). As I stated in the third paragraph of my commentary on *In Eminenti apostolatus specula,* per Canon Law (1364 – 1399), the remedy for the penalty incurred for enrolling in Masonic associations is no longer reserved to the Pope alone but can now be resolved by a priest (with the proper faculties) through the Sacrament of Penance and Reconciliation, such as other grave sins can also be (e.g., murder, theft, masturbation, and adultery).

As the Age of Indifferentism Continues

To untainted hearts, it should be unequivocally clear that faithful who enroll in Masonic associations are excommunicated *ipso facto/latae sententiae,* that is, no longer in full communion with the Catholic Church, under having incurred a grave sin. This has been the consistent teaching of the Catholic Church since Pope Clement XII's 1738 *In Eminenti apostolatus specula.* Since the access to the remedy of this grave sin has changed, the gravity of the sin itself has not.

Nevertheless, the Masonic lobby in the Catholic Church has never relented in trying to cloud, mislead, and bury this dogmatic prohibition. Even the reaction to Ratzinger's *Quaesitum Est* was that it was null in the void because it was promulgated the day before the Code of Canon Law went into effect. However, such a sophistic dismal of the truth would have been their same response if *Quaesitum Est* had been promulgated just one hour after it had been promulgated.

The enemies of the Catholic Church never rest, never sleep, and never stop plotting. There has never been a heresy known to the Church that has died. The last four great waves against the

Catholic Church, Protestantism (1517), Freemasonry (1717), Communism (1917), and now Homosexualism are all still fully alive in the world today. The rumors of the death of the latter three have been gravely exaggerated. There may be no council to come that will save us; no religious order will come to evangelize us; the Church remains full of the wheat and the tares, the penitent and the perishing. The enemies of Christ Jesus are attempting to adorn His Bride with gold chain necklaces, from which he hangs shiny medals with Pachamama on them, thus, announcing to the world their indifferentism and hatred of Christ and His Church.

In this Age of Indifferentism, the faithful should keep the writings of Popes in their hearts and minds regarding the dangers of Freemasonry and reflect on the day and night. Apply what we have learned about how Satan has used Freemasonry to persecute the Catholic Church and to supplant its authority. Since the agency, associations, and tactics that the Evil One uses constantly adapt to whatever men allow, the end goal to remove the name of Jesus Christ from the world, just as His name has been removed from the Masonic lodge, has never changed. There is power in that name, and it is a power that evil one needs to have eliminated because it is an existential threat to him. Therefore, the encouragement remains the same from the beginning: with humble prayer and fasting, keep the love and truth of Christ Jesus in your mind, tongue, and heart.

> **"Be alert and of sober mind. Your enemy, the devil, prowls around like a roaring lion looking for someone to devour."**
> *One Peter* Five-Eight

Appendix A

Anderson's Constitution of 1723
Ancient Charges of a FREE MASON
The Ancient Records of Lodges beyond the Sea

To Be Read At The Making of New Brethren, or When The Master Shall Order It. THE GENERAL HEADS, viz.:

I. Concerning GOD and RELIGION.

A Mason is oblig'd by his Tenure, to obey the moral law; and if he rightly understands the Art, he will never be a stupid Atheist nor an irreligious Libertine. But though in ancient Times Masons were charg'd in every Country to be of the Religion of that Country or Nation, whatever it was, yet 'tis now thought more expedient only to oblige them to that Religion in which all Men agree, leaving their particular Opinions to themselves; that is, to be good Men and true, or Men of Honour and Honesty, by whatever Denominations or Persuasions they may be distinguish'd; whereby Masonry becomes the Center of Union, and the Means of conciliating true Friendship among Persons that must have remain'd at a perpetual Distance.

II Of the CIVIL MAGISTRATES SUPREME and SUBORDINATE.

A Mason is a peaceable Subject to the Civil Powers, wherever he resides or works, and is never to be concern'd in Plots an Conspiracies against the Peace and Welfare of the Nation, nor to behave himself undutifully to inferior Magistrates; for as Masonry hath been always injured by War, Bloodshed, and Confusion, so ancient Kings and Princes have been much dispos'd to encourage the Craftsmen, because of their Peaceableness and Loyalty, whereby they practically answer'd the Cavils of their Adversaries, and promoted the

Honour of the Fraternity, whoever flourish'd in Time of Peace. So that if a Brother should be a Rebel against the State he is not to be countenanced in his Rebellion, however he may be pitied as any unhappy Man; and, if convicted of no other Crime though the Loyal Brotherhood must and ought to disown hi Rebellion, and give no Umbrage or Ground of political Jealousy to the Government for the time being, they cannot expel him from the Lodge, and his Relation to it remains indefeasible.

III Of LODGES.

A Lodge is a place where Masons assemble and work; Hence that Assembly, or duly organized Society of Masons, is call'd a Lodge, and every Brother ought to belong to one, and to be subject to its By-Laws and the General Regulations.

It is either particular or general, and will be best understood by attending it, and by the Regulations of the General or Grand Lodge hereunto annex'd. In ancient Times, no Master or Fellow could be absent from it especially when warned to appear at it, without incurring a sever Censure, until it appear'd to the Master and Wardens that pure Necessity hinder'd him.

The persons admitted Members of a Lodge must be good an true Men, free-born, and of mature and discreet Age, no Bondmen no Women, no immoral or scandalous men, but of good Report.

IV Of MASTERS, WARDENS, FELLOWS and APPRENTICES.

All preferment among Masons is grounded upon real Worth and personal Merit only; that so the Lords may be well served, the Brethren not put to Shame, nor the Royal Craft despis'd: Therefore, no Master or Warden is chosen by Seniority, but for his Merit. It is impossible to describe these things in Writing, and every Brother must attend in his Place, and learn them in a Way peculiar to this Fraternity: Only Candidates may know that no Master should take an Apprentice unless he has Sufficient Employment for him, and unless he be a perfect Youth having no Maim or Defects in his Body that may render him uncapable of learning the Art of serving his Master's Lord, and of being made a Brother, and then a Fellow-Craft in due Time, even after he has served such a Term of Years as the Custom of the Country directs; and that he should be descended of honest Parents; that so, when otherwise qualifi'd he may arrive to the Honour of being the Warden, and then the Master of the Lodge, the Grand Warden, and at length the Grand Master of all the Lodges, according to his Merit.

No Brother can be a Warden until he has pass'd the part of a Fellow-Craft; nor a Master until he has acted as a Warden, nor Grand Warden until he has been Master of a Lodge, nor Grand Master unless he has been a Fellow Craft before his Election, who is also to be nobly born, or a Gentleman of the best Fashion, or some eminent Scholar, or some curious Architect, or other Artist, descended of honest Parents, and who is of similar great Merit in the Opinion of the Lodges.

These Rulers and Governors, supreme and subordinate, of the ancient Lodge, are to be obey'd in their respective Stations by all the Brethren, according to the old Charges and Regulations, with all Humility, Reverence, Love and Alacrity.

V. Of the MANAGEMENT of the CRAFT in WORKING.

All Masons shall work honestly on Working Days, that they may live creditably on Holy Days; and the time appointed by the Law of the Land or confirm'd by Custom shall be observ'd. The most expert of the Fellow-Craftsmen shall be chosen or appointed the Master or

Overseer of the Lord's Work; who is to be call'd Master by those that work under him. The Craftsmen are to avoid all ill Language, and to call each other by no disobliging Name, but Brother or Fellow; and to behave themselves courteously within and without the Lodge.

The Master, knowing himself to be able of Cunning, shall undertake the Lord's Work as reasonably as possible, and truly dispend his Goods as if they were his own; nor to give more Wages to any Brother or Apprentice than he really may deserve.

Both the Master and the Masons receiving their Wages justly, shall be faithful to the Lord and honestly finish their Work, whether Task or Journey; nor put the work to Task that hath been accustomed to Journey.

None shall discover Envy at the Prosperity of a Brother, nor supplant him, or put him out of his Work, if he be capable to finish the same; for no man can finish another's Work so much to the Lord's Profit, unless he be thoroughly acquainted with the Designs and Draughts of him that began it.

When a Fellow-Craftsman is chosen Warden of the Work under the Master, he shall be true both to Master and Fellows, shall carefully oversee the Work in the Master's Absence to the Lord's profit; and his Brethren shall obey him.

All Masons employed shall meekly receive their Wages without Murmuring or Mutiny, and not desert the Master till the Work is finish'd.

A younger Brother shall be instructed in working, to prevent spoiling the Materials for want of Judgment, and for increasing and continuing of brotherly love.

APPENDIX A

All the Tools used in working shall be approved by the Grand Lodge.

No Laborer shall be employ'd in the proper Work of Masonry; nor shall Free Masons work with those that are not free, without an urgent Necessity; nor shall they teach Laborers and unaccepted Masons as they should teach a Brother or Fellow.

VI. Of BEHAVIOR.

1. In the LODGE while CONSTITUTED.
You are not to hold private Committees, or separate Conversation without Leave from the Master, nor to talk of anything impertinent or unseemly, nor interrupt the Master or Wardens, or any Brother speaking to the Master: Nor behave yourself ludicrously or jestingly while the Lodge is engaged in what is serious and solemn; nor use any unbecoming Language upon any Pretense whatsoever; but to pay due Reverence to your Master, Wardens, and Fellows, and put them to Worship.

If any Complaint be brought, the Brother found guilty shall stand to the Award and Determination of the Lodge, who are the proper and competent Judges of all such Controversies (unless you carry it by Appeal to the Grand Lodge), and to whom they ought to be referr'd, unless a Lord's Work be hinder'd the meanwhile, in which Case a particular Reference may be made; but you must never go to Law about what concerneth Masonry, without an absolute necessity apparent to the Lodge.

2. BEHAVIOR after the LODGE is over and the BRETHREN not GONE.
You may enjoy yourself with innocent Mirth, treating one another according to Ability, but avoiding all Excess, or forcing any Brother

to eat or drink beyond his Inclination, or hindering him from going when his Occasions call him, or doing or saying anything offensive, or that may forbid an easy and free Conversation, for that would blast our Harmony, and defeat our laudable Purposes. Therefore no private Piques or Quarrels must be brought within the Door of the Lodge, far less any Quarrels about Religion, or Nations, or State Policy, we being only, as Masons, of the Universal Religion above mention'd, we are also of all Nations, Tongues, Kindreds, and Languages, and are resolv'd against all Politics, as what never yet conduct'd to the Welfare of the Lodge, nor ever will.

3. BEHAVIOR when BRETHREN meet WITHOUT STRANGERS, but not in a LODGE Formed.

You are to salute one another in a courteous Manner, as you will be instructed, calling each other Brother, freely giving mutual instruction as shall be thought expedient, without being ever seen or overheard, and without encroaching upon each other, or derogating from that Respect which is due to any Brother, were he not Mason: For though all Masons are as Brethren upon the same Level, yet Masonry takes no Honour from a man that he had before; nay, rather it adds to his Honour, especially if he has deserve well of the Brotherhood, who must give Honor to whom it is due, and avoid ill Manners.

4. BEHAVIOR in presence of Strangers NOT MASONS.

You shall be cautious in your Words and Carriage, that the most penetrating Stranger shall not be able to discover or find out what is not proper to be intimated, and sometimes you shall divert a Discourse, and manage it prudently for the Honour of the worshipful Fraternity.

5. BEHAVIOR at HOME, and in Your NEIGHBORHOOD.

You are to act as becomes a moral and wise Man; particularly not to let your Family, Friends and Neighbors know the Concern of the Lodge, &c., but wisely to consult your own Honour, and that of the ancient Brotherhood, for reasons not to be mention'd here You must also consult your Health, by not continuing together too late, or too long from Home, after Lodge Hours are past; and by avoiding of Gluttony or Drunkenness, that your Families be not neglected or injured, nor you disabled from working.

6. BEHAVIOR toward a Strange BROTHER.

You are cautiously to examine him, in such a Method as Prudence shall direct you, that you may not be impos'd upon by an ignorant, false Pretender, whom you are to reject with contempt and Derision, and beware of giving him any Hints of Knowledge.

But if you discover him to be a true and genuine Brother, you are to respect him accordingly; and if he is in Want, you must relieve him if you can, or else direct him how he may be relieved; you must employ him some days, or else recommend him to be employ'd. But you are not charged to do beyond your ability, only to prefer a poor Brother, that is a good Man and true before any other poor People in the same Circumstance.

Finally, All these Charges you are to observe, and also those that shall be recommended to you in another Way; cultivating Brotherly Love, the Foundation and Cap-stone, the Cement and Glory of this Ancient Fraternity, avoiding all wrangling and quarreling, all Slander and Backbiting, nor permitting others to slander any honest Brother, but defending his Character, and doing him all good Offices, as far as is consistent with your Honour and Safety, and no farther. And if any of them do you Injury you must apply to your own or his Lodge, and from thence you may appeal to the Grand Lodge, at the Quarterly Communication and from thence to the annual Grand Lodge, as has been the ancient laudable Conduct but when the Case cannot be otherwise decided, and patiently listening to the honest and friendly Advice of Master and Fellows when they would prevent your going to Law with Strangers, or would excite you to put a speedy Period to all Lawsuits, so that you may mind the Affair of Masonry with the more Alacrity and Success; but with respect to Brothers or Fellows at Law, the Master and Brethren should kindly offer their Mediation, which ought to be thankfully submitted to by the contending Brethren; and if that submission is impracticable, they must, however, carry on their Process, or Lawsuit, without Wrath and Rancor (not In the common way) saying or doing nothing which may hinder Brotherly Love, and good Offices to be renew'd and continu'd; that all may see the benign Influence of Masonry, as all true Masons have done from the beginning of the World, and will do to the End of Time.

AMEN, SO MOTE IT BE

Appendix B

Masonry Dissected
by
Samuel Pritchard

Being a Universal and Genuine Description of All its Branches from the Original to this Present Time. As it is deliver'd in the Constituted Regular Lodges. Both in City and Country According to the Several Degrees of Admission.

Giving an Impartial Account of their Regular Proceeding in Initiating their New Members in the whole Three Degrees of Masonry.

I. ENTER'D 'PRENTICE,
II. FELLOW CRAFT.
III. MASTER.

To which is added, the Authors Vindicantion of himself
By Samuel Prichard, Later Member of a Constituted Lodge.

The Author's Vindication of himself.

LONDON:

Printed for J. WILFORD, at the Three Flowered Laces behind the Chapter Homes near St. Paul's, 1730.

Samuel Pritchard maketh Oath, that the Copy hereunto annnexed is a True and Genuine Copy in every Particular.

Fur' 13. Die Oct.
Sam. Pritchard
1730. coram me,
R. Hopkins,

Dedication to the Rt. Worshipful and Honourable Fraternity of Free and Accepted Masons Brethren and Fellows.

IF the following sheets, done without Partiality, gains the universal applause of so worshipful a Society, I doubt not but its general Character will be diffused and esteemed among the remaining Polite Part of Mankind:

Which, I hope will give entire Satisfaction to all Lover's of Truth, and I shall remain, with all humble Submission, the Fraternity's

Most Obedient
Humble Servant,
Sam. Pritchard

MASONRY DISSECTED.

THE original Institution of Masonry consisteth on the Foundation of the Liberal Arts and Sciences; but more especially on the Fifth, viz. Geometry. For at the Building of the Tower of Babel, the Art and Mystery of Masonry was first introduc'd, and from thence handed down by Euclid, a worthy and excellent Mathematician of the Egyptian, and he communicated it to Hiram, the Master-Mason concern'd in the Building of Solomon's Temple in Jerusalem, where was an excellent and curious Mason that was the chief under their Grand-Master Hiram, whose Name was Mannon Grecus, who taught the Art of Masonry to one Carolos Marcil in France, who was afterwards elected King of France, and from thence was brought into England in the Time of King Athe Stone, who order'd an Assembly to be held once every Year at York, which was the first Introduction of it into England, and Masons were made in the Manner following.

Tunc unu r ex Senioribus teneat Librum, ut illi vel ille ponant vel ponat Manus fupra Librum; tum Præcepta debeant legi. i. e. Whilst one of the Seniors holdeth the Book, that be or they put their Hands upon the Book, whilst the Master ought to read the Laws or Charges.

Which Charges were, That they should be true to one another without Exception, and should he obliged to relieve their Brothers and Fellows Necessities, or put them to labour and reward them accordingly. But in these latter Days Masonry is not composed of Artificers, as it was in its primæval State, when some few Catechetical Questions were necessary to declare a Man sufficiently qualified for an Operative Mason.

The Terms of Free and Accepted Masonry (as it now is) has not been heard of till within these few Years; no Constituted Lodges or Quarterly Communications were heard of till 1691, when Lords and Dukes, Lawyers and Shopkeepers, and other inferior Tradesmen, Porters not excepted, were admitted into this Mystery or no Mystery; the first fort being introduc'd at a very great Expence, the second fort at a moderate Rate, and the latter for the Expence of six or seven Shillings, for which they receive that Badge of Honour, which (as they term it) is more ancient and more honourable than is the Star and Garter, which Antiquity is accounted, according to the Rules of Masonry, as delivered by their Tradition, ever since Adam, which I shall leave the candid Reader to determine.

From the Accepted Masons sprang the Real Masons, from both sprang the Gormogons, whose Grand-Master the Volgi deduces his

Original from the Chinese, whose Writings, if to be credited, maintains the Hypotheses of the Pre-Adamites, and consequently must be more antique than Masonry.

The most free and open Society is that of the Grand Kaihebar, which consists of a select Company of Responsible People, whose chief discourse is concerning Trade and Business, and promoting mutual Friendship without Compulsion or Restriction.

But if after the Admission into the Secrets of Masonry, any new Brother should dislike their Proceedings, and reflect upon himself for being so easily cajoled out of his Money, declines the Fraternity or secludes himself upon the Account of the Quarterly Expences of the Lodge and Quarterly Communications, notwithstanding he has been legally admitted into a Constituted and Regular Lodge, shall be denied the Privilege (as a Visiting Brother) of knowing the Mystery for which he has already paid, which is a manifest Contradiction according to the Institution of Masonry itself, as will evidently appear by the following Treatise.

Enter'd
Enter'd 'Prentice's DEGREE.

Q. From whence came you?
A. From the Holy Lodge of St. John's
Q. What Recommendations brought you from thence?
A. The Recommendations which I brought from the Right Worshipful Brothers and Fellows of the Right Worshipful and Holy Lodge of St. John's, from whence I came, and Greet you thrice heartily well.
Q. What do you come here to do?

A. Not to do my own proper Will, But to subdue my Passion still; The Rules of Masonry in hand to take, And daily Progress therein make.

Q. Are you a Mason?

A. I am so taken and Accepted to be among Brothers and Fellows.

Q. How shall I know that you are a Mason?

A. By Signs and Tokens and perfect Points of my Entrance.

Q. What are Signs?

A. All Squares, Angles and Perpendiculars.

Q. What are Tokens?

A. Certain Regular and Brotherly Gripes.

Exam. Give me the Points of your Entrance.

Resp. Give me the first and I'll give you the second.

Exam. I Hail it.

Resp. I Conceal it.

Exam. What do you Conceal?

Resp. All Secrets and Secrecy of Masons and Masonry, unless to a True and Lawful Brother after due Examination, or in a just and worshipful Lodge of Brothers and Fellows well met.

Q. Where was you made a Mason?

A. In a just and Perfect Lodge.

Q. What makes a just and Perfect Lodge?

A. Seven or more.

Q. What do they consist on?

A. One Master, two Wardens, two Fellow-Crafts and two Enter'd 'Prentices.

Q. What makes a Lodge?

A. Five.

Q. What do they consist of?

A. One Master, two Wardens, one Fellow-Craft, one Enter'd 'Prentice.

Q. Who brought you to the Lodge?

A. An Enter'd 'Prentice.

Q. How did he bring you?

A. Neither naked nor clothed, bare-foot nor shod, deprived of all Metal and in a right moving Posture.

Q. How got you Admittance?

A. By three great Knocks.

Q. Who receiv'd you?

A. A Junior Warden.

Q. How did he dispose of you?

A. He carried me up to the North-Fait Part of the Lodge, and brought me back again to the West and deliver'd me to the Senior Warden.

Q. What did the Senior Warden do with you?

A. He presented me, and shew'd me how to walk up (by three Steps) to the Master.

Q. What did the Master do with you?

A. He made me a Mason.

Q. How did he make you a Mason?

A. With my bare-bended Knee and Body within the Square, the Compass extended to my naked Left Breast, my naked Right Hand on the Holy Bible; there I took the Obligation (or Oath) of a Mason.

Q. Can you repeat that Obligation.

A. I'll do my Endeavour. (Which is as follows.)

I Hereby solemnly Vow and Swear in the Presence of Almighty God and this Right Worshipful assembly, that I will Hail and Conceal, and never Reveal the Secrets or Secrecy of Masons or Masonry, that shall be Revealed unto me; unless to a True and Lawful Brother, after due Examination, or in a Just and Worshipful Lodge of Brothers and Fellows well met.

I furthermore Promise and Vow, that I will not Write them, Print them, Mark them, Carve them or Engrave them, or cause them to be Written, Printed, Marked, Carved or Engraved on Wood or Stone, so as the Visible Character or Impression of a Letter may appear, whereby it may be unlawfully obtain'd.

All this under no less Penalty than to have my throat cut, my Tongue taken from the Roof of my Mouth, my Heart pluck'd from under my Left Breast, them to be buried in the Sands of the Sea, the Length of a Cable-rope from Shore, where the tide ebbs and flows twice in 24 Hours, my Body to be burnt to ashes, my Ashes to be scatter'd upon the Face of the Earth, so that there shall be no more Remembrance of me among Masons.

So help me God.

Q. What Form is the Lodge?
A. A long Square.
Q. How long?
A. From East to West.
Q. How broad?
A. From North to South.
Q. How high?
A. Inches, Feet and Yards innumerable, as high as the Heavens.
Q. How deep?
A. To the Centre of the Earth.
Q. Where does the Lodge hand?
A. Upon Holy Ground, or the highest Hill or lowest Vale, or in the Vale of Jehosaphat, or any other secret Place.
Q. How is it situated?
A. Put East and West.
Q. Why so?
A. Because all Churches and Chappels are or ought to be so.
Q. What supports a Lodge?
A. Three great Pillars.
Q. What are they called?
A. Wisdom, Strength and Beauty.

Q. Why so?
A. Wisdom to contrive, Strength to support, and Beauty to adorn.
Q. What Covering have you to the Lodge?
A. A clouded Canopy of divers Colours (or the Clouds.)
Q. Have you any Furniture in your Lodge?
A. Yes.
Q. What is it?
A. Mosaick Pavement, Blazing Star and Indented Tarsel.
Q. What are they?
A. Mosaick Pavement, the Ground Floor of the Lodge, Blazing Star the Centre, and Indented Tarsel the Border round about it.
Q. What is the other Furniture of a Lodge?
A. Bible, Compass and Square.
Q. Who do they properly belong to?
A. Bible to God, Compass to the Master, and Square to the Fellow-Craft.
Q. Have you any jewels in the Lodge?
A. Yes.
Q. How many?
A. Six. Three Moveable, and three Immoveable.
Q. What are the Moveable Jewels?
A. Square, Level and Plumb-Rule.
Q. What are their Uses.
A. Square to lay down True and Right Lines, Level to try all Horizontals, and the Plumb-Rule to try all Uprights.
Q. What are the Immoveable Jewels?
A. Trasel Board, Rough Ashler, and Broach'd Thurnel.
Q. What are their Uses?
A. Trasel Board for the Master to draw his Designs upon, Rough Ashler for the Fellow Craft to try their jewels upon, and the Broach'd Thurnel for the Enter'd 'Prentice to learn to work upon.
Q. Have you any Lights in your Lodge?

A. Yes, Three.
Q. What do they represent?
A. Sun, Moon and Master-Mason.
N. B. These Lights are three large Candles placed on high Candlesticks.
Q. Why so?
A. Sun to rule the Day, Moon the Night) and Matter-Mason his Lodge.
Q. Have you any fix'd Lights in your Lodge?
A. Yes.
Q. How many?
A. Three.
N. B. These fix'd Lights are three Windows, suppos'd (tho' vainly) to be in every Room where a Lodge it held, but more properly, the four Cardinal Points according to the antique Rules of Masonry.
Q. How are they situated?
A. East, South and West.
Q. What are their Uses?
A. To light the Men to, at and from their Work.
Q. Why are there no Lights in the North?
A. Because the Sun darts no Rays from thence.
Q. Where hands your Master?
A. In the East.
Q. Why so?
A. As the Sun rises in the East and opens the Day, so the Master stands in the East [with his Right Hand upon his Left Breast being a Sign, and the Square about his Neck] to open the Lodge and to set his Men at Work.
Q. Where stands your Wardens?
A. In the West.
Q. What's their Business?

A. As the Sun sets in the West to close the Day, so the Wardens stand in the Welt [with their Right Hands upon their Left Breasts being a Sign, and the Level and Plumb-Rule about their Necks] to close the Lodge and dismiss the Men from Labour, paying their Wages.

Q. Where stands the Senior Enter'd' Prentice?

A. In the South.

Q. What is his Business?

A. To hear and receive Instructions and welcome strange Brothers.

Q. Where stands the Junior Enter'd 'Prentice?

A. In the North.

Q. What is his Business

A. To keep off all Cowans and Eves-droppers.

Q. If a Cowan (or Listner) is catch'd, how is he to be punished?

A. To be plac'd under the Eves of the Houses (in rainy Weather) till the Water runs in at his Shoulders and out at his Shoos.

Q. What are the Secrets of a Mason?

A. Signs, Tokens and many Words.

Q. Where do you keep those Secrets?

A. Under my Left Breast.

Q. Have you any Key to those Secrets?

A. Yes.

Q. Where do you keep it?

A. In a Bone Bone Box that neither opens nor shuts but with Ivory Keys.

Q. Does it hang or does it lie?

A. It hangs.

Q. What does it hang by?

A. A Tow-Line 9 Inches or a Span.

Q. What Metal is it of?

A. No manner of Metal at all; but a Tongue of good Report is as good behind a Brother's Back as before his Face.

N. B. The Key is the Tongue, the Bone Bone Box the Teeth, the Tow-Line the Roof of the Mouth.

Q. How many Principles are there in Masonry?

A. Four.

Q. What are they?

A. Point, Line, Superficies and Solid.

Q. Explain them.

A. Point the Centre (round which the Master cannot err) Line Length without Breadth, Superficies Length and Breadth, Solid comprehends the whole.

Q. How many Principle-Signs?

A. Four.

Q. What are they?

A. Gututral, Pectoral, Manual and Pedestal

Q. Explain them.

A. Guttural the Throat, Pectoral the Breast, Manual the Hand, Pedestal the Feet.

Q. What do you learn by being a Gentleman Mason.

A. Secrecy, Morality and Goodfellowship.

Q. What do you learn by being an Operative Mason?

A. Hue, Square, Mould-Bone, by a Level and raise a Perpendicular.

Q. Have you Seen your Master to-day?

A. Yes.

Q. How was he Cloathed?

A. In a Yellow Jacket and Blue Pair of Breeches.

N. B. The Yellow Jacket is the Compasses, and the Blue Breeches the Steel Points.

Q. How long do you serve your Master?

A. From Monday Morning to Saturday Night.

Q. How do you serve him?

A. With Chalk, Charcoal and Earthen Pan.

Q. What do they denote?

A. Freedom, Fervency and Zeal.

Ex. Give me the Enter'd Prentice's Sign.

Resp. Extending the Four Fingers of the Right Hand and drawing of them cross his Throat, is the Sign, and demands a Token.

N. B. A Token is by joining the Ball of the Thumb of the Right Hand upon the first Knuckle of the Fore-finger of the Brother's Right Hand that demands a Word.

Q. Give me the Word.

A. I'll letter it with You.

Exam. B O A Z.   [N. B. The Exam. says B, Resp. O, Exam. A, Resp. Z, i. e. Boaz] Give me another.

Resp. J A C H I N. [N.B. Boaz and Jachin were two Pillars in Solomon's Porch. 1 Kings, chap. vii. ver. 21]

Q. How old are you?

A. Under Seven. [Denoting be has not pass'd Master.]

Q. What's the Day for?

A. To See in.

Q. What's the Night for?

A. To Hear.

Q. How blows the Wind?

A. Due East and West.

Q. What's a Clock?

A. High Twelve.

The End of the Enter'd 'Prentice's Part

Fellow-Craft's DEGREE.

Q. Are you a Fellow-Craft?

A. I am.

Q. Why was you made a Fellow-Craft

A. For the fake of the Letter G.

Q. What does that G denote?

A. Geometry, or the fifth Science.

Q. Did you ever travel?
A. Yes, East and West.
Q. Did you ever work?
A. Yes, in the Building of the Temple.
Q. Where did you receive your Wages?
A. In the middle Chamber.
Q. How came you to the middle Chamber?
A. Through the Porch.
Q. When you came through the Porch, what did you see?
A. Two great Pillars.
Q. What are they called?
A. J. B. i. e. Jachin and Boaz. - Vide 1 Kings, Chap. 7
Q. How high are they?
A. Eighteen Cubits.
Q. How much in Circumference?
A. Twelve Cubits.
Q. What were they adorn'd with?
A. Two Chapiters.
Q. How high were the Chapiters?   - Vide 1 Kings, Chap. 7
A. Five Cubits.
Q. What were they adorn'd with?
A. Net-Work and Pomegranates.
Q. How came you to the middle Chamber?
A. By a winding Pair of Stairs.
Q. How many?
A. Seven or more.
Q. Why Seven or more?
A. Because Seven or more makes a just and Perfect Lodge.
Q. When you came to the Door of the middle Chamber, who did you see?
A. A Warden.
Q. What did he demand of you?

A. Three Things.
Q. What were they?
A. Sign, Token, and a Word.

N. B. The Sign is placing the Right Hand on the Left Breast, the Token is by joining your Right Hand to the Person that demands it, and squeezing him with the Ball of your thumb on the first Knuckle of the middle Finger, and the Word is Jachin.

Q. How high was the Door of the middle Chamber?
A. So high that a Cowan could not reach to stick a Pin in.
Q. When you came into the middle, what did you see?
A. The Resemblance of the Letter G.
Q. Who doth that G denote?
A. One that's greater than you.
Q. Who's greater than I, that am a Free and Accepted Mason, the Master of a Lodge.
A. The Grand Architect and Contriver of the Universe, or He that was taken up to the top of the Pinnacle of the Holy Temple.
Q. Can you repeat the Letter G?
A. I'll do my Endeavour.
The Repeating of the Letter G.
Resp. In the midst of Solomon's Temple there hangs a G,
A Letter fair for all to read and see,
But few there be that understands.
What means that Letter G.
Ex. My Friend, if you pretend to be Of this Fraternity, you can forthwith and rightly tell what means that Letter G.
Resp. By Sciences are brought to Light Bodies of various Kinds, which do appear to perfect Sight; But none but Males shall know my Mind.
Ex. The Right shall.

Resp. If Worshipful.

Ex. Both Right and Worshipful I am, To Hail you I have Command, That you do forthwith let me know, As I you may understand.

Resp. By Letters Four and Science Five This G aright doth stand, In a due Art and Proportion, You have your Answer, Friend.

N. B. Four Letters are Boaz Fifth Science Geometry.

Ex. My Friend, you answer well, If Right and Free Principles you discover, I'll change your Name from Friend, And henceforth call you Brother.

Resp. The Sciences are well compos'd Of noble Structure's Verse, A Point, a Line, and an Outside; But a Solid is the last.

Ex. God's good Greeting be to this our happy Meeting.

Resp. And all the Right Worshipful Brothers and Fellows.

Ex. Of the Right Worshipful and Holy Lodge of St. John's.

Resp. From whence I came.

Ex. Greet you, greet you, greet you thrice, heartily well, craving your Name.

Resp. Timothy Ridicule.

Exam. Welcome, Brother, by the Grace of God.

N. B. The Reason why they Denominate themselves of the Holy Lodge of St. John's, is, because he was the Fore-runner of our Saviour, and laid the first Parallel Lime to the Gospel (others do alert, that our Saviour himself was accepted a Free Mason while he was in the Flesh) but how ridiculous and prophane it seems, I leave to judicious Readers to consider.

The End of the Fellow-Craft Part.

The Master's DEGREE.

Q. Are you a Master-Mason?

A. I am; try me, prove me, disprove me if you can.

Q. Where was you pass'd Master ?

A. In a Perfect Lodge of Masters.
Q. What makes a Perfect Lodge of Masters?
A. Three.
Q. How came you to be pass'd Master?
A. By the Help of God, the Square and my own Industry.
Q. How was you pass'd Master?
A. From the Square to the Compass.
Ex. An Enter'd 'Prentice I presume you have been.
R. Jachin and Boaz I have seen;
A Master-Mason I was made most rare, With Diamond, Ashler and the Square.
Ex. If a Master-Mason you would be, You must rightly understand the Rule of Three. And * M. B. shall make you free: *Machbenah
And what you want in Masonry, Shall in this Lodge be shewn to thee.
R. Good Masonry I understand; The Keys of all Lodges are all at my Command.
Ex. You're an heroick Fellow; from whence came you
R. From the East.
Ex. Where are you a going?
R. To the West.
Ex. What are you a going to do there?
R. To look for that which was lost and is now found.
Ex. What was that which was lost and is now found?
R. The Master-Mason's Word.
Ex. How was it lost?
R. By Three Great Knocks, or the Death of our Master Hiram.
Ex. How came he by his Death?
R. In the Building of Solomon's Temple he was Master-Mason, and at high 12 at Noon, when the Men was gone to refresh themselves, as was his usual Custom, he came to survey the Works, and when he was enter'd into the Temple, there were Three Ruffians, suppos'd to be Three Fellow-Crafts, planted themselves at the Three Entrances

of the Temple, and when he came out, one demanded the Master's Word of him, and he reply'd he did not receive it in such a manner, but Time and a little Patience would bring him to it: He, not satisfied with that Answer, gave him a Blow, which made him reel; he went to the other Gate, where being accosted in the same manner, and making the same Reply, lie received a greater Blow, and at the third his Quietus.

Ex. What did the Ruffians kill him with?

R. A Setting Maul, Setting Tool and Setting Beadle.

Ex. How did they dispose of him?

R. Carried him out at the West Door of the Temple, and hid him under some Rubbish till High 12 again.

Ex. What Time was that?

R. High 12 at Night, whilst the Men were at Rest.

Ex. How did they dispose of him afterwards?

R. They carried him up to the Brow of the Hill, where they made a decent Grave and buried him.

Ex. When was he miss'd'

R. The same Day.

Ex. When was he found?

R. Fifteen Days afterwards.

Ex. Who found him?

R. Fifteen Loving Brothers, by Order of King Solomon, went out of the Well Door of the Temple, and divided themselves from Right to Left within Call of each other; and they agreed that if they did not find the Word in him or about him, the first Word should be the Master's Word; one of the Brothers being more weary than the rest sat down to rest himself, and taking hold of a Shrub, which came easily up, and perceiving the Ground to have been broken, he Hail'd his Brethren, and pursuing their Search found him decently buried in a handsome Grave 6 Foot East, 6 West, and 6 Foot perpendicular, and his Covering was green Moss and Turf, which surprized them;

whereupon they replied, Muscus Domus Dei Gratia, which, according to Masonry, is, thanks be to God, our Master has got a Mossy House: So they cover'd him closely, and as a farther Ornament placed a Sprig of Cassia at the Head of his Grave, and went and acquainted King Solomon.

Ex. What did King Solomon say to all this?

R. He order'd him to be taken up and decently buried, and that 15 Fellow-Crafts with white Gloves and Aprons should attend his Funeral [which ought amongst Masons to be perform'd to this Day.]

Ex. How was Hiram rais'd?

R. As all other Masons are, when they receive the Master's Word.

Ex. How is that?

R. By the Five Points of Fellowship.

Ex. What are they?

R. Hand to Hand1, Foot to Foot2, Cheek to Cheek 3, Knee to Knee 4, and Hand in Back5.

N. B. When Hiram was taken up, they took him by the Fore-fingers, and the Skin came off, which is called the Slip; the spreading the Right Hand and placing the middle Finger to the Wrist, clasping the Fore-finger and the Fourth to the side of the Wrist; is called the Gripe, and the Sign is placing the Thumb of the Right Hand to the Left Breast, extending the Fingers.

Ex. What's a Master-Mason nam'd.

R. Cassia is my Name, and from a Juft and Perfect Lodge I came.

Ex. Where was dram inter'd?

R. In the Sanctum Sanctorum.

Ex. How was he brought in?

R. At the West-Door of the Temple.

Q. What are the Master-Jewels?

A. The Porch, Dormer and Square Pavement.

Q. Explain them.

A. The Porch the Entring into the Sanctum Sanctorum, the Dormer the Windows or Lights within, the Square Pavement the Ground Flooring.

Ex. Give me the Master's Word.

R. Whispers him in the Ear, and supported by the Five Points of Fellowship before-mentioned, says Machbenah, which signifies The Builder is smitten.

N. B. If any Working Masons are at work, and you have a desire to distinguish accepted Masons from the rest, take a Piece of Stone, and ask him what it smells of, he immediately replies, neither Brass, Iron, nor Steel but of a Mason; then by asking him, how old he is, he replies above Seven, which denotes he has pass'd Master.

The End of the Master's Part.

The Author's Vindication of himself from the prejudiced Part of Mankind.

Of all the Impositions that have appear'd amongst Mankind, none are so ridiculous as the Mystery of Masonry, which has amus'd the World, and caused various Constructions and these pretenses of Secrecy, invalid, has (tho' not perfectly) been revealed, and the grand Article, viz. the Obligation, has several Times been printed in the publick Papers, but is entirely genuine in the Daily Journal of Saturday, Aug. 22. 1730. which agrees in its Veracity with that deliver'd in this pamphlet; and consequently when the Obligation of Secrecy is abrogated, the aforesaid Secret becomes of no Effect and must be quite extinct; for some Operative Masons (but according to the polite Way of Expression, Accepted Masons) made a Visitation from the first and oldest constituted Lodge (according to the Lodge Book in London) to a noted Lodge in this City, and was denied Admittance, because their old Lodge was removed to another house, which, tho' contradictory to this great Mystery, requires another Constitution, at no less Expence than two Guineas, with an elegant

Entertainment, under the Denomination of being put to charitable Uses, which if justly applied, will give great Encomiums to so worthy an Undertaking, but it is very much doubted, and most reasonable to think it will be expended towards the forming another System of Masonry, the old Fabrick being so ruinous, that, unless repair'd by some occult Mystery, will soon be Annihilated.

 I was induced to publish this mighty secret for the public good, at, the Request of several Masons, and it will, I hope, give entire Satisfaction, and have its desired effect in preventing so many credulous Persons being drawn into so pernicious a Society.

Other Resources on Freemasonry at SaintDominicsMedia.COM

The Catholic Catechism on Freemasonry: A Theological and Historical Treatment on the Catholic Church's Prohibition Against Freemasonry and its Appendant Masonic Bodies

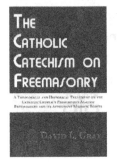

This book contextualizes the history and provides a theological analysis and commentary on the nine Papal documents, two Canon Laws, and two documents issued by the Congregation of the Doctrine of the Faith, which relate specifically to the Catholic Church's dogmatic prohibition against Freemasonry.

MASTER CLASS: The Catholic Catechism on Freemasonry: A Lecture Series on Freemasonry Through the Light of Catholicism

This course will explore the historical and philosophical foundations of Freemasonry, as well as its relationship with religion and the Catholic Church. You will learn about the meaning and symbolism of the three degrees of Freemasonry: Entered Apprentice, Fellow Craft, and Master Mason. You will also examine the various documents issued by the popes and the Congregation for the Doctrine of the Faith that condemn Freemasonry and its teachings. Finally, you will analyze how Freemasonry fits into the current global scenario of the great reset or the reordering of the world.

Made in United States
Orlando, FL
23 February 2024